Balzac, James, and the Realistic Novel

Balzac, James,

AND THE
REALISTIC NOVEL

William W. Stowe

PRINCETON UNIVERSITY PRESS

Copyright © 1983 by Princeton University Press
Published by Princeton University Press, 41 William Street,
Princeton, New Jersey 08540
In the United Kingdom: Princeton University Press,
Guildford, Surrey

Library of Congress Cataloging in Publication Data will be found on
the last printed page of this book

This book has been composed in Baskerville

Clothbound editions of Princeton University Press books are printed on
acid-free paper, and binding materials are chosen for strength and
durability. Paperbacks, while satisfactory for personal collections, are
not usually suitable for library rebinding.

Printed in the United States of America by
Princeton University Press, Princeton, New Jersey

But the greatest thing in Balzac cannot be exhibited by specimens. It is Balzac himself—it is the whole attempt—it is the method. This last is his unsurpassed, his incomparable merit. That huge, all-compassing, all-desiring, all-devouring love of reality which was the source of so many of his fallacies and stains, of so much dead-weight in his work, was also the foundation of his extraordinary power.

HENRY JAMES,
"Honoré de Balzac" (1875)

CONTENTS

PREFACE

Some readers find representational painting the best analogy for literature; others think that literature should approach the state of music. In the first view, literature teaches us how to respond to actual situations by representing such situations in words. It gives us practice in judgment and expands our sympathies. The clearest expression of this theory that I know is in the critical writings of George Eliot, and in chapter seventeen of *Adam Bede*.[1] In the second view, the literary work is primarily an artifact made of language rather than a representation of the world. We do not perceive it in the same way as we perceive the rest of the world, and the process by which we interpret it has very little to do with the process we use to interpret everyday situations. If we learn anything from literature, it is something about what language can do, and how we can use it. This way of looking at literature seems particularly appropriate to the works of such self-conscious experimenters as Mallarmé, Pound, and Robbe-Grillet.

Neither of these approaches suffices to describe the works of Balzac and James (and Flaubert and Proust and Ford and Conrad and others). In the first place, these writers see the novel as aspiring to the conditions of music *and* of painting, and demand that we interpret represented situations, as we must in a George Eliot novel, *and* textual systems, as we do in Mallarmé and Joyce. In addition, they create textual complexities that refer by analogy to the complexities of life in the world. These novelists, in other words, offer their readers moving pictures of the world, to be interpreted as if they were events in the world. They present their works as literary artifacts, with their own formal integrity, to be interpreted on their own literary terms. Finally, they fashion these works' literariness—their textuality—in such a way as to create for the reader an experience analogous to his experience of events in the world: the interpretation of the text becomes by careful plan a model for the interpretation of events in the world and a demonstration of the dynamics of interpretation itself.

It is my contention that all three of these functions are essential features of a strain of realistic novel-writing stretching from Balzac to James and beyond, and it is my purpose here to explore the interrelations of these functions in representative novels by both writers. I propose to sketch out no new *definition* of realism, but a pragmatic poetics of the mode as James and Balzac employed it, a description of the nature and the functioning of realistic texts which draws on the work of recent literary theorists, but derives mainly from the novels of Balzac and James.

These novels are all fictional narratives that set out *systematically* (i.e., consciously and intentionally) to represent the world as their readers see it, that describe and interpret social, political, and economic systems in the process of this representation, and that seek to establish themselves as complex literary systems our response to which resembles our response to the world. Their triple involvement with the notion of system suggests the term "systematic realism" as a convenient label for their common project.

If James and Balzac resembled each other in no other way, if there were no historical connection between them, they could still be profitably compared as examples of systematic realism. In fact, Balzac stands at the beginning of the nineteenth-century European realistic tradition which reaches one of its culminations in James,[2] so a comparison of their realisms ought to help us understand their individual texts, the workings and the potentials of literary realism, and the actual history of realism in the nineteenth century.

This aspect of James's and Balzac's work has not attracted much attention. Recent James criticism has focused on his language and his narrative techniques, on special problems with specific texts, or on reevaluation of his works and his oeuvre as a whole.[3] Criticism of Balzac has followed even more conventional lines, elaborating on the Marxist view that this Catholic monarchist understood almost in spite of himself the true relations of money, class, and power in early bourgeois France, or developing the Baudelairean view of Balzac as a mystic and a "visionary," or pursuing structuralist analysis in the footsteps of Barthes and Greimas.[4] Most studies of Balzac and James together have limited themselves to the search for sources of James's themes, plots, and narrative techniques.[5]

Three works stand out from the rest, however, and should be mentioned for the new critical directions they propose. Christopher Prendergast's *Balzac: Fiction and Melodrama* seeks to understand Balzac's power by examining the "despised and rejected bits of the *Comédie humaine*"[6] that have embarrassed Balzac's academic champions, claiming that these melodramatic excesses open "gaps" and "fissures" in the text which undermine Balzac's apparently common-sensical assumptions about the intelligibility and the representability of "reality." John Carlos Rowe's reading of Henry James is similar, and more explicitly pertinent to our discussion of the interpretation model (Chapter 2). For him, James's texts and the whole worlds they portray can never be finally interpreted, but must continuously be subjected to active interpretation: "The language of the literary text does not carry its reader on a magical journey toward its final revelation. Rather, the reader's voyage is a quest, an active engagement of the language of the work and a creative transposition of that language into the forms for his own understanding."[7]

Both these studies go beyond analysis and evaluation to claim that the works of James and Balzac testify to the vast, uneasy abyss beneath the smug surface of nineteenth-century bourgeois materialism. Peter Brooks makes even bolder claims for his analysis of nineteenth-century literary representation. He suggests that the literary and intellectual history of the nineteenth and twentieth centuries be understood as maintaining tension between a centered, melodramatic Balzacian/Jamesian world view in which "things" have "meanings" and interpretation leads to revelation of the truth, and a decentered Flaubertian (Derridean) world view in which each order of "things" refers to another order of "things" in an endless, pointless, but inescapable burlesque of interpretation.[8]

The extent of my indebtedness to Brooks's work is clear in what follows. It seems to me, however, that his conclusion is too schematic. As he recognizes elsewhere in his book,[9] none of James's or Balzac's novels strictly conforms to the paradigm of melodrama that he proposes, however valuable it may be for understanding the generic norms that they assume and exploit. Instead, as Prendergast and Rowe suggest, and as I argue here, these texts implicitly question their own generic assumptions by explicitly depicting the mental processes upon which these assumptions are based, and demonstrating their limitations.

The works of James and/or Balzac provide Prendergast, Rowe, and Brooks with fertile fields for the development of their particular theories of novelistic representation. They will have done the same for me if I succeed in defining the crucial similarities between the two novelists' realistic projects, in demonstrating how and why James's admiration for Balzac goes beyond a nostalgic taste for old French pictures to real, though never humble or submissive, artistic discipleship, and in clarifying the notion of realism in general.

My choice of specific texts has been dictated by their positions in their authors' careers, and by my sense that *Le Père Goriot, The American, Illusions perdues,* and *The Princess Casamassima* foreground certain fundamental problems that face the would-be realist, and that *La Cousine Bette* and *The Wings of the Dove* use the solutions to these problems to create distinct versions of a kind of "dramatic" realism which foreshadows later developments in the genre. The works of Balzac that I have neglected are too numerous to name. Among James's works I am aware that both *The Portrait of a Lady* and *The Golden Bowl* would have lent themselves well to my purpose. The choice of *The Wings of the Dove* over *The Golden Bowl* was largely a matter of personal preference. That of *The American* over *The Portrait of a Lady* was based on my admiration for the former text, and my impression that more than enough has already been written about the latter.[10]

ACKNOWLEDGMENTS

The single greatest pleasure that the publication of this book affords me is the opportunity to thank some of the friends and colleagues who have helped me write it. A. Walton Litz of Princeton is the first of these, a superb teacher, dedicated advisor, and valued friend. Peter Brooks of Yale is another: he taught me to read James and Balzac, and has criticized my work on them tirelessly and generously. Richard H. Brodhead, also of Yale, is a third: an old, old friend, and the best reader— of Hawthorne, or James, or Balzac, or me—that I know. In addition to these three, more people than I can name have helped me to shape this book, and sharpen it, and give it whatever value it has today. Victor Brombert, Robert L. Caserio, Victoria Kahn, Carol Ohmann, Richard Ohmann, Andrew M. Plummer, Mac Pigman, and Alfred Turco have all read parts of the manuscript and commented most helpfully on them. Students and colleagues at Wesleyan have provided criticism and encouragement. The university itself has provided funds for manuscript preparation.

Parts of the preface and chapter two have been published in *Texas Studies in Literature and Language;* parts of chapter one have been published in *Comparative Literature.* I am grateful to the editors of these journals for permission to reprint this material.

The list could go on and on, but it would always end with my dearest friend and most faithful supporter, my wife and more, Karin Ann Trainer.

New York City
April 1982

NOTE ON TEXTS
AND TRANSLATIONS

For the sake of convenience and uniformity I use two standard collected editions as sources for quotations from James and
Balzac. All the Balzac quotations are drawn from the new
Pléiade edition (Paris: Gallimard, 1971–1980). The English
translations are my own; for all but the simplest quotations I
have provided the French original, often with slightly more context, in the notes. All these quotations are followed by the
Pléiade volume and page number(s) in parentheses. Quotations
from James's novels are drawn from the New York Edition
(Scribner's, 1907–1909). In the case of *The American* this is an
eccentric choice, and I justify it in the proper place. All these
quotations are followed by page numbers only, except in the
case of multivolume works, for which I use "I" or "II" rather
than the New York Edition volume numbers.

Balzac, James, and the Realistic Novel

1

Systematic Realism

One clue to the similarity between Balzac's project for the realistic novel and James's can be found in their common understanding of the place of subject matter in the novel-writing process. Both writers seem to have believed they had found the appropriate subject matter ready to hand in the world. In fact, they created the "reality" they claimed to have discovered.[1]

In the preface to *Une Fille d'Eve* Balzac explains his choice of subject matter this way:

> The author does not yet know of any observer who has noticed how much French manners excel those of other countries, literarily speaking, for variety of types, for drama, for wit, for movement; in France everything can be said, everything can be thought, everything can be done. The author here does not judge, he does not reveal the secret of his political thought, entirely opposed to that of most people in France, but which we will perhaps reach before long. The time is not far off when the costly trickery of the constitutional government will be recognized. He is an historian; that is all. He congratulates himself on the grandeur, the variety, the beauty, and the fruitfulness of his subject, however deplorable it is made, socially speaking, by the confusion of the most opposing facts, the abundance of materials, the impetuosity of movements. This disorder is a source of beauties.

Therefore, it is not out of national vainglory or patriotism
that he has chosen the manners of his own country, but because that country offered, more than any other, *social man*
in more numerous aspects than anywhere else. (II, 264)[2]

Two things strike us in this passage: Balzac's insistence on "dis-
order" as a "source of beauties," and his apparently gratuitous
interpolation of his political opinions in the midst of a literary
discussion. He clearly values the great variety he perceives in
French society: he is interested in the sparkling surface, in wit,
as he says, in animation, and in spontaneity, all of which, together with a certain freedom of thought, of expression, and of
action, he finds in the Paris of his day. More important for his
literary project, however, is his perception of this society as
formless. "Formerly," he writes,

everything was simplified by monarchical institutions: social
types were clearly defined: a bourgeois was a merchant or an
artisan, a nobleman was entirely free, a peasant was a slave.
That's European society as it used to be. It didn't provide
much material for novels. (II, 263)[3]

Nowadays, however,

Equality is producing infinite nuances in France. At one time
caste gave everyone a set of features *(une physionomie)*
which took precedence over individual characteristics. Nowadays, the individual creates his own features *(physionomie)*
on his own authority. (II, 263)[4]

The implication is that if there is to be any order in Balzac's
portrayal of a society that seems to be a large and various group
of self-defining individuals, he must provide it himself.

This notion will come as no surprise to the reader of the
"Avant-Propos" to the *Comédie humaine,* in which Balzac insists as much on the active, interpretive role of the writer as on
the faithful representation of experience. Here he claims first
that the task of the would-be historian of manners is syncretic
rather than simply mimetic. Balzac wants to be the "secretary
of French society," it is true, but the kind of secretary he has in

mind would spend more time organizing and interpreting data, and putting them in shape for publication, than he would spend taking minutes:

> French Society was going to be the historian, I only had to be the secretary. By drawing up the inventory of vices and virtues, assembling the principal facts of the passions, painting the characters, choosing the principal events of Society, composing types by putting together the traits of several homogeneous personalities, I could perhaps succeed in writing the history forgotten by so many historians, the history of manners. (I, 11)[5]

Moreover, if the relatively disorganized social scene of post-revolutionary France provided a suitable body of material for this kind of secretarial activity, it was also especially liable to the kind of political and moral interpretation which Balzac thought the novelist obliged to undertake. "'A writer must have steadfast opinions in morals and in politics,'" he quotes the conservative politician Bonald as saying, and then declares that he himself writes "in the light of two eternal Verities: Religion and Monarchy, two necessities that contemporary events proclaim and toward which all right-thinking writers should try to steer our country" (I, 12, 13).[6] If Balzac intended simply to observe preexisting "facts" in order to draw deductive conclusions from them, he should ideally have been without prejudicial "steadfast opinions." If, on the other hand, he intended to write polemics in favor of the King and the Catholics, he had no business claiming to be the secretary of a formless society. If, however, his literary project required a society apparently formless, but whose hidden form he thought he had discovered, he could have it both ways, masquerading as Society's scribe, while revealing at the same time the pattern of historical development, that "political thought, entirely opposed to that of most people in France," whose secret he claimed not to intend to reveal. In the passages from the preface to *Une Fille d'Eve,* Balzac is simultaneously creating and observing such a society, projecting his desire for a suitable subject on the world around him, and claiming to have found that subject in that world.

James proceeds similarly in the preface to *The Awkward Age*. In France, he writes, the social complications which provide such a fertile field for *his* imagination could never arise, because the awkward situations which produce them have been eliminated by a strict code of social behavior. "On the other hand," he goes on,

> nothing comes home more . . . to the observer of English manners than the very moderate degree in which wise arrangement, in the French sense of a scientific economy, has ever been invoked; a fact indeed largely explaining the great interest of their incoherence, their heterogeneity, their wild abundance. The French, all analytically, have conceived of fifty different proprieties, meeting fifty different cases, whereas the English mind, less intensely at work, has never conceived of but one—the grand propriety, for every case, it should in fairness be said, of just being English. (x–xi)

English manners, it seems, with "their incoherence, their heterogeneity, their wild abundance," offered James just the kinds of socially awkward situations he found artistically stimulating. The "fifty different proprieties" of the French might be a great many, but the mind that was trained to distinguish among them was likely to be satisfied that those fifty had exhausted the moral possibilities, and to devote its energies to classification and description rather than to fresh and sensitive perception. In a society which lacks such an array of ready-made categories and proprieties, one is forced to deal with each situation as if it were totally new. One must resort to a kind of moral *bricolage,* using whatever methods, tactics, and notions are at hand, compromising a principle here, manipulating a person there, overlooking this and emphasizing that in an attempt to bring the facts of the specific situation into some acceptable relation with the general standard of propriety.

"The consequent muddle," James tells us, though "a great inconvenience for life," offered "an immense promise . . . for the painted picture of life" (xii), and we have abundant evidence in the *Notebooks* and the prefaces of his own enthusiastic encoun-

ters with the muddle and his exploitation of the promise. Time
and again James describes a situation susceptible not to organization "in the light of two eternal Verities," but to development into a complex moral and aesthetic text. In the preface to
The Princess Casamassima, for example, James says this about
the experience of walking the London streets:

> One walked of course with one's eyes greatly open, and I has-
> ten to declare that such a practice, carried on for a long time
> and over a considerable space, positively provokes, all round,
> a mystic solicitation, the urgent appeal, on the part of every-
> thing, to be interpreted and, so far as may be, reproduced.
> "Subjects" and situations, character and history, the tragedy
> and comedy of life, are things of which the common air, in
> such conditions, seems pungently to taste; and to a mind cu-
> rious, before the human scene, of meanings and revelations
> the great grey Babylon easily becomes, on its face, a garden
> bristling with an immense illustrative flora. Possible stories,
> presentable figures, rise from the thick jungle as the observer
> moves, fluttering up like startled game, and before he knows
> it indeed he has fairly to guard himself against the brush of
> importunate wings. (I, v)

And in the preface to *The Spoils of Poynton* he explains at some
length the relationship between the "germ" of his novels and
stories and their necessarily untrammeled development in his
imagination. Even more important, perhaps, we have the record
of James's characters' encounters with the muddle, and of its
more or less successful interpretation by the likes of Christopher
Newman, Isabel Archer, Maisie Farange, Lambert Strether,
and Maggie Verver.

Like Balzac, James knew precisely what kind of society his
novelistic art required, and like Balzac he simultaneously projected it on the world around him and claimed to find it in that
world. Balzac saw himself cataloguing and interpreting a post-
revolutionary society, giving form and meaning to a formless
and as yet incomprehensible welter of cases and distinctions.
James saw himself following the development of the individual

consciousness faced with a rich complexity of social, emotional, and, above all, moral conditions. Both writers stress the apparent priority of the phenomenal world, and the novelist's responsibility to represent it faithfully, yet neither abdicates for a moment his own privileged position as a mediator between the world and the reader. Both are conscious, deliberate "realists," who are at the same time conscious, deliberate artists and interpreters of experience. They use common concepts of reality to produce literary texts that will call the validity of these concepts into question. To do this, they choose subjects which might well be extensions of the world readers ordinarily perceive, and, without destroying the metonymic *vraisemblance* of the subjects, the sense that they are slices of life, transform them into metaphorical analogues for the readers' experience, related not by contiguity but by resemblance.[7]

The combination of these two tropes suggest a threefold definition of what might be called "systematic realism." James and Balzac both work methodically (systematically) to present a convincing picture of life in the world. Their realistic intentions naturally lead them to describe and analyze systems of behavior, communication, exploitation, and so on, that structure the world, and to rely, consciously and unconsciously, upon these systems to help structure their texts and to provide them with figurative language. Finally, their desire to create literary analogues for life in the world leads them to elaborate textual systems of great complexity, of purposeful particularity, and of ample power both to reproduce something like the density and the texture of experience and to involve the reader in an active process of reading and interpretation.

It is not likely to be controversial as a statement of superficial fact that both James and Balzac did intend to produce texts which created the illusion of an extension of the phenomenal world.[8] Similarly, it seems clear from their descriptions of the societies they portrayed that James and Balzac chose their material with an eye to the social structures and systems of behavior that material contained or exemplified. These two metonymic features of their novels require and will receive some exemplary illustration, but no lengthy theoretical explanations. This is not the case with the peculiar metaphoric nature of the novels, which needs further elaboration.

One very helpful way of approaching this notion of the text as metaphor is to imagine the author creating a *model* of the world in his writing. "The vast majority of works of art," writes Claude Lévi-Strauss, "are *modèles réduits,*" versions of actual phenomena which do not reduce their subjects' essential complexity, but eliminate inessential and, for the moment at least, irrelevant complications. Every art sacrifices some aspect of its subject in order to concentrate on others: painting gives up volume to concentrate on line and color; both painting and sculpture give up the temporal dimension to concentrate on spatial relations. For Lévi-Strauss, the virtue of this reduction is twofold. First, it makes its subject less formidable than it would be in the phenomenal world, and guarantees its intelligibility. At the same time, it insists upon its own artificiality, its status as the product of an artist's choices and of his craft.[9]

Furthermore, as Lévi-Strauss elsewhere argues,[10] the transformation from the sensible to the intelligible entails a transformation of the phenomenal into the systematic. The scientist, for example, in order to understand the phenomenal world as it presents itself to his senses, must first simplify his impressions by eliminating their extraneous aspects, and then relate the results of this simplification to each other, to the corpus of already existing data, and to his theoretical hypothesis. He must, in other words, systematize his simplified sense impressions. The result of his work need by no means be "simple" in the sense that it is easy for the layman to understand, but it should be intellectually more manageable than the welter of sense perceptions which the phenomenal world presents. It is in effect a metaphor for these perceptions and for that world, a declaration of similarity between them and a set of intellectual constructs which science has already created or is in the process of creating.

The artist, like the scientist, does not imitate life in the sense that he creates a substitute for life or a faithful reproduction of life. He rather presents one of many possible complex metaphors for life, homologous to human experience without being identical with any given human experience. These metaphors are *"modèles réduits"* of life in that they eliminate certain aspects of life which the artist considers extraneous to his purposes; they are systems in the sense that they organize the hurly-burly of phenomena into a coherent set of lines, of shapes, and of colors, or, in the case of the fictional text, into plots, into sets of images and themes, and into coherent verbal patterns. "Miniaturization"[11] of experience leads to enrichment of understanding by transforming the nonhuman complexity of phenomena into a man-made complexity. It represents preexisting phenomena, it organizes them by means of independently existing structures, and in so doing it creates a new phenomenon and a new structure. The purpose of the work of art is therefore to render its subject more richly intelligible than it would be as a phenomenon in nature or in society, and at the same time to be richly intelligible itself.

It is this notion of intelligibility that distinguishes Lévi-Strauss's definition of the work of art as a model from similar definitions. Martin Price, for example, outlines the advantages of seeing the literary work as a model of the world in much the same way as Lévi-Strauss. The model, he writes, "encloses a section or isolates a dimension of reality upon which we wish to concentrate our attention, and it frees it of distracting irrelevance." Whereas in scientific practice, furthermore, the model "exists for the sake of studying what it represents," the literary model demands to be enjoyed for its own sake and therefore, like a ship in a bottle, a toothpick cathedral or, to be fair, a painting or a sculpture, produces what Max Black calls a "harmless fetishism" in its admirers.[12]

Where Lévi-Strauss moves beyond Price is in his examination of what makes the model especially susceptible to study and even to fetishistic admiration. "The intrinsic value of the reduced model," he writes, "is that it makes up for the loss of sensual dimensions by the addition of intelligible dimensions."[13] Furthermore, when Lévi-Strauss calls a model intelligible, he does not mean to suggest that it can be understood once and for all, but rather that it invites a process of understanding, an active engagement of intellect. His "intellectual artifact" is not a product ready for consumption, but rather the trace of a process which the perceiver of a work of art is invited to retrace and in effect to relive. The *modèle réduit* is not only an object to be contemplated, but a machine for thinking.

James's notion of the nature of the work of art is inversely related to Lévi-Strauss's. While Lévi-Strauss's definition of the *modèle réduit* would include even the most complex of James's texts, it seems more useful to regard those texts as the traces of a process of elaboration rather than a process of reduction. James begins with a single element—a character, a situation—and develops from it an intelligible textual model. He prefers an organic metaphor of growth to a mechanical one of reduction; he sees the artist as starting with the tiniest "kernel" of a "real" situation and elaborating it into a complex system, rather than starting with all of life and reducing it to such a system. The purpose of the artistic process, however, and its result, are for both quite similar. James's simple "kernel" is no more intelligible in itself than Lévi-Strauss's infinitely complex "reality": in both cases the artist's job is to make them so.

The process of rendering his small subject intelligible involves for James the realization that "the art of interesting us in things. . . can *only* be the art of representing them," and that "this relation to them, for invoked interest, involves his accordingly 'doing'; and it is for him to settle with his intelligence what that variable process shall commit him to."[14] Once "the subject is found and . . . the problem is then transferred to the ground of what to do with it the field opens out for any amount of doing."[15] "Doing" a subject, for James, means presenting it, elaborating on it, and, most important, transforming it from futile local fact into a metaphor for more general human experience.

Perhaps the richest record of the "doing" of such a kernel begins with a morsel of gossip "related to me last night at dinner at Lady Lindsay's by Mrs. Anstruther-Thompson,"[16] and ends, triumphantly, in "the little drama of my 'Spoils,'"[17] *The*

Spoils of Poynton. The case of the sensitive "deposed" mother making off with those prized possessions that now legally belong to her son "is all rather sordid and fearfully ugly," James writes, "but there is surely a story in it."[18] It lends itself, "this case (the case I should build on the above hint)," to the most artful *doing,* the provision of "circumstances, details, intensifications, deepening it and darkening it all," the rendering intelligible of "the terrible experience of a nature with a love and passion for beauty . . . domiciled in . . . the kind of house the very walls and furniture of which constitute a kind of *anguish* for such a woman as I suppose the mother to be."[19]

From the merest hint, therefore, from a few idle words at dinner, there springs into James's mind the sense of a possible text, of the representation of just the right house and just the right lady to convey just the right sense of futile anguish. The necessarily *textual* nature of such a conception is underlined by James's retelling of the anecdote in his preface to the novel. Here his interlocutor enters into the actual details of the situation, details for which James "had absolutely and could have, no scrap of use," which reminded him once again of "the fatal futility of Fact," the "classic ineptitude" with which life never fails to develop "the excellent situation" in just the wrong way.[20]

The anecdotal kernel, then, is meaningless in itself, and can produce the stupidest, the most banal "factual" developments. The artist's work, for James as for Lévi-Strauss, is to make this kernel intelligible by constructing around it a text which is an ideally ordered whole, and an invitation to active participation in a process of intellection.

The emphasis in both James and Lévi-Strauss is on the possibility and the process of rendering experience intelligible. Although Balzac was not so active a theorist as James, and is therefore a little harder to pin down on these matters, it seems clear from his ambition to emulate the great natural scientists Buffon and Saint-Hilaire by writing the natural history of French society of his day that he, too, wished to provide his readers with an intelligible version of the world as he saw it.[21] Whether the realistic artist thinks in terms of analysis, systematization, and classification, or of the representation of life and the intensification of consciousness, his problem is how to accomplish this goal while remaining faithful to experience itself. To *render* experience is difficult enough: to render it intelligible is even harder. To do both, simultaneously, was Balzac's goal in the *Comédie humaine,* and James's in all his fictions.

To accomplish this goal, both writers developed systematic versions of realism: they made texts the experience of which is analogous to, but in Lévi-Strauss's sense simpler than, the experience of life, and they did so by reflecting, creating, and deploying certain cultural, social, and textual systems. As it happens, the novels whose prefaces helped us understand their authors' general goals also provide schematic examples of their novel-writing practice. *Une Fille d'Eve* and *The Awkward Age* are not their authors' best works, but in them Balzac and James develop certain characteristic techniques more fully and more explicitly than anywhere else.

In *Une Fille d'Eve,* Balzac presents an historically verifiable analysis of the structure of social systems in France around 1830, and uses this analysis to help create a particular kind of textual intelligibility.[22] He does this by describing the three social milieux that the main character knows and finds oppressive in such a way as to suggest the possibility, even the logical necessity, of a fourth, whose actual existence she discovers and whose temptations bring her close to ruin.

Madame de Vandenesse, née Marie-Angélique de Granville, has left the frigidly pious home of her mother, a great magistrate's wife, to preside over her new, titled husband's more liberal, elegant establishment. In Félix de Vandenesse she finds an affectionate partner who has enjoyed his grand passion and his youthful extravagances and is ready to devote himself to his wife's happiness. Her sister, meanwhile, has made a less fortunate match, accepting the great *arriviste* banker, "un sieur Ferdinand *dit* du Tillet" ("a gentleman who calls himself Ferdinand *du* Tillet" [II, 275]), and a very large marriage settlement, in part as a means of compensating the family for the large dowry it gave Marie-Angélique. "Thus," as Balzac puts it, "the Bank had repaired the damage done to the Magistracy by the Nobility" (II, 275).[23] The result for Madame du Tillet, however, is unhappy. True, her establishment is luxurious, but it is as loveless as her mother's; it is rich but tasteless, characterized by the kind of factitious elegance that can be purchased *en bloc* from a fashionable interior designer.

The Bank, then, is vulgar and loveless, the Magistracy, or at least its female manifestation in Madame de Granville, puritanical and loveless, and the Nobility moderate, cultured, and affectionate. This ternary system of oppositions would seem complete and satisfactory as it is presented in the first three chapters of the tale if it were not for three things: the hint that Madame de Vandenesse is not so happy as she ought to be, the fact that a whole segment of rich Parisian society is missing from it; and the fact that the ternary system is actually a quaternary system with one quadrant missing.

The model here is simple. Whenever two sets of mutually exclusive qualities are used to describe a field of possibilities, each of which must be characterized by two terms (x or not-x and y or not-y), four categories result: x and y; x and not-y; not-x and y; not-x and not-y. Suppose, for example, that Professor W is stodgy and a profound thinker, Professor X is stodgy and superficial, and Professor Y lively and superficial. These three characterizations suggest the possibility that there exists a Professor Z who is both lively and profound. Similarly, in the first three chapters of *Une Fille d'Eve* Balzac describes three ménages, two as cold and loveless, the first—du Tillet's—in terms of objects and surfaces, and the second—Madame de Granville's—in terms of moral ideals, and one—Vandenesse's—as warm and loving, also in terms of moral ideals. What is missing from this array of possibilities, and from Balzac's description of Parisian society so far, is a warm, loving milieu described in terms of surfaces and objects. Balzac presently fills this lack with an account of the demimonde of journalists and actresses personified by Raoul Nathan and his mistress, Florine, and symbolized by her magnificent establishment.

Florine's world is opposed to the world of Madame de Granville as Vandenesse's is opposed to du Tillet's. It combines the concern for objects, surfaces, and display of the banker with the affection of the nobleman, and has no room for either the moderation or the cold morality of the judge's puritanical wife. Its passionate vulgarity attracts Marie-Angélique much as the empty quadrant tempts the logician, analyst, or reader to fill it in. Furthermore, the process by which she learns the truth about this world's place and her own in the Parisian social system parallels the task that the text asks the reader to undertake in order to do its richness justice.

Madame de Vandenesse falls in love with Raoul Nathan, demimondain and journalist, out of boredom and curiosity: Balzac represents her fascination with this figure from a foreign social and moral milieu as the inevitable result of her own unmixed purity and her husband's generosity and elegance. Fallen by chance into the perfect marriage with a man who has exhausted his first violent passions but retains his youth and his capacity for affection, Marie-Angélique becomes under his direction the perfect wife. She has freedom and security, good taste and unchallenged social position, but she is bored. In his scheme for wedded happiness, Félix has left the dynamics of desire out of account. By anticipating and fulfilling all his wife's wishes, he has only heightened for her the allure of the unknown, and made her infatuation with its representative all but inevitable.

Luckily, Félix de Vandenesse discovers his wife's infatuation in time to show her its folly and realize his own shortsightedness. As a result of her husband's enlightened reaction to her flirtation, Marie-Angélique gains that mature marital happiness of which her earlier state was only an imitation.[24]

The lesson of Balzac's four-part analysis of society is not that one quadrant or another should or could exist independently, but that we can only appreciate any possible way of life in the context of other possible ways. His text moves from static analysis reminiscent of his own earlier *"physiologies"* to narrative, from the social taxonomy which he thought was his special strength to the dynamic description of social process at which he really excelled. At the same time it demands progressively more of the reader. Content in the first few chapters with our recognition of its acute analysis of various social milieux, it soon demands to be seen not only as a representation of social structure and personal growth, but as a demonstration in purely literary terms of the process of maturation that its protagonist undergoes. Like Marie-Angélique de Vandenesse, the reader of *Une Fille d'Eve* is presented with an oversimple view of the world, and taught how to supplement it, to make up for its inadequacies. In addition—and here lies Balzac's genius—he is presented with a text which asks to be read first as simple analysis, then as narrative, which demonstrates the inadequacy of its own apparent first assumptions as it demonstrates the inadequacy of its characters' first views of the world. The experience of reading *Une Fille d'Eve* resembles the experience that the text describes: the text is not only a picture of reality; by demanding to be read in progressively more complex ways it provides its readers with a literary analogue for the experience of learning. It renders experience intelligible by recreating it in its own literary medium.

The Awkward Age, too, makes experience intelligible, but despite the care it takes to present a believable picture of an unmistakably *fin-de-siècle* London milieu,[25] it focuses on the development of the interpretive faculty rather than on the outcome of any particular interpretation. In *Une Fille d'Eve* the reader and main character arrive in analogous ways at suitably sophisticated views of society and of the text. *The Awkward Age* leads the reader to reflect on the process of interpretation by creating a model in which various kinds of interpretation can be tested.

A great deal of the interpretation in *The Awkward Age* is idle, trivial chatter, the vapid pastime of the bored rich, with Mrs. Brookenham using her skill at this game to get what she wants out of the people she interprets. Against this background of trivial and/or interested interpretation, however, two sincere interpreters stand out, one successful and one a failure.

The successful interpreter, Mr. Longdon, an elderly gentleman and former admirer of Mrs. Brookenham's mother, is at present marveling at the phenomenon of that lady's daughter, a girl who, at the awkward unmarried age of eighteen, is by necessity emerging from the security of the nursery and schoolroom just as he is by choice emerging from the security of his country retreat. Mr. Longdon finds London's new, breezy informality awkward at best, in comparison with the customs of an earlier age. Comparing Nanda Brookenham and her grandmother, Longdon admits to the young lady that "'nothing could be less like her than your manner and your talk.'"

> Nanda looked at him with all her honesty. "They're not so good, you must think."
> He hung fire an instant, but was as honest as she. "You're separated from her by a gulf—and not only of time. Personally, you see, you breathe a different air." (152)

The gulf yawns as wide, of course, between Nanda and Mr. Longdon as it does between Nanda and her grandmother, but the young woman is confident it can be bridged. "'You'll get used to me,' she said with the same gentleness that the response of her touch had tried to express; 'and I shall be so careful with you that—well, you'll see!'" (154) As it turns out, Nanda is right. The gulf is bridged, and she and Mr. Longdon meet on her side of it, determined to cope with their modern circumstances in an unprejudiced, even an unprecedented way.

Mr. Longdon is the novel's great success[26] because he interprets a strange world boldly, discarding an outdated set of proprieties and recognizing the true value behind Nanda's "modern" freedom. Mr. Vanderbank, on the other hand, is its great failure. The first few lines of the book humorously depict him "interpreting" the weather according to a set of fixed principles:

> Save when it happened to rain, Vanderbank always walked home, but he usually took a hansom when the rain was moderate and adopted the preference of the philosopher when it was heavy. On this occasion he therefore recognised as the

servant opened the door a congruity between the weather and
the "four-wheeler" that, in the empty street, under the glazed
radiance, waited, and trickled and blackly glittered. (3)

While James and his readers enjoy a masterful sketch of a London scene—that waiting, trickling, glittering four-wheeler is
magnificent—Vanderbank "recognizes a congruity" between
atmospheric conditions and a mode of conveyance. Unfortunately for him, furthermore, his attitudes toward people are no
more imaginative than his fixed, categorical perception of the
weather. Despite his exposure to modern ways, he cannot rid
himself of a combination of hereditary delicacy and rigid self-
confidence which is his great strength and his great weakness.
He cannot, more specifically, bring himself to propose marriage
to a young person who he thinks has been spoiled by her pre-
cocious knowledge of the world of loose talk and French novels,
and therefore retreats into official busyness at the end of the
novel, leaving the scandalous world behind, and abandoning his
friendship with Nanda and Mr. Longdon, who comment sadly
on his failure, and illuminate for the reader their own special
success:

> "Everything's different from what it used to be."
> "Yes, everything," he returned with an air of final indoc-
> trination. "That's what he ought to have recognised."
> "As *you* have?" Nanda was once more—and completely
> now—enthroned in high justice. "Oh, he's more old-fash-
> ioned than you."
> "Much more," said Mr. Longdon with a queer face. (544)

Nanda and Mr. Longdon and, to some extent, Mitchett, interpret the chaotic world, its incoherent heterogeneity, its "wild
abundance" just the way James thought the modern English
novelist had to, by using a kind of moral *bricolage*, based on
sincerity rather than on fifty different proprieties. Vanderbank
attempts to impose a preexisting set of values on this world, and
he fails.

Une Fille d'Eve teaches the reader *what* Balzac believes experience teaches his characters, by inviting him to live their experiences with them, vicariously. *The Awkward Age,* on the other hand, demonstrates *how* experience teaches, and how best to profit by its lessons. Considering these novels as examples of their authors' systematic realism does not preclude interpreting them in other ways, as vehicles for philosophic views, signs of economic developments, expressions of individual anxieties, or whatever. It does, however, help us focus at one and the same time on their representational claims and their status as textual models which, by opening themselves to a particular kind of interpretation, can teach readers alternate ways of understanding events in the world. It is also, I would claim, a generous kind of reading, granting each novel's claim to be telling a certain kind of truth, and acceding to each text's demands for careful, serious attention to the program it sets out for its readers.

Balzac and James share a common set of literary traditions, forms, and purposes; they are both concerned with the faithful representation of the world as they see it, with the textual simulation of systems in that world, and with the production of literary systems which are convincing analogues of worldly experience and contribute through their superior intelligibility to a new and an active interpretation of the world. Like all representational works of art, their texts are models of the world, and since models by their nature eliminate some elements in order to concentrate on others, they are selective, emphasizing and exploring particular structures of experience rather than attempting to reproduce experience itself.

I hope that so far even those readers—certainly the majority—who are skeptical about the need for yet another discussion of realism will find my formulation of systematic realism plausible. Its great advantage, to my mind, is precisely that it does *not* propose a new definition to rival those of Auerbach or Lukacs, Fanger or Levin. Instead, it suggests a general understanding of realism which can accomodate various ideological positions and provide workspace for the interpretive tools of various schools of literary criticism.

My own original purpose in wielding these tools in this context was simply to demonstrate how particular texts function as intelligible models of experience, to show how several complex realistic novels work. In the course of my investigation, though, I discovered something else: that the shapes of Balzac's career and of James's are congruent, and can be defined by their choosing to explore similar patterns of experience at similar stages of their artistic development.

I have chosen three such patterns to discuss here; they are important throughout Balzac's and James's oeuvres, but I examine them in pairs of texts which help me trace the course of their authors' careers, as well as their use of particular structures of experience. In *Le Père Goriot* and *The American*, both in their ways *Bildungsromane*, experience is seen in terms of the process of *interpretation*, while in *Illusions perdues* and *The Princess Casamassima* the crucial process is *representation*. In *La Cousine Bette* and *The Wings of the Dove*, Balzac and James develop their visions of experience as *drama:* the characters in these novels are seen as consciously or unconsciously playing conventional roles, and the action is conceived as a series of dramatic scenes. In their progress from examining how characters come to understand their experience to studying how some parts of experience can stand for other parts to seeing life as a series of more or less consciously enacted scenes, Balzac and James describe intriguingly parallel courses, reflecting as it seems to me a common sequence in the ways people come to understand their worlds.

2

Interpretation:
Le Père Goriot and
The American

In some forms of the novel of education the projected reader learns the same lessons as the main character: how to behave in society, say, or how to use one's native grit, pluck, and, of course, honesty, to turn a tidy profit in some great free-enterprise jungle. In other, more sophisticated forms, the reader maintains a certain distance from the characters, and learns a different though related set of lessons. In both cases, however, the reader ideally takes part in, rather than simply observing, an educational process.

In *Le Père Goriot* and *The American* the reader learns one set of lessons—on social and moral interpretation—alongside the main character, and another—on textual interpretation—independently. So these novels provide two kinds of pleasure, vicarious participation in the lives of Eugène de Rastignac and Christopher Newman, and active engagement with problems of literary interpretation. They share the preoccupation of Proust's *A la recherche du temps perdu* with the narrative, thematic, and metaphorical potential of a "closed" system of aristocratic society, and use the confrontations of their heroes with such a system to define the generic outlines of their plots. Even more than in Proust, the emphasis in these two novels is on social success, on their heroes' attempts to "crash" the social system, to break into it, and even, in Christopher Newman's case, to break it down.[1]

Le Père Goriot

In *Le Père Goriot,* Eugène de Rastignac is cast as a romantic quester, a latter-day knight attempting to enter the magical precincts of the faubourg Saint-Germain. The poor student imagines himself going into society "in order to conquer patronesses for himself" and provides himself with the arms necessary for his "social conquests" in the form of a letter of introduction to his cousin, the vicomtesse de Beauséant, "one of the most exalted figures in the aristocratic world" (III, 75,76).[2] Having "conquered the right to go everywhere" (III, 76) by appearing at the vicomtesse's ball, he uses the "magic wand" of his social connections (III, 102) to gain the acceptance of the aristocratic comte de Restaud. His success is short-lived, however; he has only to mention the fact that he has seen "le père Goriot" (III, 101) leaving the comte's house to experience the effect of another "wave of the wand" (III, 102)—his own summary dismissal and eventual exclusion from the house.[3] He goes, therefore, to his cousin, and asks her to become his fairy godmother:

> "If you knew my family's predicament," he continued, "you would enjoy playing the role of one of those fabulous fairies who amuse themselves by dispersing the obstacles that confront their godchildren." (III, 108)[4]

She agrees, and provides him with a kind of talisman in the form of the knowledge he needs to succeed in society. He does not, in the course of this book, achieve the success he had dreamed of, but he does at least enter the lists of the ambitious. Delphine de Nucingen becomes his mistress in both the carnal and the courtly-romantic sense, and provides him with all he needs for worldly victory:

> "In days gone by didn't ladies give their knights armor, swords, helmets, coats of mail, horses, so that they could go out and fight in tournaments in their names? Well, Eugène, the things I am offering you are the arms of the times, nec-

essary tools for anyone who wants to make anything of himself." (III, 229)[5]

The quest motif here suggests two opposite but compatible responses. The reader can and probably does identify with the quester, experiencing his failures and successes, and learning the lessons he learns about Parisian society. At the same time the anachronistic nature of the quest image distances the reader and sets Rastignac's story in its literary and historical context. Drawing back from this story, the reader must judge the young man's actions in the double contexts of a fairy-tale world where virtuous knights receive talismans from fairy-godmothers and enchanted swords from haughty mistresses, and of nineteenth-century Paris, where political and economic success is based on birth and socio-sexual alliances. The effect is partly that of the ironic mock-heroic, which stresses the pettiness of one society by relating it to the (usually imaginary) grandeur of another: Rastignac is not accepting a coat of mail and an enchanted sword from Delphine, but a charmingly furnished bachelor apartment and the promise of monetary support; he is no *preux chevalier* but a *dandy entretenu*. This aspect of the story also suggests, however, that Rastignac's version of romantic questing is the only one left for Balzac's contemporaries, and that it is in its way as serious as the old heroic romances. Rastignac does eventually become an important politician, and Delphine's gifts have all the efficacy if not the outward form of swords and armor. The mixing of rhetorical levels, the use of heroic metaphors in a vulgar social context, can serve to stress the dullness of everyday life, but it can also remind the reader that the quotidian has its dignity, its utility, and even, if we look at it aright, its glamor.[6] Similarly, the explicit emphasis on the literary context of Rastignac's actions reminds the reader that the text as a whole should be understood in its relation to literary tradition.

The double focus established by Balzac's use of the quest motif continues throughout the novel, with the reader constantly shifting from identification with Rastignac in his quest to more distanced judgment of that quest. At the beginning, Balzac carefully identifies Rastignac with the reader by casting him as the reader's guide to the *truth*[7] of the story:

> Without his observant curiosity and the skill with which he managed to introduce himself into the salons of Paris, this story would not be painted in such true colors, colors that it certainly owes to his shrewd mind and his desire to penetrate the mysteries of an appalling situation which was being as carefully concealed by those who had created it as it was by its victim. (III, 56)[8]

Responding to passages like this one, Roger Kempf aptly describes Rastignac as a "reader in the book," an apprentice interpreter, familiarizing himself with the signs of Parisian life and the systems into which they are organized, inviting the actual reader to join him in his interpreting.

Balzac relies on a bold set of terms to remind us that the world is always at first illegible, that every career begins with an apprenticeship to language, that before speaking or presenting oneself in society, it is a good idea to practice reading words, glances, attitudes, modes of dress, fine hands, everything that demonstrates a right or a privilege.[9]

Rastignac must learn to read society so that he can create an effective social role for himself: he must learn the syntax and the vocabulary of the language of gesture, implication, and dress, so that he will never again misunderstand the message implied in Madame de Restaud's "air that wise men knew enough to obey" or in the eyes of Maxime de Trailles, who "looked from Eugène to the countess in a manner calculated to get rid of the intruder" (III, 97).[10] He must, furthermore, make himself aware of the "secret" arrangements and the scandals that lie just beneath the surface of the life of the most elegant houses, so that he can avoid by design the kind of gaffe he makes at Madame de Restaud's by referring to "le père Goriot" and the kind he avoids by chance at Madame de Beauséant's by arriving at precisely the first moment of the day at which she is by common consent "visible" (III, 105).[11]

This far the reader follows Rastignac closely, learning with him to interpret the codes of the novel's society. There is more interpretation in *Le Père Goriot* than Rastignac realizes, however, and more truth is revealed through his actions than he will ever learn. Having acquired from Rastignac a zeal for interpretation, the reader, guided by Balzac's voice in the novel, surpasses the hero's interpretive skill. The literal "truth" of Madame de Restaud's liaison with Maxime de Trailles is trivial, after all, and the knowledge that the comtesse prefers to conceal her relations with old Goriot, her father, is not a very impressive result of Rastignac's social research. The young man's blunder into the service corridor of the Restauds' mansion, however, and the glimpse he catches there of old Goriot, reveal more to the reader than they do to his intrepid surrogate in the text. As Peter Brooks suggests, the blunder resembles the theatrical device—an overheard conversation, an intercepted letter—by which the audience at a melodrama discovers the villain's perfidy. It reveals the shabby economic and emotional exploitation upon which glittering Parisian society is based, and the moral decay that this exploitation embodies.

> [I]t brings a new totalistic vision whereby superstructure reposes on substructure, ihe sordid realities of labor and economic exploitation become visible through the veneer of manners. . . . Uncovering the structure of society is simultaneously discovery of the true ethical terms of the drama: Goriot's exploitation and betrayal by his children. There is no separation for Balzac between socio-political truth and ethical truth: the sinister structuration revealed in the former domain points directly to a moral degradation.[12]

The reader of *Le Père Goriot* may or may not understand Rastignac's discovery in these terms. Rastignac himself certainly does not, at least not immediately, and I think in its full moral implications, never. Rastignac turns out therefore to be questing after truth in more important ways than he realizes, and in

more ways than the conventional young-man-from-the-prov-
inces plot suggests. He is a system-crasher in that he is a young
man on the make, who wants to be admitted to the Parisian
monde of power and glamor; he turns out also to be a system-
crasher in that he reveals, sometimes without realizing it, the
secret springs of the system, the depths of suffering and of crime
without which the upper reaches of society could not exist.

In one sense, then, the reader has an advantage over Rastignac in that he can reinterpret Rastignac's interpretations and
discoveries. In another sense, though, these interpreters are
faced with a common problem and learn their lesson about it
together. The problem has to do with inhabiting, imaginatively
or "actually," a Balzacian world in which every detail has
meaning and cries out to be interpreted.

Rastignac, for his part, lives in a world of superinterpreters.
In society, as we have seen, gestures and tones of voice convey
important messages to the knowing, and the briefest lapses in
decorum can reveal a whole generation's shameful tale of in-
humanity and exploitation. At the pension, too, interpretation
is rampant. Bianchon does long-distance phrenology, Goriot
can tell where the flour in a loaf of bread was made by sniffing
the finished product, and all the inmates speculate about the
meaning of Vautrin's dyed sideburns and the story behind Goriot's mysterious visits from ladies and his gradual
impoverishment.

The reader has been invited by Balzac into this same world,
but he knows more about it than Rastignac and is aware, of
course, of its fictive and textual as well as its "real" nature. The
particular kind of textuality that the reader is confronted with,
and its special relation to interpretation, are evident in the following description of Madame Vauquer, the landlady at the
pension:

> Her face, fresh as the first frost of autumn, her wrinkled eyes
> whose expression goes from the conventional smile of the bal-
> lerina to the bitter scowl of the bill-discounter, her whole per-
> son, in short, explains the pension, as the pension implies her

person. There is no prison without its warder; you couldn't imagine the one without the other. This little woman's unwholesome plumpness is the product of this life, just as typhus is produced by the unhealthy air of a hospital. Her knitted woolen petticoat, just a little longer than her overskirt, itself made of an old dress whose padding is coming out through tears in the frayed material, sums up the salon, the dining room, the little garden, announces the kitchen, and foreshadows the boarders. (III, 54–55)[13]

The key words in this passage—*explain, imply, sum up, announce, foreshadow*—suggest a logical connection between Madame Vauquer's appearance and the nature of her establishment and its inmates which may gain the reader's intuitive assent but which cannot stand up to rigorous analysis. That the pension as a whole should imply Madame Vauquer as a consistent part of itself is reasonable enough, but Balzac's variations on this simple synechdochic relationship are harder to follow. The very first statement of the relationship—"her person explains the pension"—is an intensification before the fact of the simpler synecdoche: a whole may *imply* its part and the part may even *imply* the whole, but the notion of the part's *explaining* the whole is more troublesome, and the sense of Balzac's assertion that Madame Vauquer explains the pension is elusive. The next two sentences are straightforward enough as examples of relations between parts and wholes, and effects and causes, but they depend for their significance in the context on a metaphorical relation to Madame Vauquer and her life at the pension. The existence of a jail certainly implies the existence of a jailer to keep it, and the symptoms of typhus imply its causes, but how Madame Vauquer's life is like the vapors issuing from a hospital, and how her pallid flab is like typhus, is not so easy to determine. The brisk self-assurance of the synecdoches, however, imparts some of its authority to the metaphors: the reader who readily admits the necessity of these relations between a part and a whole, and a cause and an effect, is likely to assent to the contiguous assertions of similarity as well.

Balzac's technique here is to lull the reader's logical defenses
with a series of indisputable statements, and then follow them
with other, apparently related but logically dubious statements,
which gain credibility by contagion. The effect of this technique
is a sense that the passage is uniformly intelligible even if it is
not uniformly logical. The reader may not know exactly what
it means that Madame Vauquer's person explains her establishment, any more than he understands how that lady's knitted
petticoat sums up her salon, her dining room, and her little garden, announces her kitchen, and foreshadows her guests. What
he does know, after reading this passage, is that the details in
this text possess an extraordinary power of signification which
is not limited by the rules of common sense and strict logic.
There is hardly anything in *Le Père Goriot*—no detail, no gesture, no speech or character—which cannot be understood as
implying or explaining, summing up, foreshadowing, or an-
nouncing some other detail, some event in the past or the future,
or even some ultimate metaphysical "meaning." The fact that
these implied details, events and meanings are not always verifiable in the text does not detract from the apparent importance
of the act of tracking them down, of interpreting the world
within the text, and the text itself.

So Rastignac and the reader are faced, the one with a world,
the other with a world and a text, that demand interpretation
and promise to repay the interpreter's zeal. It is not surprising,
then, that Rastignac's desire to crash the empirically verifiable
metonymic code of social behavior, to read complex causes in
barely perceptible effects, and to catch the whole set of relationships implied by a single speech or gesture spills over into an
attempt to understand the metaphysical, metaphorical significance of his actions and his choices, and that the reader is
tempted to follow him in his efforts. The final result is the same
kind of interpretation that has Madame Vauquer's petticoat
summing up her whole establishment, and the lesson that both
Rastignac and the reader learn has to do with the limitations of
this kind of interpretation.

After his early lesson in cracking social codes and deciphering
sublinguistic messages, Rastignac's interpretive efforts come to

center on a set of decisions and the value-choices they seem to embody. These interrelated decisions are posed as fairly simple choices between two alternatives, but in each case other factors complicate the choice and demonstrate the inadequacy of the binary model.

The first opportunity for choice comes when Madame de Beauséant suggests a sophisticated alternative to Rastignac's naive model of the *grand monde* as a fortress which will open its doors to the combination of his native boldness and his aunt's letter of introduction. The glittering surface of society, she says, its elegance, politeness, and apparent homogeneity serve only to camouflage its incredible complexity and its bitter perfidy. To succeed in this world one need not simply be bold and well-born, but understand and take advantage of a system of liaisons, jealousies, and hatreds. "'You want to succeed; I will help you. You will plumb the depths of feminine corruption; you will measure the breadth of man's miserable vanity'" (III, 115–116).[14] Specifically, Madame de Beauséant recommends that Rastignac gain the favor of Goriot's daughter, Delphine de Nucingen, by giving her access to the exclusive world of the faubourg Saint-Germain in the form of an invitation which Madame de Beauséant will provide. "'If you present her to me . . . she will adore you. Love her afterwards if you can; if not, make use of her'" (III, 116).[15]

Rastignac is astonished but not quite convinced by his cousin's cynical exposition of sexual politics. He hits on a way of testing her analysis but cannot for the moment conceive of any but a naively heroic response if she is right. Madame de Beauséant has told him that his blunders at Madame de Restaud's have shut her doors to him forever.

> "I'll go," he said to himself, "and if Madame de Beauséant is right, if I am kept out . . . I . . . Madame de Restaud will find me in every salon she visits. I'll learn to fence, to shoot a pistol! I'll kill her Maxime for her!" (III, 117)[16]

Of course, Madame de Beauséant's analysis proves correct, but Rastignac quickly abandons his murderous intentions. He cannot so easily give up his quester's ambition to succeed by

virtuous means, however, so he decides to follow both Madame
de Beauséant's advice and his own professional program: "Rastignac resolved to blaze two parallel trails to fortune, to rely on
science and on love, to be a learned doctor and a man of fashion"
(III, 118).[17]

Before he can put his resolution into action, however, Rastignac is confronted with another set of choices. "'I am going to
clarify your position,'" Vautrin tells him, "'but I am going to
do so with the superiority of a man who has seen, after examining the things of this world, that there are only two courses to
choose from: stupid obedience, or revolt'" (III, 136).[18] Vautrin's
rhetoric is impressive, and his authority is increased by his un-
canny knowledge of Rastignac's family affairs and his promise
to help him get the money he needs. "'What do I have to do?'"
is the young man's first response to his would-be protector, and
then, when he finds that it is a matter of a favorable marriage,
"'But where would I find a girl?'" (III, 143) Only with Vautrin's answer to this question does Rastignac begin to understand the full, the horrible implications of his revolt. Victorine
Taillefer, Vautrin explains, has a single brother standing between her and her father's fortune. "'If it were God's will to
take his son from him, Taillefer would recognize his daughter!'" What Vautrin proposes is to take on "the role of Providence," to "'command the will of God'" ("'faire vouloir le bon
Dieu'" [III, 144]).[19]

> "I have a friend I'm devoted to, a colonel in the army of the
> Loire who has just gotten a post in the royal guard. He listens
> to my opinions, and he's made himself an ultra-royalist. He's
> not one of these imbeciles who stick to their opinions. . . .
> He'd put Christ back on the cross if I told him to. On a single
> hint from his papa Vautrin he will quarrel with this char-
> acter who doesn't send his poor sister so much as a hundred
> sous, and . . . " (III, 144–145)[20]

"'Quelle horreur!'" cries Rastignac, but Vautrin goes on to explain that this crime would be hardly any worse than those
committed daily in society, crimes which Rastignac has seen re-

vealed in the world of Madame de Beauséant and the former demoiselles Goriot. "'The only difference between what I'm proposing and what you will do one day in any case is blood'" (III, 145).[21]

What Vautrin is proposing is that Rastignac ally himself not, or at least not exclusively, with the system of jealousies, intrigues, and social exploitation outlined by Madame de Beauséant, but with the underground system whose hired assassins stand at the disposal of the *homme supérieur,* the successful master criminal. He has complicated the choice proposed by Madame de Beauséant, which in return complicates the deceptively simple binary choice *he* has proposed.

Of the four options so far presented, one—heroic action—has been discredited, and another—respectable bourgeois professionalism—shown to be unrewarding. The two that remain, Vautrin's revolt and Madame de Beauséant's cynical sexual exploitation, form not a binary opposition but a barely distinguishable pair of options.

These options are further complicated by two factors, Rastignac's feelings about Delphine and Victorine, and his urge to label Goriot good and Vautrin evil. The first of these factors concerns Rastignac alone, and demonstrates the limitations of abstract analysis in decisions involving human affections. Rastignac pities Victorine, who is herself in love with the dashing young man from the provinces. He is also infatuated with Delphine, who sees in him the possibility of the grand passion she has missed with her husband and her lover. To choose Vautrin's plan would be to liberate an innocent, long-suffering maiden by the quasi-murder of her worthless brother, and to gain a fortune. To follow Madame de Beauséant's advice would be to free a beautiful, sophisticated married woman from a painful situation, and to gain a protectress. Seen this way, Rastignac finds it an impossible choice, so he looks for some other way to define it. His attempt to label the two options with qualities he imputes to two of their sponsors[22] is of special interest in that it parallels the reader's attempt to interpret an important symbolic aspect of the text.

Rastignac begins his interpretation of Goriot, his attempt to assign him a meaning and—even more important—a value, by discovering the facts about the old man's past and piecing causes and effects together to produce a verifiably "true" picture of his character. At the same time he is speculating about the "meaning" of Goriot in the world and in the text, and the process of interpretation soon broadens to include metaphorical speculation as well as metonymical reconstruction.

The first thing Rastignac finds out about Goriot after catching a glimpse of him at Madame de Restaud's is that he is indeed her father and the father of Madame de Nucingen, that he gave each of his daughters five or six hundred thousand francs in dowry, keeping only a few thousand a year for himself, and that he has been exiled by both his royalist sons-in-law since the Restoration of the Bourbon line. Later, when the sisters appear in all their ill-got splendor at Madame de Beauséant's ball, Rastignac has a vision of the suffering Goriot that demonstrates how much he has learned since that day. Rastignac has himself been reluctant to attend the ball, because he is worried about his elderly neighbor's health, and because he knows, and heartily regrets, that the old man has sold his last, most precious possession, and mortgaged his pension, to redeem Madame de Restaud's diamonds and pay for her ball gown. That night, as her father lies dying, Anastasie de Restaud goes to the ball, magnificently dressed, "displaying all those diamonds, which must have burned her very flesh" (III, 266).[23] Rastignac attends as well, but his pleasure in all the magnificence is spoiled, since he sees "under the two sisters' diamonds, the poor cot where old Goriot was lying" (III, 266).[24]

This much is empirically verifiable in the world of the novel, but it tempts Rastignac to further, riskier kinds of interpretation. Like the narrator in the description of the Maison Vauquer, and like any reader out to assign meaning to a text, Rastignac leaps from metonymic interpretation to metaphoric, from judgments about the *causes* of Goriot's misery and the *source* of his daughter's finery to judgments about what these facts represent. In this project, as I have suggested, Rastignac's interests as he sees them and the reader's as the text defines them practically coincide, and it is sometimes difficult to decide whether the narrator is reporting on an interpretation made by Rastignac, or suggesting one for the reader. The interpreter *in* the text and the interpreter *of* the text run parallel for a while, and the final decision reached by the one can be read as a lesson in interpretation by the other. For both Rastignac and the reader, Goriot is an inhabitant of the emblematic moral universe of the Maison Vauquer as well as a backdoor participant in the affairs of the *beau monde.* The old man's career in the pension, his gradual climb from roomy quarters on the *premier* to a sordid room on the *troisième,* and his simultaneous fall in the esteem of the hostess, exemplifies the rigid hierarchy which that lady enforces, a hierarchy which in itself suggests an interpretation of the pension as a model of the world, a metaphor for the human condition. Bianchon the medical student and Goriot himself suggest the old man's symbolic position in this model: he is an ironic figure for God or Christ, much the same way Rastignac is an ironic version of the romantic quester. "'He has only one bump,'" says Bianchon to Rastignac, explaining his phrenological analysis of Goriot, "'the bump of paternity; he will be an *Eternal* Father'" (III, 119).[25] A few pages later, Goriot takes up the image, comparing himself quite sacrilegiously to *God* the father:

> A father is with his children the way God is with us. . . . Well, when I became a father I understood God. He is completely everywhere, since all creation came from him. Monsieur, I'm like that with my daughters. Only I love my daughters better than God loves the world, because the world is not so beautiful as God, but my daughters are much more beautiful than I. (III, 160–161)[26]

The note of sacrilege sounds more strangely in Goriot's next theological allusion—"'I, I who would sell the Father, Son, and Holy Ghost to spare those two a single tear!'" (III, 177)[27]—but the effect is still to reinforce Rastignac's sense of something godlike in the old man. The reader might, of course, dismiss all this

as sentimentality on the part of Rastignac and Goriot, if it were
not for the fact that the narration itself contributes to the pattern, and so suggests that it is part of the meaning not only of
the story but of the text as well:

> He looked at her with an air of superhuman sadness. In order
> to paint this Christ of Paternity well enough, we would have
> to look for comparisons in the images that the princes of the
> palette have invented to paint the passion suffered for the
> good of the world by the Saviour of men. (III, 231)[28]

But this is too much. Just as Madame Vauquer's shabby petticoat cannot logically sum up her pension, so Goriot cannot be
Christ or even a convincing Christ-figure. He is, after all, a pathetic old *vermicellier* who has rather foolishly sacrificed himself for his daughters. The meaning of old Goriot in Rastignac's
experience and in the text of the novel cannot be determined by
any deeper analysis of Goriot's *character,* which persists in its
"realistic" inconsistency: Goriot's "meaning," like that of any
other semantic unit, is a function of his opposition to other units.

Over against Goriot, and significantly complicating the world
of the pension, is Vautrin. If Goriot is a shabby, monomaniacal
Christ-figure, Vautrin is a somewhat more elegant incarnation
of the devil, and if Rastignac's discoveries about Goriot reveal
the mercenary and selfish underside of society life, his temptation by Vautrin, and the subsequent revelation of Vautrin's
identity, suggest an alternative system of heroic criminality. Just
as Goriot is associated for Rastignac and for the reader with
Christ, so Vautrin is associated, sometimes for the reader alone
and sometimes for the reader and Rastignac, with the devil.
Rastignac calls Vautrin "that demon" (III, 184) and the red-
headed tempter himself refers to Rastignac as "a pretty prey for
the devil" (III, 185).[29] And in case there is still any doubt, the
narration comments that when Vautrin is taken into custody by
Gondureau and his men, "his glance was that of the fallen
archangel who wants perpetual war" (III, 219).[30]

So Rastignac is presented with two alternative paths to social
success, paths which he and the reader are both tempted to label

as the frankly diabolical and the naively angelic. To marry Victorine would be to accept Vautrin's devilish patronage and to exploit an innocent creature who loves him and whom he pities. To choose Delphine, to live in her little paradise,[31] would be to accept the patronage of the Christ-like Goriot and to gratify the love of a creature whom others have made to suffer, and whom he has come to love. Such a choice would be easy, as easy, say, as the choice of the way of life of Félix de Vandenesse over those of Madame de Granville and Ferdinand du Tillet, but it would imply the kind of simple, positive interpretation of the text, and of the world it represents, which may lead to the discovery of *facts* about society and its members, but which is not justified in the assigning of *values* to individual characters. These characters *seem* to demand to be interpreted in the same way as the details of social life, and Rastignac's and the reader's instinct is to give their interpretation the same kind of credence. Balzac, however, does not allow either Rastignac or the reader to persist in *believing* that the metaphysical interpretation of characters is as easy as the reading of social codes.

Goriot's money, as Rastignac has discovered, is no less, if not quite so directly, tainted as Victorine's would be: he made it by speculating in wheat during the famine of 1793. Goriot, furthermore, as the reader must realize, is a credible Christ-figure only by contrast with Vautrin. He suffers and dies not to save lost sinners, but to buy happiness for his own daughters. Vautrin is a devil, surely, and a convicted criminal, but the match he proposes between Rastignac and Victorine seems the opposite of diabolic: both are young and still fairly innocent; Victorine is clearly in love with Rastignac, who is not indifferent to her. They could even be imagined at this point turning into a couple of *bons bourgeois,* using the fruits of Vautrin's crime and the knowledge that Rastignac has obtained in society to gain power to promote honest politics and good causes.

Balzac, however, does not want things so neat. It would be easy to imagine a version of *Le Père Goriot* which would include both the deconstructions of Rastignac's original view of the social system, and yet avoid linking Victorine with either of them. Vautrin could come up with some other scheme, and so make her Rastignac's obvious choice. The result would be a representation of society as a set of complex but static structures in which characters found their places. Balzac uses his angelic-diabolic imagery here precisely in order to avoid this, and to produce in its stead a representation of society and a definition of the text as a set of loosely defined frames for the characters' actions and the readers' interpretations. The effect, as Brooks points out, is to disturb what would otherwise be a neatly conventional set of values. The comfortable choice of an unspoiled Victorine does not exist for Rastignac: "Victorine has been chosen by Vautrin as the vehicle of his scheme, which allows Rastignac by bipolar opposition to place Delphine in the virtue column."[32] The "virtue column," however, is far from unsmirched, and holds no temptation of bourgeois complacency. In choosing Delphine, Rastignac chooses moral indeterminacy, adultery, and social climbing, all under the aegis of Goriot's dubious divinity. He chooses, that is, not to have chosen but to go on choosing,[33] and he is able to do this because Balzac has created a world and a textual system that imply the necessity of risky, speculative, metaphorical interpretation as well as safer, even if ever so complex, code-reading, and are therefore actively intelligible rather than finally understood. He has created, in other words, a text that asserts its indeterminacy while it asserts its representative validity: *"All is true"* (III, 50),[34] to be sure, but truth does not imply determinacy of meaning or of value.

Le Père Goriot is a realistic novel which represents and interprets "the world as it is," while maintaining a critical distance from that world and from the processes of interpretation that occur in it, and leading the reader to interpret and to judge those processes rather than simply to follow them. It remains tentative about the systems of interpretation it proposes for itself, criticizing in one place the very readings it in other places seems to suggest. As a model for experience, *Le Père Goriot* performs three functions: it convinces us of its own faithfulness to the look of things as they are; it demonstrates the influence of money and social standing on a certain kind of social life; and it teaches us the uses and the limitations of interpretation.

The American

The American is a very different kind of text from *Le Père Goriot*, but it develops the same ironic complexity of superimposed interpretations. Despite his careful portrayal of historical conditions in French and American society, [35] his use of a similar set of social and intertextual systems and a similar plot structure, James never had Balzac's desire to "represent human feelings, social crises, and all the hurly-burly of civilization" (III, 47);[36] his ambition was instead to "get into the skin" of his characters,[37] to create "a consciousness (on the part of the moved and the moving creature) subject to fine intensifications and wide enlargement,"[38] and to represent the world as such a consciousness would perceive it. In *The American,* James combines his own textual representation of human consciousness with an analysis of interpretation much like that in *Le Père Goriot.*

Christopher Newman and Eugène de Rastignac are both outsiders confronting a system of behavior, of social relations, and of communication, which is at first incomprehensible to them, and which they desire in one way or another to penetrate. In describing Newman's situation, James uses two of the same sets of metaphors that Balzac uses in *Le Père Goriot,* the conceptual metaphor of the hero as interpreter, and the generic-structural metaphor of the plot as quest-romance.

Newman suggests the archetypal white knight in much the same way that Rastignac suggests the valiant, untried *chevalier.* He is the stranger from the west country, unsullied by the scandals of city life and far above suspicion of mercenary motives, the Duke of California, who grants "lands and houses free of rent," so rumor has it, "to all newcomers who'll pledge themselves never to smoke cigars" (320). Associated, as George Knox points out, with images of spring, dawn, vigor, and fertility,[39] he is a potential Parsifal, a revitalizer of the fortunes and a revivifier of the blood of the Bellegardes. He is also, of course, the new man of his surname, setting out, like his explorer-name-sake in reverse, to explore the Old World. Finally, he is the handsome prince come to rescue the fair lady immured in the gloomy castle by her evil mother and older brother, the real-life version of the savior of the beautiful Florabella in Claire de Cintré's story, who carried his mistress away to the Land of the Pink Sky, where "she was so happy that she forgot all her troubles and went out to drive every day of her life in an ivory coach drawn by five hundred white mice" (217).[40]

But Newman fails as a hero of romance: he loses his bride without understanding why, and he realizes only at the last moment that his planned vengeance on the Bellegardes is doomed to failure. The elements of the conventional romance plot emphasize his failure by evoking and then contradicting a common literary pattern of success. In doing so they point up both his basic goodness and his incomplete understanding of his situation.

Charles Feidelson suggests the nature of Newman's failure in his examination of James's fascination with the Romantic hero as "Man of Imagination." James's "problem," according to Feidelson, "is to shadow forth the Romantic hero within the weird disguise of a late nineteenth-century social type."[41] In his conception of Christopher Newman he approaches this problem by creating a Romantic anti-hero, a man described in heroic terms but unable to accomplish heroic deeds, a knight who chases his mistress into a convent rather than carrying her off to the Land of the Pink Sky. Newman's success as a Romantic hero would have involved his imaginative penetration of the world of the Bellegardes. His failure therefore is a failure of imagination: he simply cannot comprehend the differences between his own ways of living and those of the Bellegardes. In his later novels, Feidelson suggests, James hesitates between "the idea of imputing imagination to someone in order to reveal his intelligible character and story and the idea of devising a character and story in order to display the dynamics of a totally imaginative life."[42] In this text, James devises instead a character and a story which reveal the devastating effect of an insufficiently developed imaginative life. Difficult as it was for James later in his career to portray the Man of Imagination in the guise of the gentlemanly editor from Massachusetts or an ailing New York heiress, he managed to make a failed Romantic hero of the Man of Little Imagination in *The American,* and to suggest the importance of the imagination in the process.

Just how he did this begins to be evident in his use of the metaphor of the hero as interpreter. Like Eugène de Rastignac, Christopher Newman is confronted with a series of problems in interpretation, but unlike his Balzacian predecessor, Newman sees these problems as hindrances to *acquisition* rather than to *understanding.* Whereas Rastignac's ambition was to succeed at any price (*"Parvenir!* parvenir à tout prix!" says Vautrin [III, 139]) in the society that is at first so foreign to him, Newman's is more simply to soak up the best it has to offer in the way of music and pictures ("'First-class music and first-class pictures?' says Tom Tristam. 'Lord, what refined tastes!'" [28]), to take a great many notes on such subjects as Count Egmont and the streetcars of Brussels, to "improve his mind" in some vague, Victorian way (100), and perhaps to carry off a wife, provided she is "the best article in the market" (49).

Given this consumer's perspective on the world, then, Newman thinks at first that he need only make himself understood in order to get what he wants, and sees no reason for penetrating the deeper mysteries of language or society. When Monsieur Nioche, prompted by his rapacious daughter, Noémie, suggests that he study French—"A little practice in conversation. . . . The conversation of the best society" (12)—Newman replies that he is not so sure about conversation, but it would be useful to know a few words: "'I can't fancy myself reeling off fluent French!' Newman protested. 'And yet I suppose the more things, the more names of things, a man knows, the better he can get round'" (12).[43] In fact, Newman's ability to get what he wants in a foreign language is prodigious, considering the long conversation he carries on with Mademoiselle Nioche on the strength of a single word, *"combien"* (5ff.). Even in lan-

guages "of which he had formally not understood a word," he
is able to "emerge from dialogues . . . in full possession of the
particular item he had desired to elicit" (86). For him, however,
language is only a tool for the most straightforward communication. He is not used to writing, he says, since "in America I
conducted my correspondance altogether by telegrams and by
dictation to a shorthand writer" (103), and he has "never read
a page of printed romance" (39).[44] When he is faced with the
more subtle, connotative language of words and gestures and
glances by which the Bellegardes and their friends communicate, he misses certain signs completely and is baffled by those
he does notice. When he accepts the Bellegardes' "handsome
proposal" to give a grand engagement party, he fails "to catch
a thin sharp eyebeam, as cold as a flash of steel, which passed
between Madame de Bellegarde and the Marquis and which
we may presume to have been a commentary on the innocence
displayed in the latter clause of his speech" (285).[45] When he
sees Claire in public, just before they announce their engagement, she signals to him, but to no avail:

> But Madame de Cintré, as she gave him her hand, gave him
> also a look by which she appeared to mean that he should
> understand something. Was it a warning or a request? Did
> she wish to enjoin speech or silence? He was puzzled, and
> young Madame de Bellegarde's pretty grin gave him no in-
> formation. (275)

Unlike Rastignac, furthermore, Newman never understands
the importance of active social interpretation for the success of
his project. Rastignac knows that he must fathom the secret
workings of Parisian society. Newman, by contrast, is content
to sit back and be amused by the antics of his foreign friends,
whom he sees as performers in a great comedy of manners, actors speaking lines learned by heart and hiding their "true
selves" beneath conventional masks:

> He sat by without speaking, looking at the entrances and
> exits, the greetings and chatterings, of Madame de Cintré's

guests. He felt as if he were at the play and as if his own speaking would be an interruption; sometimes he wished he had a book to follow the dialogue; he half expected to see a woman in a white cap and pink ribbons come and offer him one for two francs. (144)

She was so high yet so slight, so active yet so still, so elegant yet so simple, so present yet so withdrawn! It was this unknown quantity that figured for him as a mystery; it was what she was off the stage, as he might feel, that interested him most of all. (145)

He is convinced that all the Parisians he likes—Monsieur Nioche, Valentin, Claire—are plain decent folks under their masks and makeup, that they are, as Richard Poirier puts it, "imprisoned Americans"[46] whom he must try to set free. Conversely, he is confident that all he needs to do in order to attain his goals in society is to learn a few rules of etiquette and deportment, just as he was able to get along in foreign languages by learning a few key words and the names of all the things he wanted. "'I want,'" he says,

"always to do, over here, what's customary, what you've been used to. You seem more lost without what you've been used to than we are. If there's anything particular to be done let me know and I'll make it right." (156)

As the plot continues to thicken, however, even Newman realizes that he is missing something. "'It's a pity,'" he says, "'that I don't wholly catch on. I shall lose some very good sport'" (162). He loses, of course, not only some sport but the whole game. By proudly parading the old Marquise up and down her well-populated rooms on his brash American arm, he virtually forces her to break off her daughter's engagement. By insisting that Claire herself be clear about a set of feelings and motivations that just cannot be reduced to terms simple enough for him to understand, he convinces her that marriage between them is impossible. "'You told me the other day that you were afraid of your mother,'" he says. "'It must have meant some-

thing. What therefore *did* it mean?'" She replies that she is
sorry to have said such a thing, and he asks what it is that her
mother does to her. "'Nothing,'" she replies.

> "Nothing that you can understand. And now that I've given
> you up I mustn't complain of her to you."
> "That's no reasoning!" cried Newman. "Complain of her,
> on the contrary, for all you're worth. To whom on God's
> earth *but* to me? Tell me all about it, frankly and trustfully,
> as you ought, and we'll talk it over so satisfactorily that you'll
> keep your plighted faith." (410–11)

No frank talk can avail to make Newman understand Claire,
however: he remains literal-minded, and she, to him, inscruta-
ble: "'I'm afraid,'" she says, "'of being uncomfortable.'" And
he replies, "'And you call marrying me uncomfortable?'"
(411). His final formulation of the situation is simplistic, and
her final resolution accentuates Newman's inability to understand her. "'I know what your feelings are,'" Newman says:

> "they're perversities and superstitions! They're the feeling
> that after all, though I *am* a good fellow, I've been in busi-
> ness; the feeling that your mother's looks are law and your
> brother's words are gospel; that you all hang together and
> that it's a part of the everlasting great order, *your* order, that
> they should have a hand in everything you do. It makes my
> blood boil." (415)

A little later Claire announces that she is "going out of the
world . . . into a convent," and he is dumbfounded:

> But still he hardly understood. "You're going to be a nun,"
> he went on; "in a cell—for life—with a gown and a black
> veil?"
> "A nun—a blest Carmelite nun," said Madame de Cintré.
> "For life, with God's leave and mercy." (418)

Newman's sally into the society of the faubourg Saint-Germain
and his quest for a wife fail because he cannot even imagine

how different the Bellegardes are from his frontier and Wall Street friends, or how important this difference is to them.

While *Le Père Goriot* functions as a model of society, a machine for thinking about and coming to understand the social and moral life of Restoration Paris, *The American* functions as a model for misunderstanding, and a machine for contemplating the nature of understanding itself rather than the object understood. As in *Le Père Goriot,* the opening pages of *The American* cast the reader as an expert interpreter. The difference is that James's narrator assumes that his reader is a connoisseur and a psychologist of human types, while Balzac's assumes that his is a student of Parisian social topography. The result in both cases is to establish at the outset a simple model of interpretation whose inadequacies will later be revealed.

When Newman is discovered in the opening pages paying a dutiful visit to the Louvre, he is described in such a way as to evoke benevolent amusement and a vague sense of superiority on the part of the sophisticated reader, the "observer with anything of an eye for local types" (2) whose knowledgeable co-operation the text assumes. Such a reader, the kind who either is or would like to think himself familiar with the Salon Carré and "Murillo's beautiful moon-borne Madonna" (1), can be imagined smiling indulgently at Newman's zeal in seeking out "all the pictures to which as asterisk was affixed in those formidable pages of fine print in his Bädeker" (1), mildly disapproving of his unceremonious posture, and congratulating himself on being the equal and the collaborator of his describer, clearly a man of the world who knows which ottomans were where in the Louvre in 1868, and can spot a "shrewd and capable person" by observing his "physiognomy" from a considerable distance.

James reinforces this sense of collaboration and superiority in his reader by judging Newman quite candidly himself, and explicitly including the reader in his judgment:

We have approached him perhaps at a not especially favourable moment; he is by no means sitting for his portrait. But

listless as he lounges there, rather baffled on the aesthetic
question and guilty of the damning fault (as we have lately
discovered it to be) of confounding the aspect of the artist with
that of his work (for he admires the squinting Madonna of
the young lady with the hair that somehow also advertises
"art" because he thinks the young lady herself uncommonly
taking), he is a sufficiently promising acquaintance. (4)

"We" see that the Madonna squints and that the young lady is
guilty of "a great deal of vivid by-play" calculated to draw attention to herself; we see that Newman is about to be duped by
a pretty face into a foolish purchase, and we probably wince a
little at his all-too-typical American crassness, the limitation of
his French vocabulary to one word, "Combien?" and his willingness to use it unblushingly on an unknown "young lady" in
a public place. The comedy continues as Newman rather gra-
tuitously explains that he is interested in the Madonna even
though he is "not a real Catholic" (6), and then misinterprets
the copyist's "flush of incredulity" (6) at his interest in her me-
diocre work as a sign that "he had offended her."

> She was simply trying to look indifferent, wondering how far
> she might go. "I haven't made a mistake—*pas insulté,* no?"
> her interlocutor continued. "Don't you understand a little
> English?" (6)

The young lady sizes Newman up, and asks for two thousand
francs for her copy, which is, she says, "extremely *soigné.*"
Newman apparently agrees with her judgment, and James allows himself and his reader a little more ironic amusement at
his hero's expense:

> The gentleman in whom we are interested understood no
> French, but I have said he was intelligent, and here is a good
> chance to prove it. He apprehended, by a natural instinct, the
> meaning of the young woman's phrase, and it gratified him
> to find her so honest. Beauty, therefore talent, rectitude; she
> combined everything! (7)

Finally, lest there be any doubt about the lady's talent and Newman's taste, she assures him that her picture "'shall be finished in perfection' ... and to confirm her promise she deposit[s] a rosy blotch in the middle of the Madonna's cheek" (7).

In these first pages of *The American,* the reader is invited—indeed challenged—to understand and to "place" Christopher Newman in much the same way that the reader of *Le Père Goriot* is called upon to understand and place the Maison Vauquer. The illusion in both texts is that the subject—the pension and French society; Christopher Newman and human motivation—is essentially knowable, and that the reader and the author share the means—a familiarity with Parisian geography, architecture, and interior decoration for *Le Père Goriot,* and a certain sophisticated savoir-faire and sensitivity for *The American*—to know them completely. James's project for *The American,* however, will not allow him to present Christopher Newman as a simple object of satire, and the reader who begins by gloating over his superiority to Newman's philistinism soon discovers a disturbing reflection of himself in the sadly comic figure of Mr. Babcock of Dorchester.

Even before Newman meets Babcock, James suggests that his hero's unorthodox brand of tourism is as admirable as it is unmistakably amusing. Newman's tastes are catholic, rather than uniformly bad, and he can be as "greatly struck" by "the beautiful Gothic tower of the Hôtel de Ville" in Brussels as he is by that city's streetcar system. True, his appreciation takes the form of acquisitiveness—he wonders "if they mightn't 'get up' something like it in San Francisco" (86)—and he does see the world as "a great bazaar where one might stroll about and purchase handsome things" (87), but his curiosity and his good humor are boundless, and he enjoys his tour as few travelers can boast of having done. "There is sometimes nothing," James writes, mingling his habitual superiority to Newman with a tinge of admiration,

> like the imagination of those people who have none, and
> Newman now and then, in an unguided stroll through a for-

eign city, before some lonely, sad-towered church or some angular image of one who had rendered civic service in an unknown past, had felt a singular deep commotion. It was not an excitement, not a perplexity; it involved an extraordinary sense of recreation. (89)[47]

Mr. Babcock is the perfect foil for Newman in this regard, since he has an exaggerated notion of his duty to official culture, and enjoys no "sense of recreation" whatsoever. He regards the world as a bowl of hard nuts to crack, and lavishes his nutcracking attention about equally on obligatory works of art and on his relationship with his disturbing traveling companion. Indeed, it is his practice often "to retire to his room early in the evening for the express purpose of considering it conscientiously and, as he would have said, with detachment" (91). For all his consideration, however, Babcock cannot understand Newman, and he finds this "distressing." Newman fails to see the problem. "'Don't I understand you?'" he asks. "'Why, I hoped I did. But what if I don't; where's the harm?'" (95). Babcock, exasperated, goes his own way, pausing to write Newman a letter enjoining him to "remember that Life and Art *are* extremely solemn" (98).

The businessman's easy, apparently random ramble across the continent with his Baedeker, his acceptance of, indeed, his liking for, everything, make an attractive alternative to the clergyman's compulsive pilgrimage, with his sack of digestive hominy in his luggage, across a Europe which "in his secret soul he detested" (92). The contrast becomes even more evident when it develops that Newman has truly enjoyed the monuments he has visited, learning something about art and keeping his sense of proportion and self-irony in the process. "'If you want to know everything that has happened to me these three months,'" he writes Mrs. Tristram,

> "the best way to tell you, I think, would be to send you my half-dozen guide-books with my pencil marks in the margin. Wherever you find a scratch or a cross or a 'Beautiful!' or a

ing American, but he has also by now been reminded of the advantages and the attractions of simplicity.

These two aspects of Newman's simplicity are put to the test in his confrontation with the Bellegarde family, and the melodramatic plot that results is a demonstration that even the most honest, the most open, the frankest good will cannot make up for lack of sympathetic imagination in the face of an alien social system. The interest, however, lies not in the conclusion but in the process of demonstration.

James's descriptions of Newman's first encounters with the Bellegardes are marvelous studies in uneasiness. On his first successful visit to the Rue de l'Université, for example, Newman spends some uncomfortable minutes accumulating metaphors for his own awkwardness, and the long paragraph in which James enumerates these metaphors suggests one of those moments of social silence which seem, to the social *ingénu,* at least, never to end. Newman first imagines himself an explorer in unknown territory: "He had an unusual, unexpected sense of having wandered into a strange corner of the world." Then he thinks of that strangely disconcerting feeling that "one feels in missing a step, in an ascent, where one had expected to find it." Next he imagines himself a violent intruder "in the grey depths" of this forbidding house, and an intruder, furthermore, who is rather embarrassed not to remember why he has broken in: "She seemed enveloped in triple defences of privacy; by what encouragement had he presumed on his having effected a breach?" Finally, he sees himself as a swimmer drowning in "some medium as deep as the ocean" who "must exert himself to keep from sinking." He is saved, in the end, from this "fit of sharp personal embarrassment," by a kind glance from Madame de Cintré, a glance which frees him from his rush of mental metaphors and makes him comfortable enough to act out his own habitual metaphor of American ease: "He performed the movement frequent with him and which was always a symbol of his taking mental possession of a scene—he extended his long legs" (114–15).

This paragraph can be seen as emblematic of all of New-

'So true!' or a 'Too thin!' you may know that I've had som one or other of the sensations I was after. . . . I carry abou six volumes of Ruskin in my trunk; I've seen some grand ol things and shall perhaps talk them over this winter by you fireside. . . . '*L'appétit vient en mangeant,*' says your prover and I find that the more sweet things I taste the more greedil I look over the table." (103–104)[48]

Christopher Newman is not *simply* a philistine, not *only* rich American boor out to purchase the Continent; he is, as eve Babcock notices, "one of nature's noblemen" (91), a mor likeable and a more vital character than the thin-blooded criti who finds him lacking in moral seriousness. This does not mak him a man of the world by anyone else's standards, however and to drive this point home James introduces another characte into the last few sentences of Newman's description of his trav els, an Englishman, "'a very bright man who writes in the Lon don papers and knows Paris nearly as well as Tristram'" (104– 105)—and who is soon to be disappointed in Christopher New man. "'He pronounced me a poor creature, incapable of the jo of life—he talked to me as if *I* had come from Dorchester'" (105).

Newman is neither bon vivant nor Puritan, and he cares ver little what the Puritans and the bons vivants think of him "'Which of my two critics was I to believe?'" he wonders. "' didn't worry about it and very soon made up my mind the don't know everything'" (105).[49] James had written a little ear lier in the chapter that although Newman had set out to im prove his mind, "he would have felt a certain embarrassmen a certain shame even—a false shame possibly—if he had caugh himself looking intellectually into the mirror" (87). Impatien with Babcockian sententiousness, Newman rejects both intro spection and the analysis of the motives of others: Newman' critics certainly "don't know everything," but they probably d know something, and Newman quite willfully refuses to fin out what this might be. The reader is thereby confirmed in hi first impression of Newman as the aggressively uncomprehend man's meetings with the Bellegardes, though from this point on his anguish will stem from intellectual and emotional frustration rather than awkwardness, and his desire to take "mental possession of the scene" will never be truly satisfied. On the contrary, the more he sees of the noble family, the less he understands them, and the more he suspects that there is something positively evil about their mysterious way of life. This sense of evil begins with his view of the Marquis and his mother as Claire's moral jailers, restricting her to the "hereditary shade" and "equivocal gloom" of "that inconvenient and ill-warmed house," when she should be disporting herself in "the sun and the air" of "the great world—*his* great world, not the *grand monde* as there understood" (244–45).[50] Soon Newman is thinking of the pair as "out-and-out rascals" (246) and dramatizing their sins with remarkable vividness. The old Marquise, according to him, is "a bad, bold woman." "'I shouldn't wonder,'" he says, "'if she had done some one to death.'" Her son is even worse, for he lacks her "rage of passion." "'If he has never committed murder he has at least turned his back and looked the other way while some one else was committing it'" (246–47). At this point Newman's imaginative flights seem to be the counterpoints of his enthusiastic speeches in praise of Claire's goodness and simplicity and his own. He is a compulsive labeler who would like to make the kind of judgment about the Bellegardes that Rastignac is unable to make about Vautrin or Goriot, Victorine or Delphine: he would like to label them unequivocally *evil*.

This desire becomes all the more insistent when the Bellegardes break off the engagement, and Newman begins to realize how poorly he understands their way of life. His first reaction is absolute disbelief, expressed in an incongruously comic American expression:

"Why can't she marry me?"—and he looked all at them.
Madame de Bellegarde never moved in her seat, but her consciousness had paled her face. The Marquis hovered protectingly. She said nothing for some moments, but she kept

her keen clear eyes on their visitor. The Marquis drew himself up and considered the ceiling. "It's impossible!" he finely
articulated.
   "It's improper," said Madame de Bellegarde.
   Newman began to laugh. "Oh, you're fooling!" he ex-
claimed. (363–64)

His amusement, however, soon changes to outrage at the duplicity of these honorable aristocrats, and horror at the methods
he thinks they must have used to force Claire to bend to their
will.

   Newman shook his head heavily. "This sort of thing can't
   be, you know. A man can't be used in this fashion. You not
   only have no right that isn't a preposterous pretence, but you
   haven't a pennyworth of power."
   "My power," Madame de Bellegarde observed, "is in my
   children's obedience."
   "In their fear, your daughter said. There's something very
   strange in it. Why should anyone be afraid of you?" added
   Newman after looking at her for a moment. "There has been
   something at play I don't know and can't guess." (369–70)

Something there has indeed been at play, and Newman is quite
ready to believe the worst about it. They have hurt Claire, he
thinks (372); she has tasted some "infernal potion" of threats
and hatred (376).
   This is a crucial point in the story. Newman is aching for
some concrete manifestation of the Bellegardes' evil, and James
provides it for him in the form of Mrs. Bread's allegations about
the "murder" of the old Marquis. This whole episode is too
conventionally Gothic to be convincing, which is not to say that
it is either unimportant or irrelevant to the meaning of the text
as a whole.
   It provides, in the first place, a necessary element in Christopher Newman's education. For a short time after Valentin's
hints about the skeleton in his family's closet and Mrs. Bread's

revelation of the murderous past of the old Marquise and her son, it seems as if Newman's simplistic analysis of the situation is about to be vindicated. James, his reader, and Newman himself revel for a few pages in the blessed relief of open hostility: it is difficult to resist the opportunity to hiss the proven villains and applaud the hero's vitriolic repartee. When the Marquis, for example, questions Newman's taste in pursuing the family to Fleurières, and the American replies, "'Oh, don't talk about taste! that would bring us round to yours! If I consulted my taste I certainly wouldn't come to see you'" (429), the reader's glee—mine at least—is practically audible. And after Newman has accused the Marquise directly—"'You cruelly killed your helpless husband, you know; and I'm in possession of all the facts'" (490)—he glories in the sense that he has finally *made himself felt* by the haughty pair.

His very need for this sense, however, suggests that the Bellegardes may prove impervious to his threats, and that he may have been too hasty in seizing on a means for his revenge. Newman, in fact, is so set on proving to the world that the people he has perceived as vaguely sinister from the first, and who have done him irreparable wrong, are somehow demonstrably, inescapably, publicly evil, that he jumps at what seems to him a providential concretization of their evil only to have it evaporate in his hands. Even leaving to one side the unsolvable problem of Mrs. Bread's reliability and the late Marquis' veracity—was she his mistress? did he forge the note? is the whole thing an exaggeration if not a hoax?—Newman's knowledge can ultimately do little for him beyond justifying his simple, Manichaean view of the world. The Bellegardes assert their invulnerability:

> "Your hawking that tatter about will be, on your part, the vulgarest proceeding conceivable, and, as having admitted you to our *intimité*, we shall proportionately wince for it. That we quite feel. But it won't otherwise incommode us."
> (501–502)[51]

And Newman, on visiting their friend the Duchess, practically
admits their right to do so:

> What in the world had he been thinking of when he fancied
> Madame d'Outreville could help him and that it would con-
> duce to his comfort to make her think ill of the Bellegardes?
> . . . was he to have brayed like that animal whose ears are
> longest? Whether or no the Duchess would hear his story he
> wouldn't tell it. Was he to sit there another half-hour for the
> sake of exposing the Bellegardes? The Bellegardes be deeply
> damned! He got up abruptly and advanced to shake hands
> with his hostess. (507–508)

He has realized at last that the reading of social texts is not a
matter of simple one-for-one decoding leading to some objective
truth. No matter what his piece of paper says to *him* about what
has happened in the past and what should happen in the future,
he is suddenly sure that it will say something quite different to
Madame d'Outreville. Even metonymic interpretation, Newman has finally learned, is not simply the objective reconstruction of events from clues, or the implication of causes by effects:
to know how another person will interpret a set of events or
even read a short text, one must use one's imagination to become
that person for an instant, and to read with his eyes. Newman's
failure to do this until now has been, as we have seen, the chief
cause for his failure in society. One of his small successes in the
novel is that he gains the interpretive skill and the depth of social imagination necessary to understand this failure in time to
avoid a pointless scene with the Duchess.

Even after he has taken this long first step in the process of
learning to read social texts, however, Newman clings to his
own righteousness. He retains his poor scrap of evidence as a
reminder that, "after all and above all, he was a good fellow
wronged" (528). He keeps this sense of his own goodness and
the evil of his persecutors alive during his peregrinations to
England, to New York, and to San Francisco, and returns with
it to Paris when he hears that Claire has definitively taken the
veil. Facing the "dull, plain" wall of the house of the Carmelites

he is reminded of the walls of the *hôtel* de Bellegarde in the faubourg Saint-Germain, and realizes that he can neither understand nor affect what goes on behind any of these walls, that "the woman within was lost beyond recall" (533). Sitting in the "splendid dimness" of Notre Dame, he admits the inadequacy of his simple notions of good and evil, victory and defeat:

> The most unpleasant thing that had ever happened to him had reached its formal conclusion; he had learnt his lesson— not indeed that he the least understood it—and could put away the book. . . . At last he got up and came out of the darkening church; not with the elastic step of a man who has won a victory or taken a resolve—rather to the quiet measure of a discreet escape, of a retreat with appearance preserved. (534)[52]

Despite his earlier misreadings of the texts of society and his own experience, Christopher Newman, the brash, bold American, has finally learned discretion and resigned himself to the elusive indeterminacy of such metaphysical categories as *good* and *evil*. If he has not *understood* the book, he has at least learned the significance of his lack of understanding, has acquired the imagination necessary to see himself as not understanding, and to behave accordingly. So he goes to Mrs. Tristram's, announces that he has "worked off" "a lot of troublesome stuff" (536), and tosses his scrap of paper into the grate.[53]

What Newman has learned and what James has demonstrated is the inadequacy of the American's literal-minded brand of melodrama to account for or to deal with events in the world. Even when good and evil are as clearly labeled as they are in the last 150 pages or so of *The American,* they cannot effectively serve as the exclusive criteria on which to base judgments and make choices. The melodramatic imagination may be the basis of a novelist's or a character's view of the world, but it is no substitute for that more complex and sympathetic social imagination which James's most successful characters, Lambert Strether, say, or Maggie Verver, come to possess.

The American can be seen on one level as a critique of Newman's limited sensibility, and on another as a calling into question of its own initial narrative and semantic assumptions. Newman is in the end far less a white knight than Rastignac is a
preux chevalier, and James's original antithetical characterization of the American and French adversaries in terms of innocence and experience, nature and artifice, "business" and lei-
sure, and so on, cannot make them the kinds of characters that
can hold a reader's interest. Melodrama is an essential element
in James's view of the world and in his aesthetics of fiction, but
it is too simple in its received form to provide him with the kind
of optic he requires. Sophisticated readers rejoice in opportunities to hiss the villain, but only when they come as rare and
refreshing moments of simplicity in a more complex narrative
texture. *The American* is a record of James's realization of this
fact, of his discovery, as Peter Brooks puts it,

> that to maintain the melodramatic terms of his vision and his
> presentation, in particular to maintain the conflict of polar-
> ized moral conditions, while at the same time escaping the
> limitations of overt, explicit melodrama (of the type of *The
> American*), he must make his confronted terms rich in per-
> ceived and felt possibilities while elaborately refusing desig-
> nation of their ontology.[54]

Le Père Goriot and *The American* call attention to the difficulties inherent in their own interpretation by thematizing the
problematic nature of the interpretation of social systems. Neither Eugène de Rastignac nor Christopher Newman is allowed
the simple, straightforward interpretation, the kind of moral labeling that tempts the Frenchman in his dealings with Goriot
and Vautrin, and quite undoes the American in his plotting
with Mrs. Bread. Similarly, neither *Le Père Goriot* nor *The
American* can be labeled once and for all as a "critique of early
bourgeois society" or a "failed melodrama." Both are scrupu-
lously realistic in intention and in effect: Balzac and James do
their best to represent society and their characters' experience
of it in believable and, where possible, historically verifiable

ways. Neither, however, tempts the reader to a premature, pat "understanding" of either the society or the characters. Instead, they use their characters' attempts to understand the social systems with which they are confronted to suggest the reader's analogous attempt to understand the textual system and the dynamic nature of interpretation in general. They are, in other words, models for reading and for living, realistic novels that challenge any too-easy understanding of either realism or reality itself.

Representation:
Illusions perdues and
The Princess Casamassima

We value models for their elegance and for their representational power. Model airplanes and doll-houses delight children because they are attractive and because they stand for the real thing. Mathematical formulas and computer programs please their makers by their simplicity, their efficiency, and their ability to stand for economic systems, physical laws and functions, and so on. Realistic novels attract readers by their literary qualities and by their faithful representations of human experience.

The novels of James and Balzac present their readers with two kinds of models, representing simultaneously the physical, social world, and the various processes of representation itself, the ways in which things stand for other things in our perception of the world. They are doubly mimetic, imitating in words both the surface of the world and the processes by which we relate things in the world one to another.

We have already seen how both writers examine the process of interpretation, depicting characters who must read elements of their environment as conventional signs of their emitters' desires or as natural signs of their moral qualities. Such conventional and natural signs fall into the category of what Charles Sanders Peirce calls *symbols,* signs which depend for their meaning neither on their resemblance to something else nor on

their physical reference to something else, but on their interpreter's ability and desire to decipher them.[1]

In *Illusions perdues* and *The Princess Casamassima*, representation, not interpretation, is the central process, and the differences between Balzac's and James's understandings of this
process reinforce the distinctions between their fictional methods
and their views of the world, which we began to detect in chapters one and two. In *Illusions perdues*, representation is an
iconic function, again in Peirce's sense: things and systems of
things in this novel's world resemble each other by their nature
and not as a function of the central character's perception. In
The Princess Casamassima representation is more personal:
speakers produce unfinished, meaningless sentences which represent their ignorance; the central character represents himself
to himself and to others in various guises, and perceives things
and systems of things in the world as representations of his own
fate, *symbols* in the sense that he must decode them, and *indices*
(Peirce's third and final term) in that they point at him and his
particular dilemma.

These two novels are concerned with representation in another way, too. Like all realistic novels they claim the iconic
function of conjuring up images that resemble the real world.
More than most of their writers' works, more, especially, than
most of James's, they also claim the indexical function of pointing to particular conditions at particular times and places. Indeed, they are often considered their authors' most realistic
works. Describing social problems in a straightforward manner,
they tempt the reader to see them as analyses or critiques rather
than as novels, tempt him, that is, to focus on the subject rather
than the text.

This would be a mistake. *Illusions perdues* and *The Princess
Casamassima*, despite the care they take to represent actual conditions accurately, do not strive for perfect transparency. In
them the represented economic and political systems function
textually, standing for other systems in the text as well as actual
conditions in the world, and suggesting strategies for interpreting the text as a whole.

Illusions perdues

Illusions perdues occupies its own peculiar niche among the novels of the *Comédie humaine*. The second unit of the Vautrin trilogy, it lacks the heroic framework of *Le Père Goriot* and the dark, romantic undertones of *Splendeurs et misères des courtisanes*. Gaëtan Picon captures its peculiarity when he calls it "the foremost and the least Balzacian of the masterpieces: perhaps the only one illuminated not by the deep firelight that burns behind the stained-glass windows of the *Comédie humaine,* but by the simple light of day,"[2] and relates Lucien's surrender to the dark power of Vautrin-Herrera at the end to Balzac's own decision to turn from the light of common day of the early "Scènes de la vie" to the "prodigies" and "monsters" of the *Comédie humaine*.[3]

The rhetorical differences between *Illusions perdues* and *Le Père Goriot* are already evident in their openings. Balzac begins *Le Père Goriot* simply enough with a few facts about the Maison Vauquer and its *patronne,* but by the end of the first paragraph he has claimed his privileges as author by indulging in a pseudo-conventional exhortation to his readers to take his work seriously, an exhortation which is at the same time perfectly earnest in its claim of ultimate truth ("It is so true, that everyone can recognize its elements in his own household, perhaps even in his own heart" [III, 50].)[4] and slightly ironic in its request that the reader, who has just seen Parisian civilization likened to the car of Juggernaut, not tax the author with exaggeration or "poetry" (III, 50). The effect of this consciously clever literary play is to establish a productive tension between the narrator's two roles as faithful scribe and as creator of the text. Even the reader who is not inclined to tax the narrator with poetry and exaggeration can have no doubt as to his controlling presence in the text, no illusion that its structures are merely natural, preexisting phenomena faithfully reproduced. As we have seen, this implied presence suggests that the text has a recoverable meaning, and directs the reader's attention to this meaning and the process of interpretation by which it might be discovered, to the intensely "significant" nature of represented details and the phenomenological structure of the act of interpretation.

The opening paragraphs of *Illusions perdues* suggest a different reading strategy. Their writer seems to be a modestly erudite historian rather than a novelist; their tone is slightly pedantic and more than a little conservative, combining an apparently random assortment of facts about typographical history and etymology with brief obiter dicta on the unfortunate proliferation of the "ravenous mechanical presses" (V, 124)[5] and the undependability of family feeling among the lower classes (V, 128). The very first sentence, for example, is extraordinarily laconic. This extremely long novel, dedicated to Victor Hugo, entitled, rather grandly, *Illusions perdues,* whose first book is called "The Two Poets," opens this way: "At the time this story begins, the Stanhope press and inking rollers were not yet in operation in small provincial printshops" (V, 123).[6] The first clause here admits that it is introducing a *story ("histoire"),* but the rest of the sentence asserts the historicity that this word implies, rather than its fictionality. Stanhope's press and the small provincial printshops really existed, after all, while the Maison Vauquer is a conventionally fictional setting for a novel. There is no sense here of obtrusive literary artifice, of secrets to be discovered or codes to be cracked, but just the illusion of the leisurely, unstructured chronicling of personal and social history.

This illusion is based, of course, on a naive model of representation in which a signifier—in this case the text—is a perfectly transparent vehicle for a signified—in this case the world. Representation according to this model is simple and binary: x stands for y, period. The first couple of paragraphs introduce the reader to this naive representational model by portraying the Séchard printshop as a kind of paradise of representation, a primitive linguistic setting in which words and things maintain their original etymological relationships:

Angoulême was still using wooden presses, which our language has to thank for the now obsolete expression "make the press groan." (V, 124)

The movable tray holding the form full of type to which the
sheet of paper is applied was still made of stone, and so jus-
tifiably called the "marble." (V, 124)

This Séchard was a former journeyman pressman, in typesetters' jargon, a Bear. Their back-and-forth movement, the
way they took themselves from the ink-block to the press and
the press to the ink-block, is reminiscent of a bear in a cage,
and certainly earned them the nickname. In retaliation, the
Bears named the typesetters Monkeys, because of the inces-
sant gymnastics required to snatch type out of the hundred
fifty-two little boxes that hold it. (V, 124)[7]

Language here is clearly motivated: if a part of a printing press
is called a *marble* it is because it is made of stone; if a worker
is called a *bear* it is because he typically spends most of his time
lumbering bearlike from one part of the shop to the other and
back. Language, even figurative language, here means pretty
much what it says. If it weren't for the fact that the elder Séchard cannot read and write, but has learned to judge manuscript pages in terms of the fee he can charge for printing them,
this paradise of the word would seem consistent and complete.

Séchard's illiteracy is more than an ironic detail, however, for
it extends in effect to the novel's two main characters, David
Séchard and Lucien Chardon (de Rubempré), who emerge
from their childhood paradise in the printshop as functionally
illiterate as old Séchard, but less aware of their handicap. They
can read, they think, but in fact their readings of the world be-
tray their naive belief in simple binary representation and lead
them into dangerous errors. The lesson of *Illusions perdues* is
that representation is never simple, that every signified is potentially a new signifier, and that the process goes on forever.

We begin to suspect something of this sort early on, in the
story of old Séchard. "In the calamitous period of 1793" (V,
124), we are told, Séchard, who has escaped conscription because of his age and his married state, uses his wife's savings to
buy the printshop from the widow of his former employer for
approximately half its value. Since he is illiterate, he cannot op-
erate the shop by himself, so he relies on educated fugitives from

Revolutionary tribunals who work for no wages but protection. By the time the last of these leaves, Séchard has amassed enough money to employ a regular staff and has become a miser, squeezing the last sou out of his customers and buying up the stock of ruined competitors at low prices. He sends his son to work with the Didots on the condition that it not cost him any money, and then awaits impatiently the boy's return so that he can sell out to him:

> If he had first seen David as his only child, he later saw in him a buyer, whose interests were naturally opposed to his own. He wanted to sell dear, David had to buy cheap: his son therefore became an enemy to conquer. This transformation of feeling into self-interest, which in the genteel is slow, tortuous, and hypocritical, was quick and direct in the old Bear. (V, 128)[8]

What is the reader to make of Séchard's successive exploitation of his own wife, a war widow, a nobleman and a clergyman on the run, weaker local businessmen, and finally his own inexperienced son, all recounted by the narrator in the first ten paragraphs? They certainly establish the old man as a Balzacian grotesque like Gobseck or old Grandet. They also suggest to the reader that if there is no sense of mystery at the center of this text, no kernel of meaning to be hoped for when a code is deciphered or a closed system penetrated, then perhaps the text is to be understood as a system for the multiplication of examples of certain patterns of behavior rather than for the intensification of their meaning. In other words, *Illusions perdues* can be seen as a set of represented actions whose value lies in the ways they evoke, echo, and resonate with other similar actions both within the text and in the world it purports to represent. The novel provides a panoramic representation of the world; it may seem random and chaotic at first viewing, but it is actually a coherent work of art, a complex but controlled *"modèle réduit"* by means of which represented experience may be actively understood.

Understanding, here, though, is circular rather than centripetal: the goal is not to discover hidden significance but to demonstrate resemblances. Lucien never sees through the surface to the economic basis or the moral motivations of social behavior; the reader comes to see social experience as a dynamic succession of similar events, which form differing patterns depending on the perceiver's viewpoint. Rastignac echoes early Romance in his linear determination to achieve a goal; Lucien prefigures the characters of Zola in his entrapment by a series of social systems that take him up, spin him around, and, like a series of revolving doors with single openings, leave him off just where he started.

Michel Butor suggests that the whole *Comédie humaine* is a "novelistic mobile,"

> a whole made up of a certain number of parts which we can take up almost in any order we like; each reader will trace a different course in the universe of the *Comédie humaine;* it is like a sphere or an enclosure with several doors.[9]

Illusions perdues, it seems to me, is a novelistic mobile in itself, a representation of disillusionment and social entrapment whose interest derives from the shifting relations among its parts and whose center of gravity shifts with the points at which the reader and would-be critic applies his critical pressure. It is an account of the transformation of poets' and inventors' brain-children into commodities,[10] of the corruption of Parisian publishers and theater managers, and of the consequences of personal moral weakness, each primarily by some accounts, secondarily by others.

The effect of such a conception of the text is of course to deny the possibility of a definitive reading and to suggest a kind of infinite and eventually circular multiplication of reference from smaller systems of exploitation, for example, to larger ones, which again remind us of smaller ones, and so on. If, as I believe, this is a fair representation of the way we experience the world, Balzac's *Illusions perdues* is his second most faithful novelistic representation of this experience, surpassed only by the *Comédie humaine* as a whole.

One way to demonstrate what I mean by this would be to

move from old Séchard's machinations to similar cases of the exploitation of the weak by the strong, of labor by capital, and so on, and to show how these examples reflect on and illuminate each other. Balzac's demonstration of the tendency of early capitalists to treat other people's talents as their own investable and expendable assets contributes enormously to the novel's significance as a social document. The repetition of this pattern, the way that Lucien's fate at the hands of the journalistic capitalists is mirrored by David's at the hands of the Cointets and the lawyers, by the actresses' at the hands both of the press and of the rich businessmen who keep them, and in another way by Lucien's treatment of David and his own mother and sister, all this adds to the novel's realistic density.

Georg Lukacs has examined this series of homologous exploitations so thoroughly that I see little point in going over the ground once more. Instead, I will explore another pattern, closely related to the patterns of conscious exploitation, which is embodied in the threats posed to individuals by what seem to be enormous impersonal machines or networks.

Like Eugène de Rastignac in *Le Père Goriot*, Lucien Chardon and David Séchard are confronted by complex systems that they do not understand, but that are vital to their success in the world. Lucien faces successively the social worlds of Angoulême and Paris and the politico-economic systems of bookselling and journalism, while David must deal with the intricacies of the *code de commerce* as manipulated by the rapacious Cointets and their legal minion, the aptly named Pierre Petit-Claud. Whereas in *Le Père Goriot*, the significance of Eugène's encounter with society, with Goriot, and with Vautrin lay in his attempts to interpret the social and ethical systems they individually and collectively represented, here the significance of Lucien's and David's encounters lies precisely in their failure to interpret the systems that threaten them, and in these systems' tendency to stand for nothing but each other. Lucien and David are defeated by these systems without ever understanding them, ground in the mill of a set of inescapable and ultimately meaningless conventions.

Their defeats are figured twice in the opening pages of the

text. They are suggested first by the allusion to the commercial network of printers and papermakers which connects Paris and Angoulême, a slow, inefficient medium for the transmission of technological innovation from Paris to the provinces, which is yet capable of gobbling up Angoulême's paper production to feed the voracious mechanical presses of the capital. These mechanical presses, furthermore, can be seen as metaphors for the system itself and its own impersonal, insatiable appetite not only for paper, but for ideas of a provincial inventor and, potentially, at least, for the texts of a provincial poet.[11]

Secondly, Balzac's description of the career of Lucien's father offers a metaphysical variation on the theme of the destruction of the individual by blind, impersonal forces. For the elder Chardon these forces were not printing presses or economic exploiters, but nature, chance, and death:

> Nature had made a chemist of Monsieur Chardon, Senior, and chance had set him up as a pharmacist in Angoulême. Death surprised him in the midst of certain preparations made necessary by a lucrative discovery, the fruit of many years of scientific study. (V, 140)[12]

Paper from Angoulême, then, is consumed by Parisian presses, texts from Angoulême's poets are consumed if not published by Parisian publishers, and the ideas of Angoulême's inventor are consumed by Angoulême's own capitalists. Similarly the hopes and labors of Angoulême's experimental druggist were consumed by a cruel fate, and those of his son will be smashed by a combination of systems that he does not understand.

Let us look more carefully now at Lucien's career in Paris as one manifestation of the pattern of the individual threatened by a large, impersonal force. Lucien's first encounter with the world of journalism is emblematic of his future relations with this world. Like Rastignac at Madame de Restaud's, Lucien presents himself at what he takes to be the editorial offices of one of the popular newspapers, and like Rastignac, his inexperience leads him to error. Unlike Rastignac, however, whose social gaffes lead him to an understanding of the economic and emotional truths behind the Restauds' brilliant establishment, Lucien's mistaken identification of a room *labeled* "Bureau de Rédaction" as the actual editorial office of the paper leads him nowhere. Rastignac in possession of the secret of the Restauds is on his way to an understanding of Parisian society: Lucien, having stepped boldly into what he takes to be the nerve center of the paper he wants to serve, finds a dusty, disused mock-up of an editor's office, an emptiness where he had expected to find a center. "'So where is the paper put together?'" Lucien wonders, and the porter replies, "'The paper, monsieur, is put together in the street, in the authors' rooms, at the printshop, between eleven o'clock and midnight'" (V, 333).[13] Its center, in other words, is not to be found in any one place, but shifts with the physical and ideological perambulations of the interested parties. Its secret is not a hidden fact, but a skill and a talent, a way of behaving in order to make the most of its unpredictable tides and fashions. Like *Illusions perdues* itself, a text without a center, which points its reader toward no single meaning, the newspaper cannot be pinned down either physically or, as it turns out, ideologically.

The paper, furthermore, is part of a system of political and economic debts and obligations as complex as the social world of Mesdames de Restaud and de Beauséant, but less concrete and more threatening. Lucien, for his part, makes assumptions about this system that are as naive as his predecessor Rastignac's. When, for example, the porter asks him what he wants with the editor-in-chief, he replies simply enough that he wants to become "'a contributor who works well and therefore is paid well.'" "'You're just like all the draftees who want to be field-marshals!'" replies this former military person, amused at Lucien's innocence and his ambition (V, 334).[14] Later on, Lucien's "friend," Lousteau, further ridicules the notion of the journalist as a regular, well-paid worker. He himself lives by journalism, he says, but only through dealing in payola:

"I live by selling tickets given me by theater directors in return for my favors in the paper, and books sent to me by publishers for review. Then, too, I sell off the tributes in kind brought to me by manufacturers for or against whom my editor, who gets his cut, allows me to write articles. *Carminative Water, The Cream of the Sultanas, Cephalic Oil,* and *Brazilian Mixture* pay thirty or forty francs for a scoffing article. I'm forced to bark at the publisher who gives the paper too few copies, since the paper itself takes two that the editor sells, and I need two to sell myself. If he were to publish a masterpiece, the publisher who's stingy with review copies would take a beating. It's a low business, but I live by it, like a hundred others." (V, 343–44)[15]

Lucien is unabashed by this description of the monstrously demeaning system of journalistic bribery. He perseveres, and gets his notorious big break, the chance to toss off and read an article in the presence of the editor, an article which brings the salon to its feet to applaud its brilliant young author. In the same evening, Lucien makes the conquest of a much sought-after young actress, Coralie, and Balzac is able to report that he had "one foot in Coralie's bed, and the other caught in the birdlime of the daily press" (V, 402).[16]

Even after this amazing coup, however, Lucien is far from understanding the nefarious ins and outs of the journalistic system, and seems to think he has won a permanent place in this subliterary world by the sheer power of his talent. Later the same evening Claude Vignon decries journalism as an unscrupulous and irresponsible profession, and although Lucien is present, he makes no comment and is apparently unaffected. "'The press,'" says Vignon,

"instead of performing a sacred duty became a tool of the parties; from a tool it turned into a form of trade, and like all trade it now lacks faith and principles. . . . *Collective crimes implicate no one.* A paper can allow itself the most atrocious conduct, and no one feels personally soiled by it." (V, 404)[17]

And as if this were not enough, Vignon predicts, still in Lucien's presence, that the young man's naïveté, his intelligence, and his good looks will earn him no favors in the profession, which will

use him for what he is worth and discard him when he has
served its purpose:

> "Lucien! he's handsome, he's a poet and, even more valuable
> for him, a wit. So he'll join one of those intellectual brothels
> called newspapers, he'll throw his best ideas into it, dry out
> his brain, corrupt his soul, commit in its pages those cowardly
> acts that replace in the war of ideas the strategies, pillaging,
> arson, and quick reversals in the wars of the *condottieri*.
> When, like a thousand others, he has used up his genius for
> the benefit of the stockholders, those poison-merchants will
> let him die of hunger if he's thirsty and of thirst if he's hun-
> gry. (V, 406–407)[18]

A few pages later, Finot himself, the redoubtable editor-in-
chief, initiates Lucien to his staff in terms which so flatter his
pride that he either fails to perceive or believes he can afford to
ignore the base, conniving, back-stabbing relations among his
colleagues that they imply:

> "Between ourselves, you can bring me as many as two sheets
> a month for my weekly Review, and I'll pay you two hundred
> francs for them. Don't talk about this arrangement to anyone:
> all those wounded prides would take vengeance on me for a
> new arrival's good fortune. Make four articles of your two
> sheets, and sign two with your own name and two with a
> pseudonym, so as not to seem to be taking bread out of other
> people's mouths. You owe your position to Blondet and Vig-
> non, who think you have a future, so don't botch it. And
> above all, don't trust your friends." (V, 432–33)[19]

In the end, Lucien's downfall proceeds directly from his willful
disregard for these warnings, and his underestimation of the
power of the associated journalists to stamp him out without
any one of them feeling the slightest personal remorse. When
the young man from the provinces breaks with the liberals who
launched him and rallies to the cause of the Government and
the ultras in the hopes of obtaining official sanction for his claim
to the name of de Rubempré, a move which his cynical col-

leagues would have applauded in a man like Finot (V, 433–34), they seize the occasion as an excuse for wreaking their vengeance on him.[20] "The poet's alleged treason," Balzac writes,

> was then described in the most poisonous terms and embellished with the most aggravating circumstances. . . . Everyone felt instinctively that a young, handsome, witty man whom they had corrupted was going to make it big; they therefore used all the means at their disposal to defeat him. (V, 520–21)[21]

So Lucien, the perfect dupe, falls into the trap his "friends" have laid for him, writes an article ridiculing the King and the very Garde des Sceaux who is alleged (falsely, as it turns out) to be about to grant him the letters patent of the comte de Rubempré, and finds himself accused of treachery by both sides, evicted from the ministry, hated by the liberals, and finally willing to admit he has been a fool:

> Lucien found himself on the Place Vendôme, as stupefied as a man who's just been hit on the head with a bludgeon. He returned on foot along the boulevards, trying to judge himself. He saw himself as the plaything of envious, greedy, and wicked men. (V, 538)[22]

Lucien's fall from this point on is precipitous, and it is not long before we see him bury his mistress, accept a pittance which her faithful servant earns for him by prostituting herself, and set out for Angoulême, broken.

Lucien's experience with the Parisian journalists is in many ways mirrored by David Séchard's with the bankers and lawyers of Angoulême. Both are subjected to humiliation and reduced to poverty by systems they do not understand, but David's defeat is deservedly less devastating, since his original mistakes were the products of commercial naiveté, single-minded scientific concentration, and kindheartedness, rather than self-centered, cynical ambition.

The tightfisted, old-fashioned commercial practices of David's father have made the problem of competition with more enlightened establishments inevitable for the young printer. The old man is perfectly aware of the crisis to come, and delighted to be escaping from it. In the opening pages of the text Balzac tells us that when old Séchard learned that the papermaking concern of Cointet Frères had acquired a license to print a paper in Angoulême, he rejoiced that "the conflict which would arise between his own establishment and that of the Cointets would be sustained by his son and not by himself" (V, 126–27).[23] Shortly thereafter the Cointets are alluded to again, this time in even more ominous tones:

> The name of *Cointet frères* frightened him; he saw it dominating that of *Séchard et fils*. In short, the old man smelt misfortune on the wind. His presentiment was correct; misfortune was hovering over the house of Séchard. (V, 137)[24]

So even before David takes over the family business, it is clearly headed for hard times: his neglect of day-to-day affairs in favor of scientific experiments only makes its demise more certain and more rapid. In the first weeks of his incumbency debts pile up and troubles multiply. His wife Eve, Lucien's sister, is forced to sell her wedding jewelry and silverware to pay one note, and sets out on her own to reissue a once-popular peasants' almanac. Lucien in Paris requires money, and gets it first by begging from David and Eve, then by forging David's name to some notes of hand. The time is ripe for the Cointets to deploy their forces.

Their first move is to sabotage Eve Séchard's printing project by bribing her foreman, Cérizet, with offers of a better job, money, even glory, to slow down the work until they can issue a competitor. The purpose of this maneuver is to bring the Séchards to such an untenable commercial position that they will agree to give up printing altogether, and lease their shop to the Cointets. After this has happened, and the Cointets have made the Séchards dependent for their daily bread on the rent they pay them, they can bring to bear the shabby and sinister forces

of French commercial law to accomplish their ultimate goal, the
acquisition at the least possible cost of David's valuable
invention.

It is at this point that David's plight comes more and more
to resemble Lucien's: the byways of commercial law are every
bit as treacherous as the back rooms of Parisian journalism, and
the effect on both of the "two poets" from Angoulême is comparable to the effect of the "ravenous mechanical presses" on
Angoulême's paper. One way or another, they eat them up.

The forces of law are embodied in the two-faced young law-
yer, Petit-Claud, who pretends to be representing David's interests while all along manipulating the affair for the benefit of
the Cointets, who have promised to help him make an advan-
tageous marriage.

"In the provinces, . . ." Balzac writes,

> lawyers cultivate what is known in Parisian law offices as
> *pettyfogging* [*la broutille*—"nibbling"], that mass of little
> documents that load their accounts with costs and use up
> stamped paper. (V, 587)[25]

> Ninety readers out of a hundred will be as allured by the
> following details as they are by the spiciest bit of news. And
> so once again the truth of this axiom will be proven:
> "Nothing is less well known than that which everyone
> ought to know, THE LAW!" (V, 591)[26]

Petit-Claud uses the laws concerning the rights of debtors on
David's behalf in such a way as to run him deeper and deeper
into debt while leaving him free to work on the invention that
the Cointets hope to take over once it is perfected. Balzac takes
the opportunity for one of his marvelous outraged treatises on
law and business, a treatise which makes the mechanical presses
of Paris seem benign and the motives and devices of journalists
seem absolutely transparent when compared with the malignity
and incomprehensibility of the French legal system:

> You would not believe to what extent the function of banker
> attached to the august title of creditor changes the condition

of the debtor. Thus "on the Bank" (note this expression), as soon as a bill transferred from Paris to Angoulême remains unpaid, the bankers owe it to themselves to draw up what the law calls a return account.

Puns aside, no novelist has ever invented a more unlikely account than this one, for these are the ingenious jokes authorized by a certain article of the commercial code, and whose explanation will demonstrate how many atrocities lie hidden beneath that terrible word: Legality! (V, 591)[27]

There follows an account of the manipulations which in two months raise the cost of making good one of Lucien's forged thousand-franc notes from the face value plus thirty-seven francs and forty-five centimes in fees, to a total of nineteen hundred twenty-six francs and forty-five centimes.

All this time David and Eve believe that Petit-Claud is their friend, the Cointets their honest if aggressive competitors, and their troubles due to unscrupulous middlemen and check-cashers. It takes their faithful Alsatian laborer Kolb to uncover the depth of corruption which surrounds them: "'You haf scountrelss all rount you'" ["'Vus êdes endourés de goguins'"] (V, 624), he tells them, and says they should think of hiding David away in case his enemies try to have him arrested.

This is just what they do try, and the Cointets are temporarily stymied by David's disappearance. By this time, however, Lucien has returned home, sick and in disgrace, so they and Petit-Claud can crank up their infernal machine once again, this time for use against the "celebrated author of the *Marguérites*." Petit-Claud organizes a series of tributes to Lucien, who plays directly into his hands: "The shrewdest journalist may find himself very dense when it comes to commercial matters, and Lucien was bound to become, as he did, the plaything of Petit-Claud" (V, 660).[28] The upshot of Petit-Claud's maneuvers is that David is lured out of hiding and arrested, and Lucien leaves Angoulême for the last time, with the intention of committing suicide.

As it turns out, of course, David is soon freed from jail by his acceptance of the Cointets' propositions, and from the clutches of these men of business by his ultimate indifference to commercial success. Petit-Claud "obtains" a prearranged settlement from the Cointets, and the Séchards retire to the country:

> "We owe you a great deal," said Séchard to Petit-Claud.
>
> "But I've just ruined you," Petit-Claud answered his astonished former clients. "I have ruined you, I repeat, as you will see in time, but I know you. You prefer ruin to a fortune that would perhaps have come too late."
>
> "We are not greedy, Monsieur, and we thank you for giving us the means to be happy," said Madame Eve; "and you will always find us grateful." (V, 730–31)[29]

The case of David Séchard, then, is something like the case of Lucien Chardon, which is something like the case of Monsieur Chardon *père,* and the fates of all these men resemble that of some crude raw material devoured by a giant machine, whether that machine be fate or journalistic infighting or legal hanky-panky or a "ravenous mechanical press." All these cases, furthermore, bear an undeniable resemblance to life in the world. Balzac, as we know very well,[30] was deeply involved in both journalism and printing, and constantly being prosecuted for debt. Young men of talent in the post-Napoleonic era were cynical and disillusioned, out of work and out of hope, ripe for exploitation by the newly-developing money-machines.[31] And the mechanical press itself was just being introduced to France.[32] When we try, however, to reduce all these resemblances to some kernel of meaning, if we try to get at what Balzac in his novelistic representation of recognizable patterns of events in the world was "trying to say," we are ourselves reduced to banalities. In *Le Père Goriot* the existence of some "truth" is implied by the thematization of the act of interpretation, yet the nature of that truth remains elusive. In *Illusions perdues* the truth, such as it is, is self-evident: the meek, the naive, and the trusting are likely to be ground up in the mill of the powerful, the exploitative, and the conniving. Times were bad, as Lukacs points out, for young men with illusions, and they haven't gotten much better, but can such a truism stand as the center, the purpose, the meaning of a great literary work?

The answer, it seems to me, is *no*. Any attempt to locate the "center" of *Illusions perdues* in the meaning or even the truth behind one of its themes must be doomed, like Lucien's attempt to penetrate the central editorial office of Finot's newspaper, to disappointment if not to failure. If there is any important truth in *Illusions perdues*, any permanent metaphysical value like those that Rastignac and the reader of *Le Père Goriot* are led to look for, it resides far from the trivial "center" of the journalistic or the financial world, in the cold hearths of the Cénacle poets, perhaps, or the warm bosom of the family Lucien has left behind. As for the center of the text, it shifts with the course of the narration, as the system of echoes and resonances it establishes organizes and reorganizes itself around the reader. The meaning of the text is to be found in the way that its events and characters must be read, not as signs of a hidden truth but as representations of each other and of events and characters in the world.

The importance of this meaning in the text and in the world of the novel is underlined, furthermore, by Balzac's continued attention to the nature of language. We remember that in the first few paragraphs he described the Séchard printshop as a linguistic paradise in which things mean just what they seem to mean, and signs are clearly motivated. Lucien first leaves this paradise for the provincial salon of Madame de Bargeton, where he reads some poems for a singularly unappreciative audience. Here there is hardly any communication at all, since hardly anyone is willing to give Lucien the kind of attention that is necessary for poetry:

> Poetry requires devout attention if it is to be recited properly by the voice, or grasped by the mind. An intimate bond must be created between the audience and the reader, without which those electric communications of feeling cannot take place. (V, 199)[33]

In fact, those who understand poetry try to foster in their souls the seed that the author has planted in his verses. But these cold listeners, far from breathing in the soul of the poet, were not even listening to his recitation. (V, 200)[34]

When Lucien reads his most impassioned piece, a thinly disguised love poem to Madame de Bargeton, Madame Zéphirine (Fifine) de Sénonches declares in a most exasperatingly knowing way, "'After all, it's just phrases, and love is poetry in action'" (V, 205).[35]

The desire to understand is absent from this salon, but the intention to communicate remains: the listener may be dull, but the language itself still carries a meaning. In the world of Parisian journalism, language is devalued even further, until it becomes little more than a means of filling pages, pages that together form a newspaper which is very likely sold in large quantities to subscribers who only buy it to insure that it will not slander them. Communication is by definition impossible, because the writer is no longer a sender of messages but a composer of copy. Lucien learns this lesson slowly. When Lousteau suggests that he take his revenge on Raoul Nathan by writing a deprecatory article on his novel, a second edition of which is about to appear, Lucien replies,

"But what can be said against this book? It is beautiful."
"Come now, my friend, learn your trade!" Lousteau said, laughing. "Even if the book were a masterpiece, it would have to become under your pen a stupid bit of nonsense, a dangerous and unhealthy work."
"But how?"
"You change the beauties into faults."
"I am incapable of such a tour de force." (V, 442)[36]

Lousteau goes on to demonstrate what he means by extemporizing a critical review of the novel. Lucien is baffled and believes, despite what has just been said, that Lousteau actually dislikes the book in question, and that he himself has misjudged it.

Listening to Lousteau, Lucien was stupefied. At the words of the journalist the scales fell from his eyes and he discovered literary truths which he had not even suspected. "But what you are saying is full of reason and insight," he cried. (V, 444–45)[37]

So Lucien writes the article, and Nathan is suitably humiliated. Lousteau reports this fact, and suggests that Lucien do something to mollify his colleague:

"We saw Nathan this morning. He is in despair. But you're going to do him up an article praising him to the skies."

"What? After my article against his book you want . . ." asked Lucien.

. . . .

"You really believed what you wrote, then?" Hector asked Lucien.

"Yes."

"Well, my boy," said Blondet, "I thought better of you than that." (V, 456–57)[38]

Unfortunately for Lucien, he finally catches on to the blatant hypocrisy of the journalistic system, so that when he is forced to write a negative review of his former friend d'Arthez's novel, which he admires, he is able to turn one out. Utterly despondent, he carries the review to d'Arthez, who works a kind of reverse magic with it, making it express, even in its negative terms, the respect Lucien feels for the work. The resulting text is no less hypocritical than the first one in its superficial criticism of d'Arthez's novel, but it is somewhat more authentic in its underlying attitude. Lucien's writing the review at all, however, remains an act of bad faith, for which he is publicly humiliated by another member of the Cénacle, Michel Chrétien. The whole episode teaches Lucien a limited lesson about the use of language *in journalistic reviews,* but he does not carry over what he has learned about the written word to his experience with the spoken word, and when he returns to Angoulême he is every bit as bamboozled by Petit-Claud's flattery as he had been by the false friendship of the journalists.

If language cannot be relied upon to convey meaning, either because its receiver is not willing to pay attention to it or because its sender has no meaning to convey, or because it has degenerated from an original, simple state,[39] then perhaps the best thing to do with it is to multiply examples of its possible functions and patterns, to craft these examples as carefully as possible, and to arrange them in such a way that they reflect and resonate with each other, creating a verbal mobile whose significance lies not in its elusive center but in the relationships it suggests, however fleetingly, among its parts.

This is what Balzac has done with his words, his plot, and his characters in *Illusions perdues,* and the result is a text which takes its place among other objects in the world as a reflector and a refractor, an optical instrument to help its user see relationships among the systems it represents and creates and those he experiences. "The question of representation," writes Peter Brooks, "is at the very heart of *Illusions perdues,*"[40] and while we may wonder whether *Illusions perdues* has any heart at all, we can agree with Brooks's estimation of the importance of representation. *Illusions perdues* is a lesson in representation just as *Le Père Goriot* is a lesson in interpretation: it is a textual representation of a "reality" which is itself constituted by sets of events that come to represent one another in Balzac's and the reader's perception. The significance of the represented systems in *Illusions perdues* lies not in some truth that they represent but in the fact of representation itself and the role it plays in our perception of a world—fictive or actual—in which things are never only what they are but always also analogues, reminders, and representations of other things. The success of the novel depends on its brilliant combination of verisimilitude, social criticism, literary complexity, and aesthetic integrity in a text so richly representational that any single element of it—the theater, journalism, society, business, love, family relations—can be seen as suggesting all the others without sacrificing one jot of its own particularity.

The Princess Casamassima

The success of *The Princess Casamassima* depends upon a similar combination of effects, and if James's novel falls short of Balzac's triumph and his own earlier and later triumphs, it is because of the difficulty he had in balancing the claims of the social, the moral, the political, and the aesthetic. Like *Illusions perdues* in the *Comédie humaine*, *The Princess Casamassima* has a special place in the James canon, sharing with its predecessor, *The Bostonians,* an attention to the details of mundane experience and the observable features of political movements which is missing from the rest of James's novels. Lionel Trilling may have been exaggerating when he declared that "of all James's novels these are the two which are most likely to make an immediate appeal to the reader of today" and found in them a prescient vision of the effects of "wars and concentration camps" on man's understanding of human nature,[41] but it is nonetheless true that they come as a surprise to the reader who thinks he understands James's oeuvre as it develops from *The American* and *The Portrait of a Lady* to *What Maisie Knew* and *The Ambassadors*. Representation has its place in these texts, of course, and in such shorter works as *The Spoils of Poynton, The Europeans,* and *Washington Square,* but in *The Bostonians* and *The Princess Casamassima* it usurps the central position.

Both these novels were written in the mid-1880s, a period when James was interested in the activities of the French Naturalists. He had met Flaubert and his circle as early as 1875, but his interest in the group did not flower into print until the period surrounding his trip to Paris in 1884, in which he wrote "The Art of Fiction" (1884), the essay on Daudet (1883), and, stretching it a little, that on Maupassant (1888), not to mention *The Bostonians* and *The Princess Casamassima*. The actual in-

fluence of these men on James has been discussed in some detail
by Lyall H. Powers in *Henry James and the Naturalist Movement* and by Philip Grover in *Henry James and the French
Novel*. It is most often summed up in James's own words to
William Dean Howells in a letter from Paris in February 1884:

> I have been seeing something of Daudet, Goncourt and Zola;
> and there is nothing more interesting to me now than the ef-
> fort and experiment of this little group, with its truly infernal
> intelligence of art, form, manner—its intense artistic life.
> They do the only kind of work, today, that I respect; and in
> spite of their ferocious pessimism and their handling of un-
> clean things, they are at least serious and honest. The floods
> of tepid soap and water which under the name of novels are
> being vomited forth in England, seem to me, by contrast, to
> do little honour to our race.[42]

Not surprisingly, James seems most impressed in this passage
with the Naturalists' attention to "art, form [and] manner."
They are for him primarily artists; their great advantage over
their British counterparts is the care they take with style and
technique. The group's hallmark for general readers, of course,
is its choice of subject matter and its faithful representation of
the look of the world. In the 1880s, under their direct influence,
James interested himself for a while in these matters, too.

He was, in the first place, simultaneously disgusted and fascinated by the Naturalists' "unclean" subjects, subjects that re-
pelled him, it should immediately be noted, not by their sexual
or moral unconventionality but by their vulgarity.[43] James himself had already written about adultery (Madame Merle), bas-
tardy (Pansy Osmond), and genteel prostitution (Noémie
Nioche), but always by implication rather than sordid description, and always among the well-washed classes. What he ob-
jected to in Zola was not so much the morals of the characters
as their odor:

> M. Zola's uncleanness is not a thing to linger upon, but it is
> a thing to speak of, for it strikes us as an extremely curious

phenomenon. In this respect *Nana* has little to envy its predecessors. The book is, perhaps, not pervaded by that ferociously bad smell which blows through *L'Assomoir* like an emanation from an open drain and makes the perusal of the history of Gervaise and Coupeau very much such an ordeal as the crossing of the Channel in a November gale; but in these matters comparisons are as difficult as they are unprofitable, and *Nana* is, in all conscience, untidy enough.[44]

He did balk, too, at unrestrained sensuality, and was later to castigate Maupassant for paying too much attention to man's sensual nature and not enough to his intellectual and moral capacities,[45] but his main objection to the Naturalists was their unfortunate predilection for the *low* and the *ugly*. One way of understanding *The Princess Casamassima* is as an attempt to meet the Naturalists on their own ground without mimicking their vulgarity, to "do" a *low* subject without descending to sordidness or sensuality.

The Naturalists' subjects were not only unclean, however, but panoramic and, above all, closely related to actual places and social conditions. By the time James wrote "The Art of Fiction," he was clearly eager to work with such material, if only to prove that even the most unlikely subject could be beautifully "done." Furthermore, he was ready for a change. The international theme had provided him with a successful novel in *The American,* a popular short story in "Daisy Miller," and any number of minor pieces, before culminating in *The Portrait of a Lady,* a text which combined the thematic appeal of the "American girl" with the literary sophistication of the interpretation model discussed above in connection with *The American.* It was time he tried his hand at something more panoramic, at something with the "pictorial quality" of Daudet. His first attempt was to be a text "as local, as American, as possible, and as full of Boston: an attempt to show that I *can* write an American story"[46]—*The Bostonians*. His second, which followed hard upon it, was *The Princess Casamassima*.

Despite the marvelous set pieces on Cape Cod and Olive's

view of the Back Bay, and the Balzacian description of Basil Ransom's New York lodgings, *The Bostonians* is finally less panoramic than elegiac. The Boston it depicts is not the modern city, home of the Irish immigrants, poor dressmakers, and rising shopgirls, as well as Beacon Hill suffragettes, but rather the former home of Emerson and Garrison and "Eliza P. Moseley," a spiritual city threatened by profound intellectual ennui.[47] It is only in *The Princess Casamassima* that James attempts a specifically naturalistic panorama of city life, a panorama whose "prime idea was unmistakeably the ripe round fruit of perambulation" (I, v) and observation, rather than any preconceived idea of Englishness or Londonism.

Before examining this panorama directly, however, it will be helpful to look at one other issue raised by James's encounter with the Naturalists, the problem of the epistemological status of representation and its moral and aesthetic value. Representation, for James, was at least as much a matter of imagination as of observation. Mere observation, he believed, was neither a sufficient nor even a necessary prerequisite for successful representation. The important thing was what he called "experience," the conscious play of the mind with even the most insignificant bits of observed material:

> Experience is never limited, and it is never complete; it is an immense sensibility, a kind of huge spider-web of the finest silken threads suspended in the chamber of consciousness, and catching every air-borne particle in its tissue. It is the very atmosphere of the mind; and when the mind is imaginative—much more when it happens to be that of a man of genius—it takes to itself the faintest hints of life, it converts the very pulses of the air into revelations. The young lady living in a village has only to be a damsel upon whom nothing is lost to make it quite unfair (as it seems to me) to declare to her that she shall have nothing to say about the military.[48]

Experience, in other words, is not composed of events alone, or even primarily, but of events and the preexisting patterns—the spider-webs in the chamber of consciousness—by which we

grasp and order them. This is not to say that James underesti-
mated the importance of getting one's facts right—indeed, he
made at least one Zolaesque fact-finding excursion in preparation for writing *The Princess Casamassima*[49]—but only to suggest that the act of representation, whether to oneself in the processes of imagination or to others in literary texts or political
theories, is essentially an act of mind, not an unconscious
reflection.

The moral and aesthetic values of *literary* representation
were for James the great discovery of the French Naturalists,
whose special kind of *modernité* he described this way:

> It is partly physical, partly moral, and the shortest way to
> describe it is to say that is a more analytic consideration of
> appearances. It is known by its tendency to resolve its discov-
> eries into pictorial form. It sees the connection between feel-
> ings and external conditions, and it expresses such relations
> as they have not been expressed hitherto. It deserves to win
> victories, because it has opened its eyes well to the fact that
> *the magic of the arts of representation lies in their appeal to
> the associations awakened by things.*[50]

The "entertainment" to be derived from the Naturalists, that
"miraculous enlargement of experience"[51] that James enjoyed
in the world of Daudet, resulted from the combination of the
aesthetically pleasing multiplication of pictorial forms and the
morally enlightening revelation of the relation of these forms to
one another and to patterns of human behavior. As we have
seen, this is just the kind of entertainment afforded by *Illusions
perdues*.

The question of the moral and aesthetic value of *nonliterary*
representation is also important for James, so important, in fact,
that he deals with it only in fictional texts, where his characteristic irony and lightness of touch allow him to discuss the problem without making pronouncements on it. Madame Merle and
Gilbert Osmond in *The Portrait of a Lady*, for example, create
representations of themselves for variously mercenary and aesthetic ends, and their activity comes to seem artificial, sterile,

and even wicked. Gabriel Nash, on the other hand, declares in *The Tragic Muse* that his life is his best work of art, yet remains vital, sympathetic, and certainly no more sterile than Julia Dallow or Mr. Carteret. Olive Chancellor in *The Bostonians* represents the world to herself and Verena Tarrant in one way and Basil Ransom represents it in an opposing way. Both believe in their representations, but also use their versions of the way things are and ought to be as tools to gain the love and respect of the confused young girl. Hyacinth Robinson, as we will see, is finally overcome by his own and other people's representations of the ways of the world.

The "magic of the arts of representation," then, was clearly on James's mind in the mid-1880s, as he was planning and writing *The Princess Casamassima*. Twenty years later, in the preface to the New York Edition of the text, his perspective has changed somewhat, and his attention is focused more narrowly on the representation of states of mind. Here he writes that

> the figures in any picture, the agents in any drama, are interesting only in proportion as they feel their respective situations; since the consciousness, on their part, of the complication exhibited forms for us their link of connexion with it.
>
> . . . .
>
> I confess I never see the *leading* interest of any human hazard but in a consciousness (on the part of the moved and moving creature) subject to fine intensification and wide enlargement. (I, vii–viii, xii)

What sets *The Princess Casamassima* off from James's other "social" novels of the 1880s is its particular liability to description from either perspective: the panorama it represents is wider, though not necessarily richer, than theirs, and its central character can boast a more complicated consciousness than Basil Ransom or Nick Dormer and a more fully represented one than Olive Chancellor or Julia Dallow. The resultant doubleness is an essential element of *The Princess Casamassima;* indeed, it can be argued that Hyacinth Robinson's precarious position between anarchism and aristocracy parallels James's own wavering between Naturalism and the more subjective psychological impressionism he was eventually to adopt, and is emblematic of the ambiguous nature of the text itself, whose descriptions of low life and subtle analyses of feelings and impressions can seem irrelevant and indispensable by turns.

The Princess Casamassima is a successful experiment on several levels of textual representation. It succeeds first of all in conveying the impression of the "objective" representation of details, the painting of scenes of London life. The description of Millbank Prison, "got up" à la Zola, is the most celebrated example of this strain. James's "grey stony courts, in some of which dreadful figures, scarcely female, in hideous brown misfitting uniforms and perfect frights of hoods, were marching round in a circle" (I, 46) are the most strikingly naturalistic details in all his fiction. Equally impressive, and equally unexpected to the reader of both the earlier and the later James, are his remarkably specific account of Pinnie's "showroom," and his report on the deliciously low and immoral Hennings, surely the closest he ever came to the stench of *L'Assomoir*.

Passing in after her guest she found the young lady already spread out upon the sofa, the everlasting sofa covered in a tight shrunken shroud of strange yellow stuff, the tinge of which revealed years of washing, and surmounted by a coloured print of Rebekah at the Well, balancing in the opposite quarter, against a portrait of the Empress of the French taken from an illustrated newspaper and framed and glazed in the manner of 1853. (I, 58)

The freedom and frequency of Mrs. Henning's relations with a stove-polisher off the Euston Road were at least not a secret to a person who lived next door. . . . The little Hennings, unwashed and unchidden, spent most of their time either in pushing each other into the gutter or in running to the public-house at the corner for a pennyworth of gin, and the borrowing propensities of their elders were a theme for exclamation. There was no object of personal or domestic use which Mrs. Henning had not at one time or another endeavoured to elicit

from the dressmaker; beginning with a mattress, on an occasion when she was about to take to her bed for a considerable period, and ending with a flannel petticoat and a pew-
ter teapot. (I, 63–64)

The language here is all James's, to be sure, but the scenes are
as common and as detailed as a Zola could have wished them.
In other places, James is at pains to reproduce the speech of the
common folk:

There were men who kept saying, "Them was my words in
the month of February last, and what I say I stick to—what
I say I stick to"; and others who perpetually enquired of the
company, "And what the plague am I to do with seventeen
bob—with seventeen bloody bob? What am I to do with
them—will ye tell me that?" (I, 338–39)

"Perpetually enquired of the company" is James again, but the
attempt at common speech seems honest enough.

The same could be said about James's treatment of the social
system in *The Princess Casamassima*. He seems conscientiously
intent on presenting a picture of all the relevant social classes
and the relations among them. From the unwashed sordidness
of the Hennings to the shabby poverty of Pinnie and Mr. Vetch,
from the working-class comforts of the Poupins to the petty-
bourgeois gentility of the ugly harp-playing Miss Crookendens,
to the various representatives of the aristocracy, dissolute Captain Sholto, angelic Lady Aurora, the insipid Miss Marchant,
and the Prince and the Princess themselves, James aptly fills
the slots of the social world and chronicles the nuances of class
consciousness. Millicent Henning, for example, is a defiantly
respectable young shopgirl, proud of never having worked with
her hands (I, 62) and surprised that her friend Hyacinth has
decided to "follow a trade" (I, 67). She admires the upper
classes (II, 329) and is more than willing to be patronized by
them, especially as they are embodied in the form of Captain
Sholto. Pinnie and Rosy Muniment share this lower-class admiration for the aristocracy, which Rosy expresses early in the

text in a sentence which might later be endorsed by Hyacinth himself. "'I haven't the least objection to seeing the people improved,'" she all self-importantly announces, "'but I don't want to see the aristocracy lowered an inch. I like so much to look at it up there'" (I, 146). Lady Aurora, on the other hand, is ashamed of her rank and its perquisites, while the Princess finds them tiresome. Meanwhile the anarchists at the "Sun and Moon" blame their unfortunate positions on the upper classes, and the leaders like the mysterious Hoffendahl plot their overthrow.

All through his description of these various social classes James draws fine distinctions and uses them ironically to deflate his characters' pretensions. Poupin, for example, is a flaming Communard with a comfortable bourgeois *intérieur* in Lisson Grove. When the Princess sells all she has to give to the poor (retaining her Italian maid, but keeping her hidden), Paul Muniment comes to visit and tells her she's "'got a lovely home'" (II, 230). The wealthy Miss Marchant betrays abject mental poverty in her "conversation" with Hyacinth: "She had . . . a beautiful voice and the occasional command of a few short words. She asked Hyacinth with what pack he hunted and whether he went in much for tennis, and she ate three muffins" (II, 29).

James's representation of society is so conventionally comprehensive, and his irony so equally distributed among the social classes, that he seems as documentarily objective here as he undoubtedly meant to be in his picture of the Millbank prison and his reproduction of common speech. When he comes to describe the anarchist movement, however, he is at a disadvantage, because it is by its nature not subject to his observations and researches. A workers' meeting at the "Sun and Moon" is one thing, but the ins and outs of what James suggests is an international conspiracy are quite another, and James would have been betraying his readers' trust if he had pretended to give them a true representation of such a secret system. A provincial lady may imagine life in a garrison in a general way, and even be convincing about it. A conservative novelist in London, on the other hand, is well advised not to commit himself on the subject of international conspiracy: it would be too easy for those in the know to prove him wrong and deride his error. His solution to the problem is to depict only what he later called "the suggested nearness (to all our apparently ordered life) of some sinister anarchic underworld, heaving in its pain, its power and its hate; a presentation not of sharp particulars, but of loose appearances, vague motions and sounds and symptoms, just perceptible presences and general looming possibilities" (I, xxi). W. H. Tilley has argued very convincingly that James could have gotten and probably did get all the information he needed about the anarchists from the pages of the *Times* of London, and we need not attach too much importance to Tilley's attempts to "identify" Hoffendahl and even Hyacinth Robinson himself with actual revolutionary figures to profit from his assertion that the number of rumors about anarchist plots in the 1880s was exceeded only by their vagueness.[52] James's representation of the anarchist movement does not pretend to be an exposé of things as they are, a true account of an actual political and organizational state of affairs, but rather a view of a contemporary phenomenon which would be recognizable to his audience because it was the only view that they themselves, as respectable *Times*-readers, could have. The artisans' meetings at the "Sun and Moon" are perfectly appropriate in this context: most of the known anarchists were artisans, and such political meetings are so much a part of the public's conception of underground movements as to be the common coin of the political novel.

The brilliance of James's representational scheme becomes evident when he goes behind this relatively innocent and public manifestation of the anarchic passion to suggest its hidden and ubiquitous power. He does this by having his characters intimate in vague and mysterious language that they know a great deal more than they will specify. The conspirators, Poupin, Vetch, Muniment, and later even the Princess, cultivate a mystifying form of reference which suggests that they know what

they are talking about, hides their ignorance if they do not, and
leaves the reader free to imagine the vast network of potential
terrorists to which they refer.

A case in point is Hyacinth's introduction to the very notion
of a conspiracy at the Poupins'. In the course of presenting Hyacinth to Paul Muniment, Madame Poupin announces myste-
riously that "'it was a shame not to take in M. Hyacinthe, who,
she would answer for it, had in him the making of one of the
pure.'" More mystification follows. Monsieur Poupin wonders
if he should make Hyacinth an *"interne."* "'What do you mean
by an *interne?*'" Hyacinth asks. "'Can you keep a secret?'"
asks Muniment, and when Hyacinth wonders if it is "'a plot—
a conspiracy,'" apparently decides not to tell him. "'It's a group
of workers to which he and I and a good many others belong,'"
he says. "'There's no harm in telling him that'" (I, 115). Later
that same evening Hyacinth himself, who has learned nothing
more definite about Muniment's organization, introduces a kind
of code-response which seems to mean a great deal, actually
means very little, and can therefore be interpreted by his hearers
and James's readers in any way they choose. Lady Aurora,
Rosy Muniment informs Hyacinth, is "'a tremendous socialist
. . . worse than anyone . . . worse even than Paul.'" "'I wonder
if she's worse than me,'" is Hyacinth's response, on which Paul
exclaims, "'Hullo, I didn't know you were so advanced.'"
"'You didn't know I was advanced? Why, I thought that was
the principal thing about me. I think I go about as far as anyone.'" In this case Lady Aurora comes close to calling Hyacinth's bluff, and gives James a good chance to point out just
how much of a bluff it is. "'I should like so very much to
know,'" she says, "'it would be so interesting—if you don't
mind—how far exactly you do go.'"

This challenge was hardly less alarming than the other, for
he was far from being ready with an impressive formula. He
replied, however, with a candour in which he tried as far as
possible to sink his vagueness: "Well, I'm very strong indeed.

I think I see my way to conclusions from which even Monsieur and Madame Poupin would shrink. Poupin, at any
rate; I'm not so sure about his wife." (I, 129–30)

Hyacinth clearly has very little idea what he's talking about,
but the ensuing chapters indicate that he is at least willing to
learn. The reader too is by this time eager to know what is going
on, but, like the ordinary member of society, he is permanently
barred from the councils of the mighty and left only to imagine
what Hoffendahl's program and the extent of his influence
might be. He is also, however, continually tantalized, and this
is James's genius, by a proliferation of signifiers which the characters use on each other and which suggest a vast network of
revolutionaries which everyone wants to imply he knows more
about than he actually does. So Hyacinth questions Rosy
Muniment:

—"But isn't he tremendously deep in—" What should he
call the mystery?
—"Deep in what?"
—"Well, in what's going on beneath the surface." (I, 147)

And the Princess questions Hyacinth:

—"Do you think anything will occur soon?"
—"Will occur—?"
—"That there'll be a crisis—that you'll make yourselves
felt?"
    In this beautiful woman's face there was to his bewildered
perception something at once inspiring, tempting and mock-
ing; and the effect of her expression was to make him say
rather clumsily, "I'll try to ascertain—" as if she had asked
him whether her carriage were at the door. (I, 224)

Later on, of course, one thing, Hyacinth's vow, becomes all too
evidently specific, but the vagueness of secret meetings and of
people who "go too far" in order to know that they have "gone

far enough" (II, 276) continues, and the reader's curious but unprivileged perception of the movement is preserved.

Representation here is not the circular process of infinite substitutions that it was in *Illusions perdues,* but rather a series of linguistic feints intended to suggest that each speaker knows more about the anarchist underground than he actually does. Cryptic remarks, in other words, cover a void and project an illusion; they represent nonexistent knowledge. Behind these remarks, as behind the door of the putative editorial offices in *Illusions perdues,* there is nothing.

In *Illusions perdues* the lack of central meaning that Lucien's visit to the newspaper office embodies leads Balzac to describe the world as a collection of equivalent systems, each of which resembles the others but none of which provides meaning for the others. In *The Princess Casamassima* this same lack of central, knowable meaning leads James to concentrate on representation as a mental process rather than a quality of things in the world, as a conscious mental act when we use some medium of communication to represent a thought or a physical object, whether or not that thought or object actually exists, and as a necessary element of perception when we understand sensory data as representations of real or imaginary thoughts or objects.

This shift of focus from the object of perception to the process of perception—from anarchism and elegance to the way Hyacinth perceives anarchism and elegance—solves James's problem of writing a political novel which avoids both the fatal futility of fact and the dangers of portraying actual historical figures. It cannot, however, solve Hyacinth's pressing problem of which side to choose, of whether to kill himself or the Duke. When Christopher Newman and Lambert Strether return to America, when Isabel Archer returns to Rome, when Merton Densher returns, presumably, to his job at the newspaper, they are compensated for their emotional losses by gains in sensitivity: they have become wide-ranging Jamesian consciousnesses, works of art, in fact, of their own art and of James's, which they at least will live to contemplate, all solipsistically, in their exile. Hyacinth, the penniless artisan, cannot afford to become a work of art: he must choose murder or suicide, to destroy a representative of the high culture he has come to admire, or to destroy himself.

The Princess Casamassima is at least partially successful because it *represents* political movements and people's feelings about them, and *presents itself* as a carefully shaped aesthetic object, regardless of its own and its author's uncertainty as to his and its conscious purpose. Works of art and some Jamesian characters can endure this uncertainty of purpose because their only essential purpose is to *be*. Ordinary people, however, rarely have the luxury of simply being: they must be something specific and accomplish something concrete. *The Princess Casamassima* can endure as a structured compendium of representations. Hyacinth Robinson, who stands in a similar, uncertain relation to the world, cannot. Doomed by his allegorical heredity to suffer contradictory longings for beauty and for justice, for comfort and for violent revolution, Hyacinth is finally overwhelmed by his contradictory impressions of the world, by the contradictory ways in which it represents itself to him. James may very well have seen Hyacinth's dilemma as similar to his own, and it is certainly indicative of his uneasiness about this dilemma that he portrays his young man as choosing the aesthetic over the political values, and then punishing him for his choice. Still, Hyacinth dies, while James, and *The Princess Casamassima,* live on. The choice of the aesthetic is not quite the choice of art, and for all Hyacinth's similarity to James, he is no artist. His function in the text is not to produce representations but to receive them: he is finally overcome by the quantity of contradictory representations which force themselves in upon him, rather than by any anguish over the contradictory role of the artist in society.

Hyacinth's predicament is represented most clearly in the novel by his dubious but certainly mixed parentage (he is presumably the son of a loose-living low Frenchwoman and her noble English lover, whom she has been convicted of murdering). James introduces the notions of heredity and environment in typically naturalistic fashion as an explanation for the young bookbinder's extraordinary sensitivity.[53] Hyacinth himself, when he learns who his parents were, internalizes the opposition they stand for, and uses it to represent his own conflicting desires. All through the text, in fact, James, the other characters, and finally Hyacinth himself explain aspects of his character and his behavior by reference to his parentage, and use one or the other or both of his parents or their families as models—representations—of the sort of life he ought to lead.

The reader's first view of Hyacinth is of a little boy "planted" in front of a sweet-shop window, gaping at the *Family Herald* and the *London Journal,* "where he particularly admired the obligatory illustration in which the noble characters (they were always of the highest birth) were presented to the carnal eye" (I, 5). Here, presumably, is an unconscious manifestation of Hyacinth's blue blood before he even knows he has it. Even as a boy, though, Hyacinth's hereditary glory, and his duty to live up to it, are represented to him, albeit in veiled terms, by his guardian, Miss Pynsent:

> The boy proved neither a dunce nor a reprobate; but what endeared him to her most was her conviction that he belonged, "by the left hand," as she had read in a novel, to a proud and ancient race, the list of whose representatives and the record of whose alliances she had once (when she took home some work and was made to wait, alone, in a lady's boudoir) had the opportunity of reading in a fat red book, eagerly and tremblingly consulted.
>
> . . . .
>
> To believe in Hyacinth, for Miss Pynsent, was to believe that he *was* the son of the extremely immoral Lord Frederick. She had from his earliest age made him feel that there was a grandeur in his past. (I, 10–11)

Despite her reverence for the aristocracy, however, Miss Pynsent is true to her friend, Hyacinth's mother, and young Hyacinth's vague notions of himself as fulfilling an aristocratic destiny are counterbalanced by his vision of the strange dying

woman he is taken to Millbank Prison to visit, a woman he is
made to feel has some mysterious connection with himself:

> The woman had had a wicked husband who maltreated and
> deserted her; she had been very poor, almost starving, dread-
> fully pressed. Hyacinth listened to her history with absorbed
> attention and then said:
> — "And hadn't she any children—hadn't she a little boy?"
> . . . .
> — "How can she like me so much if she has never seen
> me?" Miss Pynsent wished the gate would open before an
> answer to this question became imperative. . . . "It's because
> the little baby she had of old was also named Hyacinth."
> — "That's a rummy reason," the boy murmured, still star-
> ing across at the Battersea shore. (I, 41; I, 45–46)

As Hyacinth grows up, then, conflicting images impinge on
his consciousness, representations of what he has been, and of
what he ought by rights to become. When Miss Pynsent finally
tells Hyacinth the truth about his parentage, these images lose
their vagueness and gain strength as he begins consciously to
use them as representations of his own conflicting feelings: even
when he learns that his putative father's relatives never admitted the connection, his faith in his personal iconography is
unshaken:

> That was their affair; he had long since made up his mind
> that his own was very different. One couldn't believe at will,
> and fortunately, in the case, he had no effort to make; for
> from the moment he began to consider the established facts
> (few as they were and poor and hideous) he regarded himself
> immutably as the son of the recreant and sacrificed Lord
> Frederick.
> He had no need to reason about it; all his nerves and pulses
> pleaded and testified. His mother had been a daughter of the
> wild French people—all Pinnie could tell him of her paren-
> tage was that Florentine had once mentioned that in her ex-
> treme childhood her father, his gun in his hand, had fallen in
> the bloodstained streets of Paris on a barricade; but on the

other side it took an English aristocrat to account for him, though a poor specimen had apparently had to suffice. (I, 174)

What is important for Hyacinth and for James's project in *The Princess Casamassima* is not finally what is "objectively" the case but rather what seems to Hyacinth to be true and important. The business of the text comes to center in Hyacinth's consciousness, and the importance of the represented facts and systems comes to depend directly on their effect on him. Hyacinth is no aggressive interpreter like Christopher Newman nor is he such a simultaneous and only half-conscious victim and exploiter as Lucien Chardon. He is from the very beginning a passive and somewhat overawed receiver of representations, doing his frantic best to keep pace with the demands these representations place on his understanding.

Hyacinth has life represented to him—and represents it to himself—in so many different ways that he is finally at a loss to know what to *do* with it. So long as his life is fairly simple he can enjoy being overwhelmed by his impressions:

Everything in the field of observation suggested this or that; everything struck him, penetrated, stirred; he had in a word more news of life, as he might have called it, than he knew what to do with—felt sometimes as he could have imagined an overwhelmed man of business to whom the post brought too many letters. (I, 159–60)

So long as Hyacinth is a stroller in the city, called upon to accomplish nothing more than a daydream on a long Saturday evening, he can afford to be a receiver of messages from the world, a spinner of fantasies, a "youth on whom nothing was lost" (I, 169), to be sure, but only a potential artist because not yet an active user of these messages, impressions, and representations. He can imagine the world as a long Sunday afternoon at Medley *and* a succession of cold winter evenings at the "Sun and Moon," himself as a young aristocrat or at least an artist under the patronage of his "people" *and* a barricade-fighter with his grandfather, alternately, simultaneously, and with im-

punity, so long as he does not have to act or to choose. He can
entertain whatever representations of the world that Pinnie or
the Princess or Paul or even Rosy want to present him with,
amuse himself with them, even bother himself about them. The
trouble, as he begins to realize, is that all this entertainment,
openness, imagination, and representation will have got him no
closer to choice or action.

> It made him even rather faint to think that he must choose;
> that he couldn't (with any respect for his own consistency)
> work underground for the enthronement of the democracy
> and yet continue to enjoy in however platonic a manner a
> spectacle which rested on hideous social inequality. (I, 171)

His anxiety on this score builds up until one evening at the
"Sun and Moon" he imagines himself into such a state that he
succeeds in representing himself to his comrades as a man of
action, and for a few hours at least, actually becomes one. The
talk in the club goes on around him, "but he was following a
train of his own." "He was in a state of inward exaltation, possessed by an intense desire to stand face to face with the sublime
Hoffendahl, to hear his voice and touch his mutilated hand. He
was ready for anything" (I, 355). For once, Hyacinth is possessed by a single idea, a "faith transcending logic" (I, 356). He
steps outside for a moment and even his imaginative powers
seem at the service of his new-found resolve. He becomes his
own Zola and casts himself as his own hero:

> The puddles glittered roundabout and the silent vista of the
> street, bordered with low black houses, stretched away in the
> wintry drizzle to right and left, losing itself in the huge tragic
> city where unmeasured misery lurked beneath the dirty
> night, ominously, monstrously still, only howling, for its pain,
> in the heated human cock-pit behind him. Ah what could he
> do? What opportunity would arise? (I, 358)

The opportunity arises as soon as he reenters the pub. One
member of the club has been accusing the others and himself of
being cowards, full of talk but unwilling to put themselves on

the line for the cause. *"Vous insultez le peuple!"* cries Eustache Poupin, and Hyacinth rises to deliver an impassioned speech in which he declares that he, for one, is ready to do whatever is necessary to bring about the ends they all desire. As luck would have it, Hoffendahl is looking for just such a self-sacrificing young "gentleman" to devote himself wholly and irrevocably to the cause, so Hyacinth is whisked away into his presence, to make his vow of absolute obedience and promise to hold himself ready to carry out the master's one terrible order whenever he sees fit to give it.

So Book Two ends. Book Three opens with Hyacinth rising after a sleepless night, not because he is anxious about the consequences of his pledge, but because he is so excited to be at Medley, the Princess Casamassima's rented country house, and concerned "that his appearance shouldn't give strange ideas about him" (II, 3). He is. apparently, the same old Hyacinth, timid and ever open to new experiences:

> He had never in his life been in the country—the real country, as he called it, the country which was not the mere ravelled fringe of London—and there entered through his open casement the breath of a world enchantingly new and after his recent feverish hours unspeakably refreshing. . . . There was a world to be revealed to him: it lay waiting with the dew on it under his windows, and he must go down and take of it such possession as he might. (II, 3–4)

What has happened is that he has been liberated not for action but from responsibility. He has made the great sacrifice in advance and is now free, as he says, "to live each hour as if it were to be one's last . . . in extreme thankfulness for every good minute that's added" (II, 57).

Save for the death of Pinnie, his life in the next few months is a blissful series of beautiful impressions. Using his guardian's small legacy, he travels to Paris where he haunts the Louvre and treats himself to an ice on Tortoni's terrace. He continues to Venice where he amuses himself smoking cigarettes on a magenta divan in his hotel room, with "the works of Leopardi and

a second-hand dictionary . . . convenient to my hand," as he
writes to the Princess (II, 143). He justifies all his behavior by
reference to his vow, but he comes more and more to realize that
in freeing him from what he perceived as the moral necessity of
adhering to the revolutionary program, this vow has helped him
to realize that he never really believed in the revolution at all.[54]
He values in the end his impressions of the world of art and
ease more than any scheme to overthrow this world for the benefit of his comrades of the "Sun and Moon."

Back in London, Hyacinth's doubts return, and he realizes
that his vow has been no great decision but an abdication of
responsibility. He comforts himself by conjuring up an image
of the rise of democracy as a great tide, an inevitable movement
to which he has given himself up.

> . . . there was joy and exultation in the thought of surrender-
> ing one's self to the wash of the wave, of being carried higher
> on the sun-touched crests of wild billows than one could ever
> be by a dry lonely effort of one's own. That vision could
> deepen to ecstasy; make it indifferent if one's ultimate fate, in
> such a heaving sea, were not almost certainly to be submerged
> in bottomless depths or dashed to pieces on immovable rocks.
> (II, 263)

But this aesthetic view of revolution cannot satisfy him for long,
and he must face the fact that he is a backslider, an unbeliever
who passionately wishes for belief if only because it would bring
him peace (II, 405).

Hyacinth ends by paying the price of passivity, of keeping
himself open to everything and deciding nothing. For all his
being a young man on whom nothing is lost, he is no artist and
no revolutionary, since what is not lost on him is lost in him,
drowned in a sea of received impressions, tentatively accepted
representations of the world, never to emerge as part of that new
representation that would be a work of art or an act of revolt.
His representation of himself as a man of action is as futile, as
"aesthetic," and as passive as all his other acts. His final self-
assertion is, typically, an act of self-annihilation.

The Princess Casamassima is on one level a textual representation of certain social and political systems and conditions in
force at the time of its publication. On this level the book is
generally reliable, though rather unsatisfying when it comes to
the minutest particulars of political doctrine and organization,
and not a little disappointing in its choice of such a passive little
"hero" as Hyacinth Robinson. On another level it is an analysis
of the relation between political and moral commitment on the
one hand and aesthetic pleasure on the other, between the use
of representation—in role-playing, speech-making, storytelling—as a means to a higher end, and its enjoyment in and for
itself in art. Hyacinth fails as an anarchist and as an artist because he can neither ignore the contradictions inherent in this
relation, nor reconcile its two poles, because he cannot ade-
quately deal with the political and aesthetic impressions that
flood in upon him.

This most representational of James's novels stands paradoxically as a warning against allowing the passive reliance on novelistic and imaginative representations of the world, beautiful or
politically convincing as they may be, to take the place of personal decisions and actions. James represents in his prose the
world of London in the 1880s, the processes, cognitive and dis-
simulative, by which people *try* to understand or, failing that,
pretend to understand the mysteries around them. He shows
how the world represents itself to an impressionable young man
in terms of his own heredity, of political movements, class structures, and aesthetic values, and how that young man internalizes the representational process by indulging in endless day-
dreaming and theorizing, building alternative representations of
the world and his own place in it, partly at least in order to
keep the actual world and its decisions at arm's length. Hyacinth Robinson is defeated by the volume of representations he
feels obligated to process: like "the man of business to whom the
post brought too many letters" (I, 160), he is so busy processing
these communications that he never gets around to doing any
business.

"The magic of the arts of representation," James wrote in his

essay on Daudet, "lies in their appeal to the associations awak-
ened by things." This is certainly true in *Illusions perdues,*
where the fascination, the pleasure, and even the meaning of
the text derive from the multiple associations that the various
representations of social and individual behavior evoke. James,
however, never wrote an *Illusions perdues.* Intrigued as he was
by the possibilities of representation, he was suspicious of its
implicit claim to exhaustive truth. The truth for James, at this
stage in his life, at least, might be unattainable, but this was not
because it was embodied in the shifting perspective of a mobile
universe. Balzac was by national heritage a Pascalian Catholic
for whom truth might be a circle of infinite circumference and
indeterminate center. James was in a similar way an American
Protestant, imbued by the rationalism of his Scots forebears and
the independence of his Swedenborgian father with the notion
of the priesthood of all believers, the idea that every man is a
potentially successful interpreter of divine will. Balzac could
content himself, this once, with a textual model of endless and
repetitive representation, whose meaning was to be found in the
circular structure of representation itself. James could acknowledge the power of such a model, but he could not be happy with
it. Representation without effective interpretation was for him
a danger to be avoided, a danger of which the figure of Hyacinth
Robinson stands as a warning.[55] The truth for James might not
be attained, but it is always there, potentially attainable by the
character who interprets accurately and acts on his
interpretations.

Illusions perdues and *The Princess Casamassima* are realistic
texts by anyone's definition, but the models they develop for the
representation of human experience are symptomatic of the difficulties inherent in the notion of realism as textual reproduction of "the real." *Illusions perdues* presents the reader with a
disturbingly decentered model of reality, a model which would
come dangerously close to sacrificing the reassuring *vraisemblance* of interpretability[56] to the more strictly representational
truth of factual detail if it were not for Balzac's insistence on
the pattern of the devouring of the weak and unorganized by

the strong and systematic exploiters. It is a shorter step to *One Hundred Years of Solitude* or *V* from *Illusions perdues* than it would be from *Nana,* say, or *Sister Carrie;* Balzac's realism here teeters on the edge of absurdism as well as prefiguring Naturalism's detailed depiction of social and economic systems. *The Princess Casamassima,* on the other hand, develops an implicit intratextual critique of the representation of mere facts and systems, of the multiplication of sensory perceptions and intellectual discriminations, however fine and clever these may be. It is not a decentered text, but a text in search of a center, so uneasy with its status as "the ripe round fruit of perambulation" that it attempts to center itself on Hyacinth Robinson's inadequate consciousness and ends in a critique of its own hero's decentered ineffectuality. Balzac takes the circularity of representation as a given in *Illusions perdues,* and produces a prophetic vision of the sense of meaninglessness that pervades modern life. James recognizes and regrets Hyacinth Robinson's disorientation, but he sees it as an individual failure, historically and genetically determined, perhaps, but nonetheless blameworthy and punishable. Hyacinth Robinson kills himself because he has failed to reconcile the conflicting demands made on him by the world, failed to find a center for his life. Lucien de Rubempré does not kill himself because just as he had decided that he is the guilty center of all the cycles of exploitation in the text, Vautrin-Herrera appears on the scene, "rescues" the would-be suicide, and a new and even more fantastic cycle begins. Hyacinth Robinson and Henry James reach a dead end in their search for an honest, reliable center in the political life of the 1880s and the generic content of the naturalistic novel. Balzac and Lucien set out at the end of their joint venture in circularity to describe new and wider circles around an indeterminate, ever-changing, perhaps even nonexistent center.

4

Late Balzacian Realism:
La Cousine Bette

Balzac and James never ceased to be interested in the problematics of interpretation and representation, but they did sometimes, especially in their later years, produce texts which assume the complex nature of these processes without thematizing them. Such texts are less self-reflexive, less overtly meta-textual than the ones we have been examining, but they are not for this reason any less sophisticated, either artistically or epistemologically. Indeed, the two texts to which we turn now are not only among their authors' most complex and successful productions, they also represent significant new solutions to the problems of realistic writing and, despite their immense differences, point a single way for the future of realistic fiction.

Historical Problems

In 1847 Balzac finally completed *Splendeurs et misères des courtisanes,* the prodigious sequel to *Illusions perdues,* part of which had been sketched as early as 1834. In the same year he published *Les Parents pauvres (La Cousine Bette* and *Le Cousin Pons).* All three novels can be seen as attempts to solve the same set of aesthetic and commercial problems, but whereas Balzac's solution in *Splendeurs et misères* threatened to lead him away from realism, the solution embodied by *Les Parents pauvres* might well have led to a new cycle of realistic novels, had Balzac's health not failed him.

The first problem that Balzac had to face in the mid-1840s was how to go on writing novels about the complexities of contemporary life and society without simply repeating the formula of *Illusions perdues*. It would have been easy enough to continue the story of Lucien de Rubempré, multiplying examples of exploitation and of the debasement of language and values, describing different milieux and suggesting that each could be seen as representing all the others. Balzac was too restless, too innovative for this, however, and in *Splendeurs et misères* he intensified the circular representationality of the earlier text to such a degree that it seems at times to cross the line from realism to phantasmagoria.[1] The impulse to cross this line was already present in the decentered sensibility of *Illusions perdues,* but Balzac nowhere yielded to it so completely as he did in *Splendeurs et misères*. Here, as Christopher Prendergast points out, every conspiring group comes to represent every other conspiring group until "the opposition between society and outlaw, order and anarchy, dissolves into a conflict of morally indistinguisable forces, in which the roles of criminal and policeman are, in moral terms, wholly reversible."[2] Pierre Barbéris applauds this vision of the interchangeability of criminals and policemen, swindlers and bankers as a representation of the radical complicity of ambition, criminality, capital, and exploitation in the early capitalistic world of France in the eighteen thirties and forties.[3] Its cumulative effect, however, is to diminish the surface credibility of the text, so that it can seem, as Gaëtan Picon writes, that "it is no longer life that unfolds here, but its fantastic metamorphosis: a legend of blood and shadows."[4] We need not agree with Picon's rather harsh judgment of the fantastic and visionary aspect of Balzac's genius to see that in *Splendeurs et misères* the combination of this genius with a certain kind of representational realism had gone as far as it could. If Balzac were not, therefore, to produce more of the same kind of text as *Splendeurs et misères,* and yet were to continue as a realist, he would have to develop an alternative model for realistic fiction.

This problem was complicated by the fact that he also needed to produce texts which would suit the format of the *roman-feuil-*

leton. Balzac had himself introduced the practice of newspaper serialization when he published *La Vieille fille* in *La Presse* in 1836.[5] Others were quick to take advantage of his profitable method of publication, however, and they soon discovered narrative devices and techniques which helped them produce texts better suited for presentation in short installments than Balzac's more sustained pieces. By 1842, Eugène Sue had usurped Balzac's place as the king of the *feuilletonistes* with his *Mystères de Paris.* In 1844 Balzac attempted a comeback with the publication of *Modeste Mignon* in *feuilleton* form, but the choice of text was unfortunate, and the result a failure. Meanwhile, he had been working sporadically on *Splendeurs et misères,* publishing fragments in the *feuilletons* of the smaller papers, and in volume form, and fuming over the success of Sue's cloak-and-dagger *Mystères.* That Sue's writing, or at least his subject matter, influenced Balzac at this time is clear in the third part of *Splendeurs et misères,* published in 1846, which presents the life of the Conciergerie and the legal and psychological ins and outs of the process of a criminal investigation in copious Sue-esque detail.[6] Commercially, Sue's influence was salutary: Balzac's new text had a successful run in *feuilleton* form. Artistically, however, Balzac was not satisfied: as early as 1843 he had complained to Madame Hanska that he was "doing pure Sue."[7] *Splendeurs et misères* was for him a dead-end success; like James after his experiment in the theater, he longed to take up his "own old pen again."[8] In *La Cousine Bette* he takes up at least one of his old pens, and the result is a masterpiece of classical realism.

A Balzacian Solution: *La Cousine Bette*

As James learned the scenic method from the theater, so Balzac learned the lesson of successful *feuilleton*-writing from *Splendeurs et misères.* In *La Cousine Bette* he applied the method masterfully, writing short episodes calculated to produce both suspense and steady newspaper customers, and incorporating current events into the *feuilleton,* so that the news at the top of the page was sometimes barely distinguishable from the installment of fiction on the "ground floor."⁹

He attacks the separate problem of developing a new realistic manner with a strategy that combines retreat and advance, moving away from the complicated plot-structure of *Illusions perdues* and *Splendeurs et misères* while refining their textual density. The first part of this strategy makes *La Cousine Bette* resemble such classical Balzacian texts as *Eugénie Grandet* and *César Birotteau*. It is a neatly structured, closed-ended narrative, with none of the confusion or mystery of the last two Vautrin novels. Eugène Marron, reviewing *Les Parents pauvres* in the *Revue indépendante* of January 25, 1847, points out that these texts are pure Balzac, and do not represent some modification of the writer's principles to suit the taste of the time: "If he has happened to find himself in complete agreement with a public which for several years hasn't given him any great signs of affection, he is not the one who has changed his system, or made concessions."¹⁰ The public is experiencing, Marron goes on to point out, a "thirst for reality," and *La Cousine Bette* is there to satisfy it. Similarly, Gaëtan Picon classifies *La Cousine Bette* with the "great objective novels" of Balzac, and opposes it quite specifically to *Splendeurs et misères*.¹¹

For all this, however, *La Cousine Bette* is no more a new version of *César Birotteau* than it is of *Splendeurs et misères,* and Balzac's solution to the problems of the mid-forties was not simply to return to his mid-thirties manner. On the contrary, his great innovation in *Les Parents pauvres* was to combine the straightforward structure of his earlier novels with the textual density of *Illusions perdues* and *Splendeurs et misères,* and to move beyond both towards a genuinely new—albeit characteristically Balzacian—conception of dramatic realism, a conception which might in happier circumstances have marked the beginning of a new, mature "late Balzac" comparable to the "late James."¹²

The first thing to notice about the new fictional mode of *La Cousine Bette* is that it accommodates Balzac's perennial desire to chronicle the scenes and events of his day and to analyze its social, political, and economic systems. The description of the slum quarter around the Louvre in this text is as interesting a bit of social history as the pictures of the Galeries-de-Bois in *Illusions perdues* and the Palais de Justice in *Splendeurs et misères,* and Balzac insists upon its importance as part of a chronicle of the age:

> It will certainly not be out of place to describe this corner of contemporary Paris. Later generations could not imagine it, and our descendants, who will certainly see the Louvre finished, would refuse to believe that such barbarism survived for thirty-six years in the heart of Paris, right across from the palace where, throughout those thirty-six years, three dynasties received the elite of France and of Europe. (VII, 99)[13]

The description is not out of place in the text of *La Cousine Bette* for another reason, of course, since it suggests that the *quartier* is an objective correlative for the moral states of its inhabitants, notably Lisbeth Fischer and Valérie Marneffe. Still, it is important to recognize that Balzac's desire to be a chronicler continues in *La Cousine Bette,* and becomes if anything more strictly local and topical. The condition of the *quartier* of the Louvre was indeed a scandal at the time the novel appeared, and an issue likely to be discussed elsewhere in the newspaper in which it was appearing *en feuilleton.*[14]

With the figure of Crevel, Balzac moves from the depiction of topical detail to that of social movements, in this case the triumph of bourgeois commercialism, exemplified by a personal triumph which seems particularly brilliant to those readers who first made Crevel's acquaintance when he was nothing but a clerk in César Birotteau's perfumery. And in the figures of the old maréchal Hulot, the maréchal Cottin, prince de Wissembourg, and the baron Hulot d'Ervy himself, he depicts the political power enjoyed by Napoleonic heroes under the July Monarchy as well as the persistence of the Napoleonic virtues in some and their decay in others.

In the field of the analysis of manners, too, Balzac is as active here as he ever was. This is the way he has Crevel outline Hortense Hulot's matrimonial prospects:

"Given the situation you are in, there are only three ways you can marry your daughter. With my help—but you don't want it!—that's one. By finding an old man of sixty, very rich, childless, but wanting a family—it's difficult, but it does happen— . . . that's two. The last way is the easiest . . ."

Madame Hulot raised her head and looked anxiously at the former perfumer.

"Paris is the meeting-place for all those men of energy who are sprouting up like volunteers on French territory: it swarms with talented men who have neither house nor home, but the courage to do anything, even make their fortunes. . . . Well, one of these *condottieri*, as they call them, of finance or the pen or the artist's brush, is the only one in Paris capable of marrying a penniless beauty, for they have all kinds of courage." (VII, 71)[15]

The impulse behind passages like this, and there are many others in *La Cousine Bette*,[16] is substantially the same as that behind Balzac's early forays into the field of social journalism, his *Codes,* his *Physiologies,* and his *Théories,* all pretending to reveal the hidden structure of social behavior as well as the meaning of individual words and gestures.

The second essential feature of the late Balzacian mode as it manifests itself in *La Cousine Bette* is its use of the processes of intratextual representation. Representation in *La Cousine Bette* is less frenzied than it is in *Splendeurs et misères,* but just as central to the nature and the meaning of the text. Balzac, as we have seen, is still intent here on representing the world around him. He is also concerned with the ways in which elements of the text can be made to stand for each other, as they do in *Illusions perdues.* In addition, he is interested in using characters to represent clearly defined abstract qualities, and in playing these characters and qualities off against one another in a kind of allegorical drama.[17]

Balzac's use of characters and patterns of events to stand for
one another within the text can be seen in the repeated motif of
the character possessed by passion, similar in many ways to the
motif of the "ravenous mechanical presses" in *Illusions perdues*.
The baron Hulot, for example, is possessed by irresistible and
insatiable lust, which leads him from mistress to mistress, lower
and lower in the social scale, until he abandons his family altogether. When his wife discovers him working as a public let-
ter-writer in a slum district and living with a fifteen-year-old
girl, his lust so overpowers his shame that he asks to bring his
mistress home with him. Even after his apparent rehabilitation,
this same lust impels him to seduce his own kitchenmaid, dealing his wife a deathblow in the process.

Cousin Bette, too, is possessed by passion, driven to extremes
of hypocrisy, dissimulation, and cruelty by her jealousy of Adeline and Hortense Hulot and her desire for revenge. "'Adeline!'" she cries, "'Adeline, I will see you in the mud, even
lower than I am!'" (VII, 147),[18] and she does her best to carry
out her threat, conspiring with Valérie Marneffe to ruin Hulot
and destroy his family's happiness. She eventually dies of her
passion, unable to sustain the thought that the family might sur-
vive her machinations: "Lisbeth, already very unhappy about
the happiness that was shining down on the family, could not
withstand this happy event. She got worse so quickly that Bianchon gave her no more than a week to live" (VII, 448).[19]

Vicious characters are not the only ones to suffer from this
kind of possession. Adeline Hulot, the baron's wife, is obsessed
by her sense of duty and her love for her husband. "For Adeline," Balzac writes, "the baron was from the beginning a kind
of god" (VII, 76);[20] she scolds him only once, when she is about
to expire as a result of his perfidy: "on the edge of eternity, she
spoke the only words of reproach she uttered in her life" (VII,
451).[21]

The pattern of passionate obsession is reproduced in other
characters, too, with significant variations. Valérie and Crevel
are driven by colder forces, the one to accumulate vast amounts
of income and capital and the other to assert his dignity, and his

equality with or even his superiority to Hulot by taking as his mistress "a respectable woman" (VII, 162),[22] whether it be Hulot's wife or his bourgeois mistress, Valérie. They succumb in the end not directly to their own passions, but rather to the sensational jealousy of Valérie's mysterious former lover, the baron Henri Montès de Montéjanos.

Balzac's description of Montès and the means by which he takes his revenge is worth pausing over, for it illustrates another variation in the mode of intratextual representation, the *mise en abîme* by which certain episodes come to stand for important elements of the text as a whole. Montès himself represents a simpler kind of passion than that embodied by the other characters. When he returns to Paris from Brazil, his love for Valérie is unabated, but she has more complicated entanglements now, and must try to manage his enthusiasm. "'Valérie,'" he says to her, "'I have come back still faithful to you. My uncle is dead and I am twice as rich as I was when I went away. I want to live and die in Paris, near you and for you!'" "'Hush, Henri, for heaven's sake!'" is Valérie's less than impassioned reply (VII, 212).[23] Montès obeys, but he is confused. The first time he is able to converse with Valérie in private he begins by asking, "'But why don't you leave everything for me, if you love me?'" and Balzac comments on his directness by calling him "this American primitive, [*ce naturel de l'Amérique*] logical like all children of nature" (VII, 218).[24]

Direct as he is in his passions, Montès is more devious when it comes to taking his revenge. The effect of this revenge is so appropriate to the crimes of its victims, however, that it seems a direct effect of their evil living rather than the result of a complicated series of plots and manipulations. When Montès is finally convinced by the evidence presented to him that Valérie is sleeping with Steinbock and intends to marry Crevel, he declares that he will kill her, and describes his own "natural" method:

"I'll kill her!" the Brazilian coldly repeated. "So you've called me a savage! . . . Do you think I am going to imitate your countrymen's foolishness and buy some poison from the druggist? . . . I've been thinking, in the time it's taken you to get home, about what vengeance I would take if you happened to be right about Valérie. One of my Negroes is carrying the surest of animal poisons, a terrible disease that works better than any vegetable poison, and that can only be cured in Brazil. I'll have him infect Cydalise; she will give it to me in turn; and then, when death is running in the veins of Crevel and his wife, I'll be beyond the Azores with your cousin, whom I will cure, and take as my wife. We have our ways, we savages!" (VII, 417)[25]

Behind the exoticism and the sensationalism of Montès's revenge-killing by hideous venereal disease there lurks, as I have suggested, a certain justice and simplicity. Valérie, who has conspired to corrupt Steinbock by luring him into what Balzac calls the "mudhole of pleasure [le bourbier du plaisir]" (VII, 258), becomes nothing more than a "pile of mud [un tas de boue]" (VII, 432) herself. "'I am told this woman was once pretty,'" Doctor Bianchon remarks. "'Well, then, her punishment fits her crime [elle est bien punie par où elle a péché] for today she is hideously ugly'" (VII, 429). Her famous last words only confirm the justice of her end: "'Leave me to the Church! Only God can find me attractive now. I must try to make it up with him— that will be my last flirtation. Yes, I must make merciful God'" (VII, 433).[26]

So passion, in its most unadulterated, "natural" form, ravages civilized society. The venereal disease that corrupts Valérie's blood represents the corruption that jealousy, venality, and unlawful passion introduce into society. When Montès declares that he is "'the instrument of divine wrath'" (VII, 423), he really does make his obscure South American microbe seem like a scourge of God, a pestilence sent from on high to rid the world of the likes of Valérie Marneffe.

But these words also serve as a reminder that we are in a Balzacian world here and that things are not quite so simple. In the first place Montès may be an instrument of the wrath of

God, but he is also an instrument of "Mame Nourrisson," who is an instrument of Jacques Collin, who, through the mediation of the prince de Wissembourg, had made himself an instrument of the vengeance of Victorin Hulot and his family. "Mame Nourrisson" herself has declared that "'we replace Fate'" (VII, 387), and the alert Balzacian will recall that Collin had made a similar blasphemous statement in *Le Père Goriot* (III, 144).[27]

The story of Henri Montès de Montéjanos and his passionate revenge *represents* one of the themes of *La Cousine Bette,* the debilitating power of passion to destroy the human body and the human soul. At the same time it *represents* the more complicated set of mediations that stand behind it, the devious ways which passion in a "civilized" society uses to reach its ends. Another way of saying this is that Montès's story is a model for the text, related to it synecdochically as a part to a whole, to be sure, but also metaphorically, as a miniature, analogous version of the text itself.

The relation between this episode and the whole text is different from that among the various analogous episodes of *Illusions perdues* for two reasons. First, the Montès episode is no ordinary event in the communal, cultural, or legal life of the times, but an extravagant, exotic, and above all unique occurrence, in sharp contrast to its realistic, if melodramatic, context. Second, it stands in a special kind of relation to a whole of which it is not only a part but also an analogue. The "whole" of *Illusions perdues* is defined by the repetition and interrelations of its parts, so that no part of itself can be analogous to the whole. *La Cousine Bette,* on the other hand, is defined by a more classical kind of structure which *can* be reflected in one of its constituent parts. No single part of a mobile can reflect the mobile as a whole, because the mobile is defined as a set of interconnected, moving pieces. One part of a picture, or let us say of a sculpture, can, on the other hand, easily be made to serve as a smaller replica of the whole work.

This difference between the relation of parts to wholes in *Illusions perdues* and *La Cousine Bette* suggests the possibility of a third kind of representation in the latter text, a kind of rep-

resentation that can be hinted at but never sustained in the elusive framework of *Illusions perdues,* the quasi-allegorical representation by characters of abstract qualities. The implications
of this kind of representation for the realistic novel are obviously
far-reaching, and I shall discuss them at greater length presently. Let it suffice for the moment simply to notice that characters in *La Cousine Bette* do take on allegorical stature.
Montès, as we have seen, is "the Savage" (VII, 417), while
Bette is "Hatred and Vengeance without compromise" (VII,
152). Adeline is "Virtue" for Crevel and Josépha (VII, 333;
385), and Bette later acknowledges her own identity with
"Evil" in the struggle with "Good" (VII, 400).[28] In this context,
even the characters who are not specifically labeled take on allegorical significance: Hulot becomes Lust, Valérie Greed, and
so on. This kind of identification is only rarely possible in *Illusions perdues,* and then only for such characters as d'Arthez,
Eve and David, perhaps, and Carlos Herrera.

Balzac in *La Cousine Bette* makes use of various kinds of
representation without ever making representation itself a
theme of his text. He does the same with interpretation, developing techniques he has used before in ways which suggest a
new kind of realistic novel-writing. Interpretation in *La Cousine Bette* is in many ways a simpler affair than it is in most of
Balzac's earlier novels. When Hortense takes it into her head
to find out about Bette's *"amoureux,"* or when Adeline sets out
in search of her husband, the secrets they are after are simple
facts, not systems of dress, or speech, or behavior, like the ones
Rastignac and Lucien are faced with, or metaphysical dilemmas
like the ones presented by the various inmates of the Pension
Vauquer.

Furthermore, Balzac keeps his readers informed of his characters' significance and their histories, making further, deeper
interpretation unnecessary. His allegorical labels and the alac-
rity with which he outlines his characters' "biographies"
quickly satisfy our curiosity, and may well be an attempt to
grasp and hold the interest of the *feuilleton*-reading public. The
effect of the many passages beginning "This is why" *("Voici*

pourquoi"), "This is how" ("Voici comment") and simply "This is" *("Voici")* is harder to define. Sometimes these phrases introduce whole chapters of explanation, and seem to be used as devices to promote continuity and suspense.[29] At other times they provide a rather too portentous introduction to commonplace information, for example, the following:

> So she went resolutely up, not to her own apartment, but to the attic. Here is why. At dessert she had put some fruits and sweetmeats into her bag for her sweetheart, and she was going to give them to him, just like an old spinster bringing back a tasty morsel for her dog. (VII, 107)[30]

On still other occasions they introduce privileged information or the kind of generality we have come to expect to find peppered through a Balzacian text:

> In Paris, when a woman has decided to trade on her beauty, there is no reason to believe that she will necessarily make a fortune. One meets really admirable, witty creatures there, living in dreadful mediocrity, ending badly a life begun in pleasure. Here is why. It is not enough to set out on the shameful career of a courtesan with the intention of profiting from it while keeping the appearance of an honest married woman. Vice doesn't triumph easily. It has this in common with Genius, that they both demand a happy combination of circumstances to make the most of fortune and talent. (VII, 186)[31]

The result of all this is a text in which the process of interpretation, of figuring out what a character stands for or what motivates him, or of piecing together earlier events from evidence provided in fragmentary form, is just not very important for the reader, since it is all done *for* him. The text deemphasizes its need for interpretation by systematically interpreting itself.

This self-interpretation, however, may be read as a device designed by an anxious author to convince the reader that the meaning of the text is all on the surface, and therefore as a sign that there is a more important repressed, perhaps even unconscious meaning to be found beneath that surface. This is F. R. Jameson's assumption in his article on "*La Cousine Bette* and Allegorical Realism," in which he goes behind and beneath the text's own surface self-interpretations, and emerges with a brilliant analysis of what he calls the "deeper personal myth,"[32] which determines its deep structure and its latent meaning. Jameson's interpretation is indispensable for an understanding of the text and its author, but it seems to me that the locus of its meaning is essentially extra-textual, not in the sense that it is gratuitous, contrived, or forced, but in the way that the interpretation of a dream is valuable not so much for what it reveals about the dream itself as for what it reveals about the dreamer, in this case Honoré de Balzac and, coincidentally, about the interpreter, in this case Fredric Jameson.

Another way of reading the self-interpretation in *La Cousine Bette* is as a sign that its author has shifted his attention from the theme of interpretation in the text in order to focus on the processes of interpretation that the text itself embodies. To my mind, this shift marks the beginning of a period of expansion in Balzac's career as a realist, a period intrinsically no more valuable than the period of concentration which preceded it, but freer of the cares of the developing artist. It is as if realism had moved from a stage of concern for its own ontological and epistemological status (a stage which begins at least as early as Diderot and Sterne) into a stage of diminished self-consciousness, in which the conventions of realistic fiction could be taken more for granted than they had been, and used to expand the boundaries of the genre and develop the opportunities it affords for the exploration of human experience.

The Theater of the Passions

In *La Cousine Bette* Balzac uses these new opportunities to return to a theme that had always interested him, the human passions,[33] and to develop a model he had already made use of both thematically and structurally,[34] the model of the theater. Another characteristic of the "new" Balzacian novel as it is represented by *La Cousine Bette* is therefore its reliance on theatrical models of literary structure and human behavior. The reader of this text is no longer called upon to puzzle over the ambiguities of moral judgment or ponder the depressing similarities of all aspects of emerging capitalistic society, but rather to look on while Balzac produces for his entertainment and edification a drama in which Good characters and Evil, merchants and nobles, the exploiters and the exploited *act out* their natures.

Drama is the key word here. By alluding to plays and operas, by developing themes and structures common to classical French tragedy and contemporary melodrama, and by using theatrical techniques and devices, Balzac creates in *La Cousine Bette* a text which provides a kind of intelligibility more commonly associated with the theater than with the novel. In effect, he asks his readers to become an audience, to understand the action of his text, and the "real" actions it represents, as part of the dramatic interplay of human passions, and to appreciate the text itself as performance.

Like most of the *Scènes de la vie parisienne*, *La Cousine Bette* swarms with theatrical allusions. Some of these do little more than suggest a context for reading, while others seem part of a carefully worked out strategy for textual development. When Marneffe quotes Hamlet (VII, 105) and Crevel refers to the Moor of Venice (VII, 223) or the Gubetta of *Lucrèce Borgia* (VII, 235), the allusions to Shakespeare and Hugo seem little more than passing jibes at the superficiality of the characters' pretensions to literary sophistication.[35] Similarly, when an opera—Rossini's *William Tell*, for example, or Meyerbeer's *Robert le Diable*—is alluded to in connection with one of the book's actress-characters, the allusion strikes the reader as another convincing "realistic" detail of the life of the Paris of the day. When, however, Josépha counsels Hulot to assume the role of the bumbling Doctor Bartholo (of Beaumarchais's *Barber of Seville*) rather than that of Hippolyte (of Racine's *Phèdre*) (VII, 363), the reader, faced with these two alternative ways of viewing the character, is led to reflect on the rest of the text and to attempt to define it in terms of tragedy and comedy and the relations between them.[36]

The result of such an attempt will surprise no reader of *La Cousine Bette* who has also read Erich Auerbach, for although Balzac makes use of ignoble, often "low" characters involved in far from heroic actions, although he even describes two of his chapters as "Scenes from high comedy,"[37] his purposes are essentially serious. He is involved in that mixing of traditional modes, that serious treatment of themes and characters which had formerly only been treated in comic terms, which is an important part of Auerbach's definition of nineteenth-century realism.

One clue to this seriousness is the fact that the allusions to the classical tragedy of Corneille and Racine not only outnumber all the other theatrical allusions in the text,[38] but are more purposeful as well. When Hortense Hulot, in her conversation with her father about Wenceslas Steinbock, quotes Phèdre's line about her love for Hippolyte, "My ills come from far off" ("Mon mal vient de plus loin" [VII, 131]),[39] she thinks she is being brightly literary: like Phèdre, she implies, she was in love with the man in question long before anyone else suspected it. There are two other aspects of her allusion which may strike the reader, however, even if they do not strike Hortense herself. When Phèdre says that her "ills come from far off," she is referring to the *coup de foudre* with which she was struck the first time she saw Hippolyte ("I saw him, I blushed, I blanched at his sight") ("Je le vis, je rougis, je pâlis à sa vue" [I, iii]). Phèdre was seized by a power beyond her control, a power which she then struggled to defeat or at least to repress. Hortense, on the other hand, had never seen Steinbock before her encounter with him in the art dealer's shop, and her passion is entirely of her own invention: she loves him not because she is struck down by Cupid's arrow or the fatality of passion, but because he is the *amoureux* of her old cousin Bette, from whom she wants to steal him. On another level, furthermore, Phèdre's ills come from even further off, from the hatred evinced by Venus for her whole family (see I, iii), from her father's disobedience to Poseidon and the consequent birth of the Minotaur to Phèdre's mother and the eventual killing of the beast by Theseus, from Theseus' betrayal of Phèdre's sister, Ariadne, and from his marriage to Phèdre long after the birth of his bastard but recognized son, Hippolytus, to the Amazon queen Hippolyta. They come, in other words, from the sins of her father and her husband, and are a curse and an inevitability. Hortense's ills, which turn out to encompass far more than her love for Steinbock, are also brought upon her by the sins of her father and of her husband, and also seem, by the time the text is drawing to a close, to have been fated and inevitable. Her casual, almost flippant, reference to Racine serves both as an ironic comment on the relative shabbiness of her motivation and as a suggestion that the fate of the house of Hulot is somehow similar to those of the ancient houses of classical tragedy.

As if this were not enough, Josépha much later in the text picks up a line from the same tirade of Phèdre and applies it to another victim of love, the baron Hulot himself. Phèdre describes her finally-avowed passion this way:

> No longer a wish that is hidden away,
> It is Venus herself fastened on to her prey.

> [Ce n'est plus une ardeur dans mes veines câchée;
> C'est Vénus toute entière à sa proie attachée.]
>
> (I, iii)

Josépha addresses Hulot like this:

> "You! You have only ruined your own people! You have only sold *yourself* off! And then, you have an excuse, both physical and moral . . ."
>
> She struck a tragic pose and said:
> "It is Venus herself fastened on to her prey." (VII, 358)[40]

Hortense may be the immediate victim of her own spitefulness and only the ultimate and rather indirect victim of fate, but Hulot is a kind of tragic hero, a man who has risen to great dignity only to plunge to the depths of degradation through the

effects of a fatal flaw in his character, his insatiable lust. Hulot
is no more capable of controlling his desires than is Phèdre, and
his march toward degradation is every bit as inexorable, one
might even say as fated, as hers.

Another clue to the earnestness of Balzac's theatrical inspiration, and particularly to his awareness of the model of neo-
classical tragedy, can be found in the structure of his text and
the terms in which he describes it. About one third of the way
through he provides the following formal summary:

> Here ends what might be called the introduction to this
> story. This narrative is to the drama that completes it what
> the premises are to a logical proposition, or the exposition to
> a classical tragedy. (VII, 186)[41]

Exposition, complications, crisis, denouement: the familiar
terms would not be very helpful in dealing with such episodic
texts as *Illusions perdues* or *Splendeurs et misères*, but they can
be applied rather neatly to the structure of *La Cousine Bette* as
they could to that of many of the earlier, "classical" Balzacian
texts such as *Eugénie Grandet, Le Lys dans la vallée,* or *Le
Père Goriot.*[42] P. Barrière has done this job for us in his book
on Balzac and the classical tradition, and we need not agree
with the details of his analysis to appreciate its general validity.
The portion of the text that precedes Balzac's announcement
that the exposition is over constitutes for Barrière the first two
acts of the tragedy. First there is the exposition proper, in which
the characters are presented in their original groupings, the
"Hulot-Crevel family group," "the Marneffe group," and the
"Valérie-Wenceslas group."[43] Then there are the first indica-
tions of the antagonisms that will threaten this grouping: "The
passions of Crevel, Marneffe, and Bette take on the Hulot
group, using Hulot's passion as their tool."[44] A long third act
follows, leading through the machinations of all the various passions to a crisis in the ruin of Johann Fischer and the disgrace
of the baron Hulot. In the fourth act Hulot suffers the consequences of his "tragic" errors, hounded by such furies as Balzac

can embody in his undying lust and his fear of his creditors. At the same time, the passions of Bette, Valérie, and Crevel are leading them more and more rapidly down the road to disaster, as they prepare for the hideous marriage of Vanity and Greed, and as Vautrin, Madame de Saint-Estève, and eventually Victorin Hulot assume the role of fate and set in motion the "machine" that will lead to the dénouement. The dénouement itself is rapid, though not so neat as it might be. Valérie and Crevel die fitting deaths, the victims of their respective passions. Bette is ailing, but Balzac suggests that she actually dies because she cannot bear the apparent happiness of the Hulot family. Hulot, however, lives on, his lust unabated, and his seduction of the kitchenmaid with the words "My wife won't live much longer" (VII, 451)[45] leads directly to the death of Madame Hulot, a victim of her own passionate fidelity.

This is clearly no Racinian tragedy: the unities are completely ignored, there is no sense of *bienséance,* no economy of expression. There is, however, a tightness of construction, and a sense of the dramatic interplay of passions, which must surely have gained importance and definition from Balzac's awareness of the Racinian model, as it gains richness and significance from the reader's association of the two writers. What Barrière does not notice, perhaps because he has another ax to grind, is that his analysis of the plot structure of *La Cousine Bette* could apply just as neatly to a contemporary melodrama as it does to *Phèdre* or *Andromaque.* Balzac certainly had the classics of French tragedy in mind as he wrote *La Cousine Bette,* but the notion of classical theater which influences his text is necessarily mediated by his experience of contemporary theater, and especially melodrama.

Peter Brooks has examined the relations between the theatrical melodrama and Balzac's brand of realistic fiction very thoroughly, and several of the points he makes about them are pertinent to our examination of *La Cousine Bette.* The first scene of the novel, for example, is not tragic but melodramatic in conception, and even borders on the comic in execution. It does not represent a hero torn by the contrary demands of ambition and loyalty, or passion and duty, but rather a figure of perfect innocence, Adeline Hulot, threatened by a comically overblown vice-figure, the self-important Célestin Crevel, who is motivated by the desire to revenge himself on the baron Hulot and assert his own personal worth, rather than by an overwhelming passion for Adeline. This is the melodramatic *topos* of "virtue in a situation of extreme peril," though with rather more humor than Brooks leads one to believe was common in actual theatrical melodrama.[46] In the body of the text, furthermore, as in conventional melodrama, virtue is repeatedly thwarted, frustrated, and denied until Adeline Hulot develops a "nervous tic" (VII, 287) which serves as a melodramatically visible sign of the frustration of virtue. Finally, at the end of the novel, virtue seems to triumph, not as it does in comedy, by forming a new society around a newly married young couple, but as it does in melodrama, by "a reforming of the old society of innocence, which has now driven out the threat to its existence and reaffirmed its values."[47] In *La Cousine Bette* this reformed society does not last long, of course: Hulot's lust reasserts itself in the last few paragraphs, and finally destroys Adeline, as it had threatened to do throughout.

The plot structure of *La Cousine Bette* can therefore be seen in terms both of classical tragedy and of nineteenth-century melodrama. Balzac uses two even more theatrical devices to heighten our sense of the novel as melodramatic drama of the passions: his characters frequently act out their moral natures, even when they are trying to conceal them; the episodes of his story frequently lead up to melodramatic *coups de théâtre*.

Many of Balzac's characters are determined role-players, but for all their attempts to project misleading views of themselves, they always end up expressing their true natures. In the very first paragraph, for example, we discover Crevel, rather foolishly pleased with his own appearance and the spectacle he presents to curious onlookers, making his progress along the rue de l'Université, ensconced in his *milord* and decked out in the uniform of a captain of the national guard. Later in the same episode Crevel congratulates himself for the first of many times on his spectacular rise in society, his glamorous connections, and his own aristocratic pose:

> "I am a grocer, a shopkeeper, a former retailer of almond paste, eau de Portugal, and cephalic oil. People must think I was quite honored to marry my only daughter to the son of Monsieur le baron Hulot d'Ervy. My daughter will be a baroness! That's Regency, that's Louis XV, Oeil-de-Boeuf! That's wonderful!" (VII, 60)[48]

Crevel's attempt to present himself as a dashing *parvenu*, a man of energy worth any number of his social betters is as comical and as pitiful as his smugly silly appearance. He intends to project an image of elegant (albeit eclectic) libertinism and succeeds only in appearing foolish. Adeline Hulot, on the other hand, is doing her best in this episode to project and maintain an image of herself as she really is, noble, respectable, and loyal. She does this by maintaining a formality in her speeches to Crevel that is so strict as to be almost *précieux:* "'Eh bien!'" she begins, "'in order to cut short our mutual torment, I shall be brief [*Je serai brève pour abréger notre mutuel supplice*]'" (VII, 59).

> "My daughter Hortense had an opportunity to marry, an opportunity that depended entirely on you. I believed you were generous. I thought you would be fair to a woman who has cherished no image but her husband's, that you would recognize that she could not receive a man who might compromise her, and that you would hasten, in honor of the family to which you are connected, to encourage the marriage of Hortense and Councillor Lebas. . . . And you, Monsieur, you kept this marriage from taking place!" (VII, 61)[49]

Later in the episode, when Crevel presses his suit more warmly, she responds more coldly and more formally still:

> "Get out, Monsieur," said Madame Hulot. "Get out, and never let me see you again! If you hadn't forced me to discover the secret of your base behavior in the matter of Hortense's

projected marriage—yes, base," she repeated as Crevel made a gesture, "How can you burden a poor, a beautiful, an innocent girl with such unkindness?—If I hadn't been forced by my anguish as a mother, you would never have spoken to me again, you would never have entered my house again. Thirty-two years of honor and feminine loyalty will not fall to the attack of Monsieur Crevel . . ." (VII, 69)[50]

The sincerity of Adeline's performance here, and indeed the truth behind it, is made even clearer when she attempts much later in the text to replay the scene, this time taking the role of a seductress for the purpose of getting Crevel to rescue her uncle Fischer from suicide and dishonor. Her attempt is both pathetic, and, as Balzac repeatedly states, sublime; her virtue shines through her attempt at vice, and Crevel is unable to take advantage of her momentary weakness.

The majesty of virtue, its heavenly light, had swept away the woman's temporary impurity, and she appeared greater than ever to Crevel, resplendent in her own particular beauty. At that moment Adeline was sublime, like those religious figures, supported by a cross, that the old Venetians painted; but she expressed all the grandeur of her misfortune and that of the Catholic Church to which she was flying for refuge like a wounded dove. Crevel was dazzled, dumbfounded.

"Madame, I am at your service, without conditions!" (VII, 330)[51]

In their attempts at role-playing, Crevel and Adeline Hulot both end by expressing themselves as they really are, Crevel because he cannot forget what he used to be and Adeline because she cannot seem anything but what she is. Several other characters in the text *act out* their natures or the moral value Balzac seems to attach to them, in scenes which are as revealing as Adeline's attempted seduction of Crevel without being so obviously theatrical.

Hulot, as we have seen, hardly appears without labeling himself as the helpless victim of passion. Bette, too, acts out her evil nature, dressing and acting like a character from a Gothic novel:

> Anyone seeing Bette for the first time would tremble involuntarily at the sight of the wild poetry that Valérie's skill had made stand out by careful attention to this Bleeding Nun's dress and appearance. She had used heavy bands of black hair to frame the dry, olive face with its glittering black eyes. She had accentuated Bette's unbending figure. (VII, 196)[52]

And as if this were not enough, she delights in "innocently" twisting the knives in the various wounds she has helped to inflict. She savors her cousin Adeline's tears, and whenever she sees her gay and hopeful says to her, "'Expect to read my poor cousin's name in the police court news any day'" (VII, 375).[53] And in the end, of course, she dies because she cannot bear the thought of what she takes to be a "happy event" (VII, 448), the return of the baron Hulot to his family.

Of all the main characters, Valérie is probably the most conscious acter-out of her moral identity, just as she is also the most willful, the most calculating creator of such an identity.[54] She manages her admirers very handily in episodes which resemble, with their double-entendres and their hidden lovers, the swinging-door sequences of bedroom farces. "Danger was everywhere for Valérie. Foreseeing a quarrel with Crevel, she did not want Hulot in her room, where he could hear everything. And the Brazilian was waiting at Lisbeth's" (VII, 225).[55] Even more effective both as comedy and as the acting-out of Valérie's greed and her promiscuity are the scenes of the so-called "pères de la chambre Marneffe" ("fathers of the Marneffe bedroom," with a pun on "peers [*pairs*] of the Marneffe Chamber"),[56] in which she announces to each of her four lovers that he is about to become a father, and then jokes about the whole affair with her husband, who is the only one of the five "fathers" who knows very well that he can have had nothing to do with the child's conception. Valérie's final scene takes place on her deathbed where, as we have seen, she proposes to sell her body and her affections one more time, this time to God and for salvation.

The effect of all this acting-out is to heighten the reader's pleasure in the text as a presentation both of itself as an extravagant piece of verbal theater and of the human passions as actors in a "realistic" drama. The reader who can recognize Lust in Hulot, Fidelity in Adeline, Ambition in Valérie, and so on, is also in a position to grant his delighted assent to their "melodramatic" confrontations, to see them as valid versions of reality and necessary parts of the text as performance. Furthermore, the *feuilleton*-reader who is convinced that he understands the point of the story can appreciate the daily complications of its elaboration without worrying about losing the thread. If he *knows* and is continually reminded which passion each of the characters embodies, he can enjoy the scene of Adeline's confrontation with Josépha as a representation of the collaboration of what he ordinarily thinks of as opposing forces and as a theatrical tour de force at the same time.

Aside from characterization, there is another device that produces this effect, and that is the theatrical, call it even the melodramatic, event, which both delights the reader with its aptness, its unexpectedness or its emotional appeal, and stands as a fairly easy emblem of the "meaning" of the text. This device is particularly effective in the writing of installment fiction because it can serve, when the event is an emblematic scene, for example, to charge a whole installment with meaning, or, when the event is a loaded word or a *coup de théâtre*, to create the kind of suspense that is called for at the end of an installment.

We have already seen several examples of the event as scene in the death scenes of Bette, Valérie, and Adeline, for example, or the seduction scenes between Crevel and Adeline. Another scene that produces a melodramatic heightening of emotions, an outrageous juxtaposition of opposing forces, and three transparently emblematic tableaux is contained in the interview between Hulot and his daughter in the chapter entitled "The damages Madame Marneffes can cause in the bosoms of families."[57] The forces that the scene displays and that the reader can be counted

upon to recognize are the uncontrollable lust of the baron
Hulot, the naive, weak, but not altogether guiltless despair of
his daughter Hortense, the devotion of Adeline, the hatred of
Bette, and the stern practicality of Victorin Hulot. In the first
part of the scene Hulot, disguising his lechery under a thin ve-
neer of slimy worldly-wisdom, takes his full-grown daughter on
his knee and gives her a lesson in the ways of the world. The
reader knows, of course, that there is no more pitiful victim of
these ways than the baron himself, and that the guarantees he
offers Hortense for the eventual return of her husband are based
on his own mistaken faith in Valérie's attachment to himself.
He also knows that Hortense may love her husband, but that
she married him at least partly to vex her cousin Bette, and so
is not quite the spotless innocent she pretends to be. The tableau
that this pair presents to Adeline, who enters on hearing her
daughter's weeping, is therefore wildly incongruous with the
reader's knowledge of their characters. What looks like Wisdom
and Innocence is actually Lust and a combination of blind love
and spiteful jealousy. The scene is complicated by the presence
of Adeline, and the three present another speaking picture to
Bette and Victorin, who have just come in:

> At that moment Victorin and Cousin Bette came in, and
> were stupefied by the spectacle. The daughter had prostrated
> herself at her father's feet. The baroness, silent and torn be-
> tween her maternal and her conjugal feelings, looked on over-
> whelmed, tears staining her face. (VII, 290)[58]

This seems to be a typical family scene, the mother interceding
with the father on behalf of the erring daughter. What it is in
fact is something much more complex. Hortense has just rejected the role her mother has been playing vis-à-vis her father
all these years, and is both pleading with her father not to ask
her to take her husband back on any terms but those of absolute
fidelity, and asserting the moral *superiority* of her resolve not to
make the kinds of compromises he has forced on her mother.

The arrival of Victorin and particularly of Bette complicates
the scene considerably. That female personification of hatred

and spite is here disguised as a loyal family member. She declares that Valérie is a common *fille,* reveals to the baron that this *fille* has been milking him for all he is worth, and asserts that she cannot imagine what has prompted her "friend" to seduce her niece's husband, when she knows that Valérie has done this specifically to further her own revenge. "'My mind is made up,'" she says: she will leave Madame Marneffe's house immediately. The result of her apparent moral revulsion with her friend is to harden the rest of the family's opposition to the baron's relations with this woman, to heighten his own sense of guilt, practically driving him from the house. He is, in fact, on the point of leaving, and Bette is on the verge of yet another triumph when the scene ends with a marvelous tableau followed by a *coup de théâtre* which defers her revenge momentarily and calls attention to the purely visual representational power of the scene:

> "Hector!"
> The cry made the Baron turn back, and he suddenly showed his wife a face awash with tears. She put her arms around him with desperate strength.
> "Do not go away like this . . . do not leave us in anger. *I* have said nothing to you!"
> At this sublime cry the children threw themselves down at their father's knees.
> "We all love you," said Hortense.
> Lisbeth, still as a statue, looked on with a haughty smile. At that moment, Marshal Hulot came into the antechamber, and his voice was heard. The family understood the importance of secrecy, and the appearance of the scene changed abruptly. (VII, 292)[59]

The scene speaks of the irrationality of Hulot's lust and the ineffectuality of his family's pleas and remonstrances: it would reveal the family's shame even to a deaf old man like the *maréchal,* and must therefore be dissolved before he can perceive it. The reader, of course, knows what all these characters are like already: he derives some pleasure from having his understanding of them reinforced, but even more, I think, from his appreciation of Balzac's masterly multiplication of entrances and tableaux, his ability to overcharge a scene with contradictory emotions without diminishing its intelligibility. The ideal response to a particularly well-executed chapter of *La Cousine Bette* is not the "Aha!" of sudden enlightenment but the low whistle of admiration for yet another tour de force of effective storytelling.

Another kind of event that can evoke this response is the less sustained but more intense moment of the simple *coup de théâtre*. Balzac occasionally uses this device in its common theatrical form of the unexpected entrance, usually at the end of a chapter, to heighten suspense. The entrance of the maréchal Hulot had this effect in the passage just discussed, as does the manifestation of "the majestic French law . . . in the form of a nice little police commissioner accompanied by a tall, thin justice of the peace, both brought in by the Sieur Marneffe" (VII, 304)[60] at the door of the love nest occupied for the moment by Valérie and Hulot.

More often, he combines the dramatic *coup de théâtre* with a more literary kind of *coup de foudre* to produce what Martin Kanes has called the "word-event,"[61] a word or set of words so loaded with meaning or emotion that it produces an effect on the hearer out of all proportion to the intent of the speaker or the ordinary meaning of the words themselves. The physical effect of words in *La Cousine Bette* is often astonishing. Valérie, for example, completes the corruption of Bette, drives her out of her moral senses, simply by pointing out some words in a review:

> "But your cousin Hortense owns the Samson group whose lithograph appears in this Review. She paid for it out of her savings, and the Baron, in the interest of his future son-in-law, is pushing him ahead and getting him favors."
>
> "Water! Water!" cried Bette after glancing at the lithograph with the caption "Group belonging to Mademoiselle Hulot d'Ervy." "Water! My head is on fire! I'm going mad! . . ." (VII, 147)[62]

Later on Stidmann produces a similar effect on Hortense by simply mentioning the name of Madame Marneffe in connection with an evening entertainment, and thereby revealing her husband's duplicity:

> "Did you enjoy yourselves last night?" asked Hortense, for Wenceslas had not come back until one in the morning.
>
> "Enjoy? ... not exactly," replied the artist, who had wanted to *make* Madame Marneffe the day before. "One only enjoys oneself in society when one is interested in one's company. Little Madame Marneffe is excessively witty, but she's a flirt ..."
>
> . . . .
>
> Hortense grew as pale as a woman who has just given birth.
>
> "So you dined ... at Madame Marneffe's ... and not ... at Chandor's," she said, "yesterday ... with Wenceslas, and he ..."
>
> Stidman guessed that he had done some harm, without knowing what it was. The countess did not finish her sentence, but fainted dead away. (VII, 266–67)[63]

The character most subject to the power of the word-event, however, is Madame Hulot. We have seen that she dies as the direct result of an overheard conversation between the baron and the kitchenmaid, but her word-caused sufferings begin much earlier. When her husband receives a letter from her uncle, describing the desperate situation in which he has placed him, she is so surprised at the effect this letter has on him (he is "floored" as if by "an attack of apoplexy") that she decides to read it:

> The baroness came in on tiptoe. Hector heard nothing. She was able to approach, she saw the letter, took it, read it, and trembled in all her limbs. She experienced one of those nervous crises that are so violent that the body is marked by them permanently. A few days later she was afflicted with a continual trembling, for after the first moment the necessity of

action gave her that strength that can only come from the sources themselves of our vital power. (VII, 315)[64]

Later, when Bette alludes obliquely to Adeline's desperate attempt to sell herself to Crevel in order to save her uncle, she succumbs once again to the power of the word:

> "She seems to have some weapon against you! . . . ." she answered. "I don't yet know what it is, but I'll find out. . . . She spoke vaguely of some story concerning Adeline and two hundred thousand francs."
>
> The baroness Hulot slipped quietly down on the divan where she was sitting, and was taken with dreadful convulsions. (VII, 401)[65]

The effect of these word-events on the characters of *La Cousine Bette,* and on the reader who shudders to read them even before he knows what results they will produce, can be attributed, I think, to the model which Balzac has here developed of the text as a stage for the drama of the passions. The words "two hundred thousand francs" have such a devastating effect on Madame Hulot and on the reader, not only because they remind her and us of a shameful event in her past, but because they represent the most violent concatenation of powerful passions the text has to offer, the opposition within Madame Hulot herself of her own purity and her selfless desire to save her husband, the weakness and baseness of Crevel, who has apparently told Madame Marneffe of Madame Hulot's actions, and the horrible nexus of forces associated with Madame Marneffe herself, her own ambition, Hulot's lust, Crevel's prideful acquisitiveness, and so on.

I have suggested that the pleasure we get from *La Cousine Bette* derives from our satisfaction in identifying and understanding such clashes of passion and in our delight in the way Balzac manipulates them. The relative simplicity of the array of passions and their "allegorical" or "melodramatic" embodiments in *La Cousine Bette* may not require the kind of active interpretation demanded by *Le Père Goriot* or *Illusions perdues,* but it creates a stage for the production of a text which does provide us as much entertainment and intelligibility as we found in those novels. Balzac does not project a drama of the human passions in *La Cousine Bette* merely to illustrate his belief in the debilitating effects of unbridled lust, jealousy, and ambition. Stating this truism is not his purpose, but a thematic pretext for an exploration of the ways in which people express and/or try to repress the passions that drive them, and for an attempt to embody both the passions themselves and the clashes among them in an appealing narrative-dramatic text. *La Cousine Bette* is not a philosophical inquiry into the nature of good and evil, but neither is *Phèdre*. They are both, rather, dramatizations of the human passions, whose goal is not to explain their meaning but to demonstrate their effects.

By 1847 Balzac had used dramatic structures, techniques, vocabulary, and imagery in a number of tales and novels including *Une Fille d'Eve, Illusions perdues,* and especially *Le Père Goriot.* In all of these texts, however, the dramatic was but one element among many, a structural model, a source of effective narrative technique or suggestive metaphors for the characters' presentations of themselves and the reader's perception of the action. In *Le Père Goriot,* for example, Balzac effectively used the drama in all these ways, constructing his text with the rigor if not the economy of a stage play, creating exciting *coups de théâtre,* and using the vocabulary of the theater from the very first pages to give emphasis and metaphorical resonance to the notions of performance and representation in the text. In *La Cousine Bette* Balzac takes the theatrical model much further, displacing those elements of the text which it had served, those themes and world views, hints of the metaphysical and invitations to interpretation, and replacing them with a set of poses, gestures, self-dramatizations, and ironic allusions, all in the service of the profoundly simple model of life and of the text as theaters of the human passions. In developing this model, Balzac has worked himself free of the problematics of representation and interpretation not by transcending them or ignoring them, but by incorporating his solutions to them, however provisional, into his treatment of Lust and Fidelity, Ambition and Revenge, as they manifest themselves in Parisian society and as they can be manipulated and exhibited in the realistic novel as he has developed it throughout his career. *Eugénie Grandet* is a book about avarice as a passion, *La Recherche de l'absolu* is a book about intellectual obsession as a passion, but *La Cousine Bette* is a book about passion itself, a new version of *La Peau de chagrin,* which proposes and elaborates a model for the understanding of human behavior which might have taken Balzac a good distance along the road that led to Henry James and D. H. Lawrence.

5

Realism, the Drama of Consciousness, and the Text: *The Wings of the Dove*

In *The Wings of the Dove* James develops two strategies for realism which could be seen as syntheses of Balzac's techniques in *La Cousine Bette*. First, he broadens and deepens the model of the theater of the passions, combining its conventional plot structure and its tendency to allegory with his own newly-developed notions of the place of the dramatic in prose fiction. The result is what he calls a "drama of consciousness"[1] in which (1) some of the dramatic action is displaced from the stage of the world to the stage of the characters' minds, and the drama of the clash of personalities is supplemented by the drama of the development of those personalities and their self-awareness. Second, he displaces much of the interpretive complexity of *Le Père Goriot* and the representational resonance of *Illusions perdues* from the realm of represented systems to that of textual systems, thereby removing the responsibility for interpreting these systems from the characters and placing it squarely on the reader.

The result of both of these strategies is further to involve the reader in the creation of the reading experience. The drama of consciousness as James writes it, and the complex textuality he produces in his writing cast the reader as an interpreting spectator of three dramas on three different stages. We interpret the characters' actions on the stage of the world and their evolving senses of themselves on the stages of their own consciousness, and we develop *our* sense of the novel as a whole as it evolves on the stage of the text.

The theatrical model in *La Cousine Bette* is double and parallel: concrete characters and the abstract qualities they embody develop and struggle simultaneously; our understanding of virtue and vice and the triumph of one or the other gains subtlety as our views of Adeline, Valérie, and the rest gain complexity. Balzac's novel proposes that we understand life in the world in terms of the dramatic conflict of abstract principles, and that we modify our understanding of these principles by observing their various and impure embodiments in the characters. The three related dramas in *The Wings of the Dove,* on the other hand, coexist without corresponding to each other point for point. The model here is not of two parallel dramas, the abstract and the concrete, each to be understood in terms of the other, but of two divergent dramas, the surface drama of manners and the more profound drama of developing moral sensibilities, mediated and coordinated by a third, textual, drama of language and literary devices.

The Drama of Consciousness and the Drama of Textuality: Brief Histories

Like Balzac's version of the theater of the passions, James's conception of the drama of consciousness was the result of a set of personal, historical, and commercial pressures. From his earliest childhood, James had been fascinated by the theater,[2] and we know from our reading of *The American* that his interest in the modes and content of consciousness dates back at least as far as his first attempts at novel-writing.

The truly "dramatic" phase of James's fiction-writing, however, that most Jamesian phase in which the dramas of the growth of human consciousness and the clash of human passions are acted out against a background of solidly specified "reality," does not begin until the 1890s. The decisive circumstance which separates these earliest novels, and even the more specifically theatrical *Tragic Muse,* from James's later experiments in the drama of consciousness such as *The Awkward Age* and *What Maisie Knew,* and his triumphs of the early 1900s, is his prolonged struggle with play-writing and the commercial theater.

James began to write plays because he was fascinated with the literary potential of the theater and because he needed to make money.[3] The beginning of the project is marked by the following entry in his notebook, dated May 12, 1889:

> I had practically given up my old, valued, long cherished dream of doing something for the stage, for fame's sake, and art's, and fortune's: overcome by the vulgarity, the brutality, the baseness of the condition of the English-speaking theatre today. But after an interval, a long one, the vision has revived, on a new and a very much humbler basis, and especially under the lash of necessity. Of art or fame *il est maintenant fort peu question:* I simply *must* try, and try seriously, to produce half a dozen—a dozen, five dozen—plays for the sake of my pocket, my material future.[4]

For all his bold optimism, however, James suspected that his idea of *drama* and the actual conditions of the *theater* had little in common. His very first theatrical reviews had echoed with the complaint that too much attention was paid in the London theater to mime, to costume, and to stage setting, and too little to the drama, that portion of the performance which only the playwright could provide.[5] By the end of 1893, his worst suspicions had been confirmed, and he could write to his brother that the "whole odiousness of the thing lies in the connection between the drama and the theatre. The one is admirable in its interest and difficulty, the other loathsome in its conditions."[6]

James persisted in his attempts to write for the stage, however, until 1895, when the humiliating, though only partial, failure of his drama *Guy Domville* convinced him to return to his own métier and begin experimenting with a new kind of nontheatrical prose drama. The difference between what he writes in 1895 and after, and what he wrote before 1890 may be attributed in part to two modifications of his conception of the nature and the versatility of the "dramatic" in literature.

First, he has become more fully aware of the potential of the scenic in prose fiction, of the possibility of presenting the characters' actions as scenes played out before the reader's mental eye rather than bits of narrative and "psychological" analysis interspersed with conversation.[7] "I realise—none too soon—," he writes in 1896,

> that the *scenic* method is my absolute, my imperative, my *only* salvation. The *march of an action* is the thing for me to, more and more, *attach* myself to: it is the only thing that really, for *me*, at least, will *produire* L'OEUVRE, and L'OEUVRE is, before God, what I'm going in for. Well, the scenic scheme is the only one that *I* can trust, with my tendencies, to stick to the march of an action. How reading Ibsen's splendid *John Gabriel* a day or two ago (in proof) brought that, FINALLY AND FOREVER, home to me![8]

Second, James had discovered in the works of Ibsen an example of the dramatic presentation of his favorite kind of literary subject. It was all very well for him to recognize that the "march of an action" was "the thing for him to do," but "action" as it is commonly understood had never been his specialty, so it was equally important for him to realize that a state of mind could take the place of what we ordinarily think of as an action, and be effectively dramatized. Ibsen's *Hedda Gabler,* James writes in an article of 1891,

> is essentially that supposedly undramatic thing, the picture not of an action but of a condition. It is the portrait of a nature, the story of what Paul Bourget would call an *état d'âme,* and of a state of nerves as well as of soul, a state of temper, of health, of chagrin, of despair. *Hedda Gabler* is, in short, the study of an exasperated woman; and it may certainly be declared that the subject was not in advance, as a theme for scenic treatment, to be pronounced promising. There could in fact, however, be no more suggestive illustration of the folly

of quarrelling with an artist over his subject. Ibsen has had only to take hold of this one in earnest to make it, against every presumption, live with an intensity of life.[9]

The state of a character's mind, or the state of his soul, then, was not only the fruitful novelistic subject James had found it from *Roderick Hudson* on, it was a suitable subject for that kind of dramatic narrative James was presently to attempt.

We can observe James's experiments with this kind of narrative in the novels and tales of the late 1890s, and its fruition in the works of the early twentieth century. James embodies what Ibsen had taught him about the dramatic possibilities of the *"état d'âme"* in narrative which emphasizes the gradual development of self-awareness in the characters and the gradual revelation of the nature of their various consciousnesses to the actively interpreting reader. In *La Cousine Bette* the passions preexist the characters and seem to have been chosen from an array of capitalized medieval virtues and vices. In *The Wings of the Dove,* on the other hand, as, for James, in *Hedda Gabler,* the passions are not easily nameable, preexisting abstractions, but the products of the conjunction of certain specific personalities and situations. The drama of consciousness in *The Wings of the Dove* is not created solely by the clash of egos and the interaction of passions which a plot summary might suggest: it derives at least as much from James's dramatic depiction of the solitary development of these egos and passions. The reader of this text observes the former, public, drama as he would the action of a stage play. He is also invited to observe even more actively the latter, private drama, joining the characters in the process of understanding their own personalities and situations.

Like the drama of consciousness, the drama of textuality demands participation: in order to enjoy it the reader must commit himself to active reading, to constant awareness of the questions the text raises about itself. Like his interest in the drama of consciousness, James's concern for the creation of a complex textuality and the generation of active and self-conscious reading goes back to the beginning of his writing career. We have seen how he uses the reader's generic expectations in *The American* to manipulate his emotional responses and to comment on the relation between melodrama and understanding. In that text, too, he uses the fairy-tale motif and the recurring image of the high, protective wall to suggest similarities among various distinct events of the story and experiences of the hero. Even individual words and groups of words take on textual significance in early James, as, for example, the word-group dealing with language and interpretation in *The American* and that dealing with knowledge in *The Princess Casamassima.*

In *The Wings of the Dove* James makes a similar use of word groups, image clusters, and the expectations aroused by implied genre. The history of these elements of James's writing, of its textual complexity and the active reading it demands, is therefore the history of the gradual evolution of his style and manner, with no decisive events like a five-year flirtation with the theater to mark its progress.

One factor did influence the development of Jamesian textuality in the period from 1895 onwards, however, and it stands as a neat emblem of the interrelatedness of this textuality and the drama of consciousness. This is James's interest in literary symbolism, especially as he came to understand it in the dramatic works of Ibsen and Maeterlinck.[10] In an article on the occasion of the production of Ibsen's *Master Builder* in London, James comments that Ibsen may be counted upon to provide "the general interest we owe to . . . the sense of life," but that in this play he goes farther and produces another kind of interest, "that play of intelligence, that acuteness of response, whether in assent or protest, which it is the privilege of the clinging theatre-goer to look forward to."[11] This interest, the intelligent response to a theatrical version of textuality, is the result of "the mingled reality and symbolism" in the play, whose simple action is given added significance by the symbolic patterns it creates, by the sense one has of its being pervaded by an "idea . . . as difficult to catch as its presence is to overlook."[12] A dense literary texture, in other words, shakes the audience of readers and playgoers out of their customary complacency and forces them to grasp at fleeting "ideas" and to recognize the text/performance as a device not only for portraying reality but also for generating new understandings of the world.

The effect of James's exposure to theatrical symbolism was surely liberating. Leon Edel writes that "the new symbolism, especially as Ibsen and Maeterlinck used it on the stage, gave him a freedom from material things and a liberty to imagine."[13] We need only add that this freedom was always curbed by James's insistent realism, by his choice to write of American heiresses in London and Venice rather than vague princesses in Maeterlinckian "Allemonde."

James's concurrent interest in his characters' drama of consciousness and his readers' experience of the text makes *The Wings of the Dove* a novel which demands the reader's participation in the development of the characters' consciousness and the construction of a literary experience. As I suggested above, the tension between these two activities produces the particular experience of the late Jamesian text as both highly referential in its treatment of character and events, and highly literary in its creation of complex textuality.

The Cast of Characters
and the Play of Expectations

Fully the first half of *The Wings of the Dove* is devoted to a special kind of dramatic exposition in which the characters define for themselves and their fellow players not only the particular roles they will be playing, but the genre of the social drama they see themselves acting out. Instead of having conventional parts distributed among them in the process implied by the French word for "cast of characters" *("distribution")*, they cast themselves in the roles they wish to play in their own not always compatible versions of the drama of life. This process fosters all three levels of the drama, provoking conflict among the characters, productive confusion in their senses of themselves and their places in society, and continual readjustment by the reader of his notions about what kind of book he is reading, and his expectations about its progress.

In the first chapter of *The Wings of the Dove,* we find Kate Croy, walking up and down in her father's shabby, rented, sitting room, scrutinizing herself from time to time in the looking glass, adjusting her hat, examining her features, and trying to get hold of her feelings. "She tried to be sad," James writes, "so as not to be angry, but it made her angry that she couldn't be sad."[14] Unlike the sitting room itself, which rivals the rooms in the Pension Vauquer for solidity of specification and transparency of meaning,[15] and unlike Lionel Croy, whose correct English exterior she has long since seen through, Kate is something of a mystery even to herself. She is, however, in the process of taking herself in hand, of establishing her relations with her relatives once and for all, and of asserting whatever identity she and fate will together have settled on.

Kate's father inadvertently helps her in this task by reminding her of her "tangible value" (I, 8) in his own scheme for financial independence and in her rich Aunt Maud's strategy for social advancement. What she must do, she realizes, is establish her right to dispose of this value—her youth, her beauty, her refinement, her availability—herself. So she makes her father an offer she knows he cannot accept: she proposes to give up her prospects with Aunt Maud in order to live poorly and obscurely with him, her closest relative. With this single gesture, she declares herself an independent agent, moving from the category of the "worked" to the category of the "workers." Her father, who had been all magnanimously intending to "give her up with some style and state" (I, 10) to Aunt Maud's safekeeping, and to make something for himself out of the bargain, sees the tables turned on him, sees his daughter reject the role of pawn in his game and become the principal player in her own. He knows what advantage she has gained of him by offering, once and for all, to do her duty. Her offer rejected, she can cut herself loose from parental bonds and take full advantage of her rich aunt's patronage and her own wit and beauty to make her way in London society, to marry the man of her choice, and even to serve in her own way her unfortunate father and sister.

By the end of the first book of *The Wings of the Dove* Kate has established herself as the protagonist in a modern drama,

the self-possessed manipulator of social codes and behavior. At
the same time the reader has settled rather comfortably into the
context of the witty, slightly ironic social novel, the novel which,
like *What Maisie Knew* or *The Spoils of Poynton,* traces the
development of a single consciousness, and follows it through
some portion of vaguely upper-class English life, pausing now
and then for vivid description or pointed social satire.

The second book complicates this generic conception slightly
by adding a second consciousness, that of Kate's amorous admirer, Merton Densher. If Densher provides an alternate view
of the text's events, though, this view is only potentially different
from Kate's. For the moment, he sees things as she does and
plays the parts she assigns him. When, for example, Aunt
Maud invites Densher to call on her, Kate is determined to fit
him into her plan for "squaring" that formidable lady and even,
with luck, for "working" her. She impresses on him the importance of her position not only for herself but for her poor sister
and even for her disreputable father. "'My position's a value, a
great value, for them both. . . . It's *the* value—the only one they
have'" (I, 71). Furthermore, she gives him to understand that
Aunt Maud holds the key to their own beautiful future.

> "I don't see why you don't make out a little more that if
> we avoid stupidity we may do *all*. We may keep her."
> He stared. "Make her pension us?"
> "Well, wait at least till we've seen."
> He thought. "Seen what can be got out of her?"
>
> .   .   .   .
>
> "So that what you mean is that I'm to do my part in some-
> how squaring her?"
> "See her, see her," Kate said with impatience.
> "And grovel to her?"
> "Ah do what you like!" And she walked in her impatience
> away. (I, 73, 74)

What *he* likes, Densher decides, is precisely what *she* likes, and
he goes off to Lancaster Gate determined to play his part as
Kate would have him. What he disconcertingly discovers when

he gets there is that Aunt Maud has decided to play *him* as if he posed no threat whatsoever, to make him her friend, enlist him for her dinner parties, and generally to let the unfortunate but finally trivial affair run it course under her eyes. The result is a standoff between two opposing definitions of the same set of circumstances, both existing comfortably, promisingly, within the familiar framework of the Jamesian social novel.

The first two books of *The Wings of the Dove* do a fine job of introducing the drama of consciousness into the text. They involve the reader in the development of the characters' views of themselves and thus provide stages for the intenser drama of the passions they will experience, the drama one can imagine taking place in the mind of Hedda Gabler or Ella Rentheim. They also lay the groundwork for the textual drama that is to follow, leading the reader by their tone and conventional content to believe that he is dealing with a mildly satirical novel of manners. The temptation at the end of Book Two is to think that *The Wings of the Dove* will be a good, sophisticated novel of British society, with a predictable cast of characters—young lovers, rich aunt, favored suitor, and so on—and no hint of philosophical or allegorical overtones.

The opening of Book Three gradually dispels this belief and sets the reader to rethinking his conception of the text. It introduces a new kind of consciousness in the mind of Susan Stringham, and a new kind of character in the person of Milly Theale, both of which seem at first to belong to a totally different text from the one projected by the first two books.

Susan Stringham is a widowed short-story writer from New England, a lady with an active imagination, a romantic mental vocabulary, and no sense whatever of the social gamesmanship and mutual exploitation of Kate Croy's world. She understands life as an aesthetic experience rather than a struggle for personal advantage, and sees the trip through Italy which precedes her appearance in the text as the overture to a grand romantic opera, a "Wagner overture" (I, 114).[16]

Milly Theale is the perfect subject for Mrs. Stringham's imaginative flights. She is a "striking apparition," a figure out

Washington Square (Anne)

of Hawthorne,[17] perhaps, or a Pre-Raphaelite painting, but in any event "romantic" and indisputably "interesting":

> . . . the slim, constantly pale, delicately haggard, anomalously, agreeably angular young person, of not more than two-and-twenty summers in spite of her marks, whose hair was somehow exceptionally red even for the real thing, which it innocently confessed to being, and whose clothes were remarkably black even for robes of mourning, which was the meaning they expressed. It was New York mourning, it was New York hair, it was a New York history, confused as yet, but multitudinous, of the loss of parents, brothers, sisters, almost every human appendage, all on a scale and with a sweep that had required the greater stage; it was a New York legend of affecting, of romantic isolation, and, beyond everything, it was by most accounts, in respect to the mass of money so piled on the girl's back, a set of New York possibilities. (I, 105–106)

Like Kate, Milly is recently bereaved, but the result of her bereavement is no sordid division of a meager legacy, no marshaling of personal resources to sally forth into the "thick of the fray," but a kind of financial and spiritual apotheosis, a privileged position of absolute freedom and total solitude. She exists, for Mrs. Stringham, at least, on a higher plane than ordinary mortals: she need devote none of her energy and attention to the daily routine of living, but can concentrate entirely on the more exalted business of simply *being* what she is, a "princess" (I, 120). Kate Croy carefully cast herself as a character in a social drama and placed the other actors around her in their conventional positions, and James at the same time suggested to his readers that they were dealing with a certain familiar kind of novel. Now Susan Stringham casts Milly Theale as a princess in what she calls a "conventional tragedy" (I, 120), and herself as the indispensable confidante. The result in Book Three is a sense of the broad ambitiousness of a text that can include and perhaps even reconcile these two views of the world, and a nat-

ural curiosity about a possible third view, that of the mysterious
and thus far closed consciousness of Milly Theale.

James heightens both these feelings by suggesting the complexity of Milly's view of herself and the world, and the existence of levels of meaning in this book which were absent from
the first two. Milly's long meditation on the brink of an Alpine
abyss begins the heightening process. The two ladies having
stopped for the night at a mountain inn, she sets off alone across
the sloping meadow in search, apparently, of solitude and sce-
nery. Some time later Mrs. Stringham follows in mild alarm,
discovers her friend on the "dizzy edge" (I, 123) of a promon-
tory, misdoubts her intentions for a moment, and then comforts
herself with the literary (Biblical or Miltonic, it doesn't matter)
thought that though "she was looking down on the kingdoms of
the earth, and though indeed that of itself might well go to the
brain, it wouldn't be with a view of renouncing them" (I, 124).
All this is perfectly consistent with James's portrayal of Susan
Stringham, and therefore credible as an episode in the development of her understanding of her mysterious friend. What is
remarkable about the passage is that in it the *drama* of consciousness transcends the *center* of consciousness. Earnest and
intelligent as she may be, Mrs. Stringham's mind cannot long
hold the reader's attention for its own sake. When she specu-
lates on the thoughts of her mysterious companion, our interest
naturally shifts from her insights to their object, and we look for
clues that would corroborate or disprove her theories. In this
instance such clues are easy to find. When Milly returns from
what Susan has seen as a mental survey of the kingdoms of the
earth with a view to taking possession of them, she reports that
she has in fact been wondering how much of all she has she will
be able to enjoy (I, 130). She may not have been surveying actual lands to conquer, but she has been taking stock of her possibilities and deciding what to do and where to go next. Meanwhile, of course, the reader's interest has shifted decisively from
Susan's transparent consciousness to Milly's mysterious one.

While Milly has been making her decision, furthermore,
James has been suggesting that the meaning of his text is not

limited to even the most complicated drama in the consciousness of its characters. He does this by having Mrs. Stringham suggest a mythic dimension to Milly's story, and by himself asserting the textual unity of his novel through the use of verbal and imagistic echoes of earlier chapters. The mythic dimension—the implied association of Milly with Christ—is only hinted at here to be taken up later on. The textual dimension is already very important for the kind of attention it demands from the reader as well as for the meanings it suggests. It is represented here by the belated concretization of a term used earlier, and by a repeated image.

In the last line of Book Two, Kate tells Merton Densher that women have "an abysmal need" of men (I, 99). The meaning of the word *abysmal* in this context is difficult to determine: it seems too strong and a little too negative, and stands out in the reader's mind for that reason. When, early in Book Three, Milly broods over an actual abyss, the term becomes even more charged with meaning in retrospect, and begins to be seen as the first appearance of a set of related words and ideas that will echo through the text. Similarly, when Kate Croy is described as gazing out of her rooms at Aunt Maud's "from the high south window that hung over the Park" (I, 27) and contemplating her eventual descent into the "thick of the fray" (I, 32) of London society, the image is effective in calling attention to itself and impressing itself on the memory. When, therefore, Milly Theale is described a few pages later as surveying *her* future from another exalted vantage point, the relation of the two women is implied by the text without arising in the consciousness of any of its characters.

The effect of the third book of *The Wings of the Dove* is quite clearly to complicate every aspect of its drama. The book adds two potential stages for the drama of consciousness, Milly's mind and Susan's. It adds, too, a potential for overt dramatic action in Milly's projected "siege of London" and especially in her connections with Merton Densher and Kate Croy. Most important, it complicates the literary drama of the text. First it ruptures the narrative continuity. Then it challenges Kate

Croy's and the first two books' definition of the action as social drama, and the text's identity as a novel of manners, suggesting that the production to follow might be a modern-dress version of *Tannhäuser*, say, rather than *The Marriage of Figaro*. Finally, it asserts the unity of the text and the narrator's control over it by demonstrating the possibility of constructing verbal and metaphoric patterns in the context of strictly controlled center-of-consciousness narrative.

The Triple Drama:
Kate, Milly, and the Reader

In the rest of the first volume of *The Wings of the Dove* James deepens our sense of the denseness and intricacy of the social drama as Kate Croy plays it, of the drama of Milly Theale's developing consciousness, and of the reading process itself. Life becomes a more complicated affair for Kate Croy as her story progresses. She is a creature of sincere loyalties and simple desires: she knows who she is, what she feels, what she wants, and what measure of support and affection she owes to others. She is not, for all this knowledge, cold or inhuman, but her natural intelligence and a youth of strained, conniving penury have made her bitterly practical about material things, and disinclined to sentimentality. Her description, for example, of her sister Marian's squalid household is full of "her constant perception of the incongruity of things" (I, 65), a perception which she attributes to the fact that "she had seen the general show too early and too sharply, and she was so intelligent that she knew it" (I, 65). "Lucid and ironic," she knows "no merciful muddle" (I, 71). Passionately in love with Merton Densher, honestly devoted to her unfortunate relatives, she comes very quickly to view life as an elaborate, serious, and cold-blooded game of skill for high stakes. Our sense of Kate as an emotional being, at its height in her spontaneous declaration of eternal devotion to Merton Densher at the end of the second book, soon gives way to a sense of her as an interested if not an unfeeling schemer. Even her final consent to sleep with her

lover is given grudgingly as a kind of payment for Merton's
continued participation in her plot to work Milly Theale. Earlier, she had given Milly her interpretation of the London world
as a kind of warning against Aunt Maud, and Lord Mark, and
even herself, and now she is acting out this interpretation. In
London, she had said,

> the working and the worked . . . were . . . the parties to every
> relation . . . every one who had anything to give—it was true
> they were the fewest—made the sharpest possible bargain for
> it, got at least its value in return. The strangest thing, fur-
> thermore, was that this might be, in cases, a happy under-
> standing. The worker in one connection was the worked in
> another; it was as broad as it was long—with the wheels of
> the system, as might be seen, wonderfully oiled. (I, 197–98)

"The world," as Kate sees it, runs on a complicated system of
mutual, rational exploitation, operating ideally for the good of
all, but most certainly for the benefit of the person who can
contrive to "work" more often than he is "worked." She attempts to "cling to some saving romance in things" (I, 72), but
her hard-earned and hard-headed practicality makes this rather
difficult. We see very little of her consciousness after the first
few chapters, and we can only imagine the dramatic conflict
that takes place in it between her naturally warm feelings and
her conditioned, rational, disabused view of life as a mutual-
benefit con game on the model, say, of *The Way of the World.*
   This view of life is challenged and effectively displaced from
the center of the text by Milly Theale's appearance in it, by her
own confused and earnest self-image, and by Susan Stringham's
and even Kate's view of her. Life as Milly Theale regards it
from the eminence of the Alps, her fortune, and her independence, is complicated, to be sure. It is not, however, a game for
high prizes, but the prize itself, something mysterious with
which she, for all her acquaintance with death, has had little to
do, which she does not understand, and which she wishes to
seize. Life is risk for her (I, 140), it is the excitement of labyrinths to explore (I, 186) and abysses to sound (I, 187, 188). At

first the risk is all vicarious, for the pleasure of watching other people live, of seeing the labyrinths and abysses without actually venturing to involve herself in any of them satisfies her desire for life. She stands on the bank, as she puts it to herself (I, 147), and observes the complexities of feeling in London life as it rushes past. She allows her new friends to dispose of her time as they will, amused to be considered such a valuable "property" (I, 157), yet remaining aloof from the life around her, looking and being looked at, learning about others but not opening her own heart or her life to be learned about. Having lived always under the shadow of death, Milly is eager for life and yet shy of it, willing to "get into the current" (I, 147), yet deathly afraid of the consequences.

The climax of this phase of Milly's London life, the "high-water mark of the imagination" (I, 210), as she puts it, and what she later refers to as the "high-water mark of her security" (II, 144), comes at Matcham, where she is for the last time and most magnificently the unengaged observer and object of observation. Unlike Maud Lowder, who has long coveted an invitation to Matcham, Milly and Susan are there through no desire of their own, but at Lord Mark's invitation. "Their feeling was," they had told him, "that there was no place they would have liked to go to; there was only the sense of finding they liked, wherever they were, the place to which they had been brought" (I, 207). So Milly strolls through the gardens, observing no particular drama but just the "admirable picture" of the place, listening to "empty words" (I, 218), returning the "bland stares" (I, 219) of the unknown faces, running on Lord Mark's arm the gauntlet of the guests, "letting people, poor dear things, have the benefit of her" (I, 218). There are, however, more pictures at Matcham than the ones that the guests provide for each other, and Lord Mark is leading Milly to see one of these, a Bronzino portrait whose subject his American friend so strikingly resembles. As they make their way to the room where the picture is hung, Milly feels that things could not be more perfect: "Once more things melted together—the beauty and the history and the facility and the splendid midsummer glow: it was a sort of magnificent maximum, the pink dawn of an apotheosis coming so curiously soon" (I, 220). The Bronzino depicts no apotheosis, however, no Assumption into Heaven or Last Judgment, and Milly feels, standing in front of it, no sense of nearness to God, no promise of eternal life, but rather that sense of death—of life interrupted, spatialized, made static—which inhabits all pictures, those in gardens and drawing rooms as well as those on gallery walls:

> The lady in question, at all events, with her slightly Michaelangelesque squareness, her eyes of other days, her full lips, her long neck, her recorded jewels, her brocaded and wasted reds, was a very great personage—only unaccompanied by a joy. And she was dead, dead, dead. Milly recognized her exactly in words that had nothing to do with her. "I shall never be better than this." (I, 221)

Milly has been living, she realizes, the passive life of a picture, a life that seems by its avoidance of action and of emotional involvement to escape the risk of death.[18] Such a life, fine as it may be, leads to no apotheosis, but exists for its own sake and its own beauty. The illusion of immortality which it provides is possible only because all that it possesses of real life is carefully suppressed, covered over with style and good manners, "empty words" and "bland stares." Such a life *is* beautiful, but it cannot and it should not last. Milly will "never be better than this" because she will never again enjoy the beautiful illusion of timelessness and deathlessness which the last few weeks and particularly the last few hours have provided. Life, she realizes, is not a picture to be admired in a gallery: one cannot know life by standing on the bank and watching it flow past; one cannot, most of all, avoid death, which is no less present in the most beautiful picture than it is in the most violent drama. One can, however, *face* death, take real and not vicarious risks, give up the picture for the drama and *live* actively while one is able. This is of course exactly what Milly Theale is about to do, which is why she fears she will never be better in one limited

way than she was a Matcham. To *be,* however beautifully, will
no longer be her task, but rather to live. Knowing this, she turns
from the Bronzino to Kate Croy, and asks the handsome girl to
go with her to consult Sir Luke Strett, the physician who will
condemn her to an active life and an early death. "'Isn't to
"live" exactly what I'm trying to persuade you to take the trouble to do?'" he will ask her, and she will take his question as
the challenge to a new, dramatic life *sub specie mortis:* "She had
been treated—hadn't she?—as if it were in her power to live;
and yet one wasn't treated so—was one?—unless it had come
up, quite as much, that one might die" (I, 246, 248).

Milly begins exercising her power to *live* by quite willfully
shedding her identity as heiress and princess, and wandering
through streets "which she hoped were slums" (I, 249), feeling
quite like any other bewildered young woman. She comes out,
eventually, in Regent's Park, cuts quickly across the circular
road "round which on two or three occasions with Kate Croy
her public chariot had solemnly rolled," and heads for the unceremonious center of the park, "the real thing" as she calls it,
"quite away from the pompous roads, well within the centre
and on the stretches of shabby grass" (I, 250). She sits down on
a bench, preferring it to a chair "for which she would have paid,
with superiority, a fee" (I, 250), and realizes that, for "the first
time in her life," "nobody in the world knew where she was"
(I, 250). The effect of Sir Luke's kind, positive admonition to
live has been "divesting, denuding, exposing." It has "reduced
her to her ultimate state, which was that of a poor girl—with
her rent to pay for example—staring before her in a great city.
Milly had her rent to pay, her rent for the future; everything
else but how to meet it fell away from her in pieces, in tatters"
(I, 253–54).

Stripped of her friends, her history, her money, and all, Milly
is here the closest any character in James comes to what King
Lear calls "the thing itself; unaccommodated man."[19] "Di-
vested," "denuded," and "exposed," she spends her hour on the
heath, confronts man's mortal fate as it will apparently apply
to her particular case, and decides that she must live actively

while she can, must see that she gets the best possible accommodation for the rent she will be able up to the end to pay.

As a result of her decision, Milly begins ever so cautiously to participate in the game of life as Kate Croy sees it, without, however, any end in view other than the preservation of her own freedom, and the protection of her friends. She therefore lies to Kate about her own health in order to spare them both, at least temporarily, the consequence of the truth. More important, she involves herself unwittingly in Aunt Maud's scheming against Kate and Merton Densher. First she agrees to find out from Kate if Merton, whom Aunt Maud has depicted as hopelessly and one-sidedly in love with her polite but indifferent niece, has returned from America. "'I shall like to help you,'" she says; "'I shall like, so far as that goes, to help Kate herself'" (I, 270). Then, although she is certain from Kate's very appearance that Merton has indeed returned, she determines to do nothing that Aunt Maud has asked her to do (I, 274), and eventually tells her that she does not think the young man has come back (I, 284). So Milly begins to *act,* not so much for herself as for others: although she feels that she is "still in a current determined, through her indifference, timidity, bravery, generosity—she scarce could say which—by others" (I, 274), she has at least left the bank and entered the stream.

Milly's most important action at this point in the novel is not, however, her debut in the social drama, but the barely perceptible way in which she begins to open herself to the possibility of a sentimental attachment to Merton Densher. When Susan Stringham first mentioned his name, there in the inn on the Brünig when Milly had announced her decision to start immediately for London, Milly had pretended not to remember him, and then contradictorily asserted that "she might very well not have thought of London at all if she hadn't been sure he wasn't yet near coming back" (I, 138). The young man is clearly not indifferent to her, but she is just as clearly not yet willing to admit any attraction. Later, however, under the influence partly of Sir Luke's advice to live, and partly of the conviction that Merton is in love with Kate, and therefore not likely

to form a potentially painful liaison with herself, Milly admits
to Aunt Maud that she likes him. "'You do like him?'" she asks
the lady of Lancaster Gate, who replies, "'Oh dear yes. Don't
you?'"

> Milly waited, for the question was somehow as the sudden
> point of something sharp on a nerve that winced. She just
> caught her breath, but she had ground for joy afterwards, she
> felt, in not really having failed to choose with quickness suf-
> ficient, out of fifteen possible answers, the one that would best
> serve her. . . . "I did—three times—in New York." So came
> and went, in these simple words, the speech that was to figure
> for her, later on, that night, as the one she had ever uttered
> that cost her most. She was to lie awake for the gladness of
> not having taken any line so really inferior as the denial of a
> happy impression. (I, 266–67)

The extraordinary effect of these few words, this simple admission, is a clear sign of the power of Milly's defensive instincts
and the great effort she must make to overcome them and participate, even mentally, in life. As it happens, however, Aunt
Maud's half-truth about Merton's relations with Kate provides
Milly's feelings with just the kind of protective insulation they]
need in order fully to emerge into her consciousness. When she
actually meets the couple in the National Gallery, therefore, she
can give her natural liking for the journalist free rein (I, 299)
without risking her independence. She can even catch herself
wishing, against the safely established contrary fact, that her
future meetings with Densher might not be so much a natural
consequence of his acquaintance with the ladies of Lancaster
Gate as a sign of the "operation of real affinities" (I, 301).

So Milly is being prepared, by James and by her own awareness of the limits set by fate on her life, to participate in the
drama of the passions. Unlike Kate, however, Milly does not
perceive this drama as a comedy of manners, nor see its complexity as a matter of plot and counterplot. Living fully is for
her an end in itself, difficult even to imagine and therefore doubly difficult to attain. Her perception of life includes that di-

mension of painful inwardness which Kate's clearly lacks, a sense of difficulty not merely tactical and of pathos which is not only pitiable but deeply and radically terrifying.

Kate's vision of the world as a stage for her own drama of ambition is complicated by Milly's growing consciousness of "real" life as a scene to be acted rather than a picture to be observed. Fast-paced, brittle comedy of manners is complicated by the slow and supple development of the drama of consciousness. Conventional bits of comic action—Milly's chance discovery of Kate's and Merton's clandestine meeting at the National Gallery, for example—take on great significance in the growth of Milly's awareness, and the two kinds of drama contaminate each other more and more as Milly decides to chance at least limited action and involvement in the world, and Kate and later especially Merton catch glimpses of Milly's intense suffering.

Both these dramas and the interaction between them help to structure the experience of reading *The Wings of the Dove*. There is also, as we have seen, a third, purely textual drama, which modifies our understanding of the drama of manners and the drama of consciousness, which is in turn modified by them, but which never asserts that it alone holds the key to the text's single meaning. This is in part the drama of the reading process itself, the continuous, active, self-modifying definition of the text and its purposes which we have examined above. It is also the drama created by the interacting patterns of words and images in the text, patterns that necessarily arise in the thoughts and words of the characters, but that suggest a greater textual consistency than the disparities among the characters would lead one to expect. Austin Warren calls the construction of these patterns the myth-making function of James's novels, and opposes it to what he calls their dialectical, which is to say their logical, narrative, argumentative functions.[20] The effect of the myth-making function is to lead the reader to "another kind of truth to be arrived at not socially, intellectually, or analytically, but personally, intuitively, imaginatively—through images and symbols."[21]

As we have seen, the repeated images of the abyss, that terrifying emptiness yawning beneath our everyday social intercourse, suggest one such truth or meaning, while the similarity implied between Kate's and Milly's apparently very different predicaments in the two scenes in which they gaze on the world from high places suggests another. In the first volume of the novel, James and his characters suggest further "mythic" meanings by the words they use to characterize Milly Theale. One such word, which has for obvious reasons tempted readers to see in it the impossible "key" to the whole meaning of the text, is *dove*.[22]

"'Why do you say such things to me?'" Milly asks Kate when, late in Book Five, the handsome girl predicts that her friend may end by loathing her, and Kate replies, "'Because you're a dove'" (I, 282, 283). The statement triggers a number of associations in the reader's mind, one set relating to the title, the psalms, and Susan Stringham's momentary vision of Milly as Christ, and another to the animal images already used in the text,[23] of Aunt Maud as a lioness (I, 30) or an eagle or a vulture (I, 73), and of Kate as a sacrificial kid (I, 30). The significance of these associations has been studied at length[24] and there is no need to rehearse here what has been so thoroughly said elsewhere. What most of the commentators on the dove-image have missed, however, is Milly's immediate and eager appropriation of it as a model for her behavior and her view of herself in the world.[25] Kate says, "'Because you're a dove,'" and Milly feels herself

> ever so delicately, so considerately, embraced; not with familiarity or as a liberty taken, but almost ceremonially and in the manner of an *accolade;* partly as if, though a dove who could perch on a finger, one were also a princess with whom forms were to be observed. . . . She met it on the instant as she would have met the revealed truth; it lighted up the strange dusk in which she lately had walked. *That* was what was the matter with her. She was a dove. Oh, *wasn't* she? (I, 283)

If Milly's "problem" is that she is a dove, she resolves to make the best of it, lies in her most dovelike manner to Aunt Maud— "'I don't *think,* dear lady, he's here'"—and perceives "straightway the measure of the success she could have as a dove" (I, 284). She decides, therefore, to "study the dovelike" (I, 284), to use Kate's inspired perception of her to help her on with the task of living.

> That, with the new day, was once more her law—though she saw before her, of course, as something of a complication, her need, each time, to decide. She should have to be clear as to how a dove *would* act. (I, 284)

For Kate, the image of the dove seems to suggest Milly's helpless passivity, her mild willingness to be sacrificed. If Milly should come one day to loathe her friend it would be because Kate has taken advantage of her dovelike qualities to exploit her. For Milly, on the other hand, the image of the dove suggests a mask, and a model for effective action. If she can only imitate the dove, she thinks, she will be able to participate effectively in life, to get something of what she wants, without betraying her shy, gentle nature. For the reader, of course, the dove suggests much more, a whole range of symbolic values which influence his reading of the rest of the text.

Not everyone sees Milly as a dove, however. For Susan Stringham, she is first and always a "princess," a term which she uses in a general way to mean a young woman to whom others seem for whatever reason instinctively to offer tribute. Milly can be a princess, of course, only because she is rich.

> It came back of course to the question of money, and our observant lady had by this time repeatedly reflected that if one were talking of the "difference," it was just this, this incomparably and nothing else, that when all was said and done most made it. (I, 121)

Her enormous wealth has made her different from ordinary people, different even from ordinary rich people, and she can no more escape it than she can escape her red hair or her mortal illness.

> She couldn't dress it away, nor walk it away, nor read it away, nor think it away; she could neither smile it away in

any dreamy absence nor blow it away in any softened sigh. She couldn't have lost it if she had tried—that was what it was to be really rich. (I, 121)

Her function as a princess, however, does not involve the direct display of great wealth, but rather the quiet, uninsistent *representation* of a set of values which certainly includes but is not limited to money. Milly is for Kate "quite the nearest approach to a practical princess Bayswater could ever hope to know" (I, 174) because her striking appearance in the present calls up such a sad and violent past, the essence, it seems to her, of the dynamics and the scale of American life.

Her visitor's American references, with their bewildering immensities, their confounding moneyed New York, their excitements of high pressure, their opportunities of wild freedom, their record of used-up relatives, parents, clever eager fair slim brothers—these the most loved—all engaged, as well as successive superceded guardians, in a high extravagance of speculation and dissipation that had left this exquisite being her black dress, her white face and her vivid hair as the mere last broken link: such a picture quite threw into the shade the brief biography, however sketchily amplified, of a mere middle-class nobody in Bayswater. (I, 174)

For Susan Stringham, on the other hand, Milly the princess represents nothing quite so specific, but rather a combination of goodness and power which evokes, in the scene by the abyss, the image of a worldly, Satan-less Christ surveying the kingdoms of the earth and deciding she wants them all. Furthermore, Susan also perceives that one of the great disadvantages of being a princess is that she must willy-nilly spend so much of her time in her representative capacity that she has precious little left for direct contact with the "real":

Milly was the wandering princess: so what could be more in harmony now than to see the princess waited upon at the city gate by the worthiest maiden, the chosen daughter of the burgesses? It was the real again, evidently, the amusement of the meeting for the princess too; princesses living for the most part, in such an appeased way, on the plane of mere elegant representation. That was why they pounced, at city gates, on deputed flower-strewing damsels; that was why, after effigies, processions and other stately games, frank human company was pleasant to them. (I, 171)

Milly's function as representative princess is one of the things she hopes at least temporarily to escape by her active participation in the life of the world, but it is clear from other people's treatment of her that she can never escape the fact that she represents, irrespective of her own intentions, a certain social value. Lord Mark, for example, clearly considers Milly Aunt Maud's greatest social asset. When Milly remarks to him on the fidelity of that lady to her old school friend, Susan Stringham, Lord Mark suggests that her apparent generosity may be as much repayment for value received as a sign of nobility of spirit (I, 154). This value, Milly realizes, with something of a shock, is her own presence. "Milly had practically just learned from him, had made out . . . that he gave her the highest place among their friend's actual properties" (I, 157). As an American princess Milly embodies the perfect combination of representationality and vagueness of reference. Insofar as she is rich, her value is unquestioned, but insofar as she is an orphaned American it is undefinable and therefore doubly valuable. "'You can do anything,'" Kate tells her, "'you can do, I mean, lots that *we* can't. You're an outsider, independent and standing by yourself; you're not hideously relative to tiers and tiers of others'" (I, 281).

The same might be said, *mutatis mutandis,* for the mythmaking function in *The Wings of the Dove.* Like Milly Theale, the text of James's novel is obviously rich, and demonstrably representational. Furthermore, the ultimate meanings of both the princess and the text are multiple and indeterminate. Just as the suggestion that Milly is a "princess" comes to represent more in the text than any one of the characters who uses it intends, so the textual and the myth-making functions of *The Wings of the Dove* suggest, even *represent,* multiple meanings, none of which can serve in itself as a satisfactory interpretation of the text.

On the other hand, neither Milly nor *The Wings of the Dove* is quite so formless and independent as Kate's declaration and my analogy might imply. Milly may stand by herself, outside the social hierarchy, but she *needs* other people, needs Merton Densher, Susan Stringham, Sir Luke, and even Kate herself, more desperately than the practical, literal-minded Kate can realize. She cannot be defined by her relation with any one of these people or by the sum of all her human relations, but without them she would not be the woman she is. Similarly, the meaning of *The Wings of the Dove* cannot be defined by any one of its textual or mythic elements—the "abyss," the Christian parallels, "representation" itself—or by all of them together, yet it needs each of them to define its character and produce its drama on the stage of the reader's mind.

The Clash of Egos,
Merton's Expanding Awareness,
and Milly's Heroism

In the first volume (Books 1–5) of *The Wings of the Dove* James has been most concerned with describing the minds and the emotions of Kate Croy and Milly Theale, and with leading the reader to define the text as a generically and referentially complex structure of words and images. There has been drama in the development of these consciousnesses and of the reader's conception of the text, but very little overt conflict.

In the second volume, James rewards the reader's patience by describing the lurid plot Kate devises to work Milly's affection for Merton Densher, and its unexpected and unfortunate results. The reader, familiar by this time with the several stages on which the drama takes place, is ready to surrender at least part of his attention to its melodramatic plot line, all the while contemplating the three related dramas of Merton Densher's slowly expanding awareness of moral complicity, Milly

Theale's heroic efforts to live in the face of rapidly approaching death, and the text's elaboration of patterns of meaning.

Merton Densher, as becomes apparent after his return from New York, is a singularly dense young man, narrow and literal-minded in his self-imposed moral "straightness." He may have that "strength. . . for thought" (I, 51) which he claims, but the "high, dim things . . . of the mind" (I, 50) which he represents for Kate Croy are in fact so high and so dim that they never manifest themselves in the pages of *The Wings of the Dove*. Leon Edel has argued convincingly that Densher's experiences with Milly Theale represent a fusion of James's own experiences with his cousin, Minny Temple, and his long-time admirer and friend, Constance Fenimore Woolson,[26] but to say with Frederick Crews that he is "an oracle for James's own opinions"[27] is seriously to underestimate the subtlety of the author's "opinions" or to overestimate the subtlety of the character's.

By the time he wrote *The Wings of the Dove*, however, James had already demonstrated, in *The Beast in the Jungle, What Maisie Knew,* and "In the Cage," for example, the potential of the limited reflector, and his portrayal of the development of Densher's moral awareness is no less dramatic because its subject is somewhat obtuse. In fact, Densher's failure immediately to comprehend his situation and its moral implications allows James to develop his young man's more appealing features, to induce the reader to *like* Densher even as he judges him and to sympathize with the young man while he wonders when he will *finally* come to understand his moral predicament. The result for the reader is a combination of fellow feeling, suspense, and exasperation which produces several different kinds of interest in Merton Densher's moral development.

From the beginning of the second volume Merton is slow to catch on to Kate's plots, and even slower to realize and admit the moral responsibility he must accept for his participation in them. It takes him the whole of the first chapter, for example, to realize that Kate is cultivating Milly for her own purposes,

that "if she weren't a bore" she might prove a real "convenience" for the lovers.

> It rolled over him of a sudden, after he had resumed his walk,
> that this might easily be what Kate had meant. The charming
> girl adored her—Densher had for himself made out that—
> and would protect, would lend a hand, to their interviews.
> (II, 14–15)

In the next chapter Kate predictably has the devil's own time
trying to make Merton understand how he should behave in
order to make the most of Milly. Her lover's conditioned
"moral" responses to her suggestions are not in the end, however, difficult to allay: she merely asks, like a wise parent, that
he trust her.

> "You accused me just now of saying that Milly's in love
> with you. Well, if you come to that, I do say it. So there you
> are. That's the good she'll do us. It makes a basis for her
> seeing you—so that she'll help us to go on."
>   Densher stared—she was wondrous all round. "And what
> sort of a basis does it make for my seeing *her?*"
> .   .   .   .
>   "And what does it give *me,*" the young man none the less
> rationally asked, "the chance to be? A brute of a humbug to
> her?"
>   Kate so possessed her facts, as it were, that she smiled at
> his violence. "You'll extraordinarily like her. She's exquisite.
> And there are reasons. I mean others."
>   "What others?"
>   "Well, I'll tell you another time. Those I give you," the
> girl added, "are enough to go on with."
> .   .   .   .
>   "Go to see Milly," she for all satisfaction repeated.
>   "And what good will that do me?"
>   "Try it and you'll see."

"You mean you'll manage to be there?" Densher asked. "Say you are, how will that give us privacy?"

"Try it—you'll see," the girl once more returned. "We must manage as we can." (II, 24–25, 25–26, 29)

Even when the fact of Milly's illness comes to light, Densher is slow to catch its significance:

For a moment now, in silence, he took it all in, might have had it before him. "What you want of me then is to make up to a sick girl."

"Ah but you admit yourself that she doesn't affect you as sick. You understand moreover just how much—and just how little."

"It's amazing," he presently answered, "what you think I understand." (II, 56)

Merton Densher *means* well, clearly, and his failure to see the purpose of Kate's plotting is among other things a sign of his appealing naiveté and praiseworthy innocence. These two characteristics together with his natural timidity and his indeterminate social position produce in the young man a feeling of frustration and helplessness which evokes the reader's sympathy if not his unstinting admiration. The feeling first arises in Densher's relations with Kate Croy: not only does the handsome girl put him off conversationally, as in the passages just quoted, she refuses to meet him privately in his rooms or elsewhere, and so denies him the solace of physical contact and sexual fulfillment. When he poses the question of where they will meet, she puts him off with a plea to "leave her, now and henceforth, to treat them in her own way" (II, 6), and then suggests another meeting in a museum "with such happy art that his fully seeing where she had placed him hadn't been till after he left her" (II, 6). The feeling arises, too, in Densher's social dealings with Aunt Maud, both because she "keeps him down" by refusing to acknowledge the threat he poses to her plans, and because he prefers being kept down to being even falsely accused of dishonorable conduct, and is ashamed of his preference.

"Being kept down was a bore, but his great dread, verily, was of being ashamed, which was a thing distinct; and it mattered but little that he was ashamed of that too" (II, 32).

To the reader's impatience with Densher's failure to understand the morally dubious plotting going on around him is added a modicum of sympathy for his unfortunate predicament. As the story goes on, however, this sympathy is sorely tested by Densher's indecisive response to those elements of that predicament that he does come to understand.

When, for example, Aunt Maud finally makes the stakes clear to him, Densher's passivity wins out over his good intentions and he tacitly falls in with the scheme. "'Don't you understand me?'" Aunt Maud asks him, and then gives her own action and Kate's their right, their brutal name: "'I've told the proper lie for you.'" Densher leaves her house mystified, but outside, under the Bayswater stars, he has his revelation:

> He had had his brief stupidity, but now he understood. She had guaranteed to Milly Theale through Mrs. Stringham that Kate didn't care for him. She had affirmed through the same source that the attachment was only his. He made it out, he made it out, and he could see what she meant by its starting him. She had described Kate as merely compassionate, so that Milly might be compassionate too. "Proper" indeed it was, her lie—the very properest possible and the most deeply, richly diplomatic. So Milly was successfully deceived. (II, 69)

Densher's new knowledge, however, has little effect on his behavior. The morning after his revelation he visits Milly as he had previously planned to, aware of but unmoved by the way he now realizes his visit will be interpreted. "Many men," he tells himself, would have drawn a moral line, would have let their awareness of such a deception "render any further acquaintance with Miss Theale impossible" (II, 71). He, however, is too intelligent and too good for that, and he convinces himself that the easiest and most natural thing to do is also the best thing for everyone concerned.

It was that he liked too much everyone concerned willingly to show himself merely impracticable. He liked Kate, goodness knew, and he also clearly enough liked Mrs. Lowder. He liked in particular Milly herself; and hadn't it come up for him the evening before that he quite liked even Susan Shepherd? He had never known himself so generally merciful. It was a footing, at all events, whatever accounted for it, on which he should surely be rather a muff not to manage by one turn or another to escape disobliging. (II, 71–72)

Densher keeps to the same line to the end, always managing, even in the face of his own apparent understanding of the facts and their consequences, to convince himself that he is doing the right thing. He tells himself, for example, that *he* has "as yet done nothing deceptive," and then sees it "with a certain alarm rise before him that everything was acting that was not speaking the particular word" (II, 76). Still, he reasons, perhaps deception is the kindest course in this case, honesty being rather difficult and not a little embarrassing. "Wouldn't it be virtually as indelicate to challenge her as to leave her deluded?" (II, 77). Even at the end of Milly's life, when she has turned her face to the wall, Densher is able to convince himself that he has been behaving perfectly honorably with her, acting falsely, to be sure, but never doing anything so ungentlemanly and so unpleasant as Lord Mark has done in confronting her with facts.

Densher had indeed drifted by the next morning to the reflexion—which he positively, with occasion, might have brought straight out—that the only delicate and honourable way of treating a person in such a state was to treat her as *he,* Merton Densher, did. With time, actually—for the impression but deepened—this sense of the contrast, to the advantage of Merton Densher, became a sense of relief, and that in turn a sense of escape. It was for all the world—and he drew a long breath on it—as if a special danger for him had passed. (II, 265)

And in a way Densher was right, if not in principle at least in common practice. There is no easy solution to his moral muddle, and there is every reason to believe that Kate's pragmatic scheme for pleasing everyone would have succeeded despite its disregard for "the truth" had not a jealous Lord Mark intervened. Densher may be slow, but he is not evil; the reader may be impatient with him for not understanding things which the course of the narration has made obvious to *him;* he may disapprove of Densher for his casuistry and his passivity, but he is certainly caught up in the development of Densher's consciousness, and cannot ignore the young man's anguish and his fundamental good intentions.

Furthermore, as we have seen, Densher is not entirely passive or entirely amoral: indeed, his passivity and his amorality are something of a personal embarrassment to him when he catches guilty inklings of them, and he does his best to compensate for them with a kind of straightforward "manliness" which is his most affecting and at the same time his most pathetic characteristic. This is manifested first in his intermittent flare-ups of sexual desire for Kate, born, it seems, of a sense of injured masculinity. "The proof of a decent reaction in him against so much passivity," he tells himself, "was that he at least knew—knew, that is, how he was, and how little he liked it as a thing accepted in mere helplessness" (II, 176). "Whereas he had done absolutely everything that Kate had wanted," he further muses, "she had done nothing whatever that he had" (II, 177). So Densher decides to assert himself, and rents private rooms in which to do it. When it comes to the point, however, his self-assertion takes the form of a sort of bargain, an exchange of Kate's "honor" for his own. "'We've told too many lies,'" Kate tells him. "'I, my dear, have told none!'" he replies. "'Rather than lay myself open to the least appearance of it, I'll go this very night.'" Soon, however, he reconsiders:

> "I'll tell any lie you want, any your idea requires, if you'll only come to me."
> "Come to you?"
> "Come to me."
> "How? Where?"
> She spoke low, but there was somehow, for his uncertainty,

a wonder in her being so equal to him. "To my rooms, which are perfectly possible, and in taking which, the other day, I had you, as you must have felt, in view." (II, 199–200)

Before Kate agrees to the bargain, however, she on her side forces Densher to articulate his part of it as simply and as clearly as he can, lest there be any mistake about his own complicity. This is the famous scene at Milly's party in Venice, where the two conspirators plot on one side of the room while their dove-princess-victim blesses them from the other. "'If you want things named'" Kate says, "'you must name them.'"

> He had quite, within the minute, been turning names over; and there was only one, which at last stared at him there dreadful, that properly fitted. "Since she's to die I'm to marry her?"
>
> It struck him even at the moment as fine in her that she met it with no wincing nor mincing. She might for the grace of silence, for favor to their conditions, have only answered him with her eyes. But her lips bravely moved. "To marry her."
>
> "So that when her death has taken place I shall in the natural course have money?"
>
> . . . .
>
> "You'll in the natural course have money. We shall in the natural course be free." (II, 225)

So the bargain is made, and Kate carries out her part of it. In expecting the same of Densher, however, she has reckoned without a second aspect of her lover's residual naiveté, his literal-minded belief in moral "straightness." What this means for Densher is a kind of absolute moral legalism, whereby casuistry, rationalization, and self-justification are all permissible, provided one can avoid the lie direct. Densher lies to Milly directly only once, as far as we know, and even then the bald lie, which he cannot uphold, turns quickly into a much more dangerous half-truth. The question, the only one that Milly has so far posed, is simply *why* does Merton stay in Venice after Kate's departure. The journalist's lying answer is not the brash avowal of love that his hostess may subconsciously be hoping for, but rather an oblique, shy lie, which avoids the issue without, this time, avoiding the necessity of falsehood. He tells her he is at work on a book and requires quiet. Then, a little later, he is surprised into an admission that there is no book (II, 248). "'Then if it's not for your book—?'" Milly asks. "'What *am* I staying for?'" he replies. "'I stay because I've got to'" (II, 249). And then, "'Isn't it enough, whatever may be one's other complications, to stay after all for *you?*'" (II, 249–50). The point is, of course, that even though by now it may seem to Densher that it *would* be enough to stay only for Milly, he is in fact staying primarily for Kate and for himself. By answering Milly's question with a question, Densher simultaneously gives voice to his feeling for her without actually declaring it, and deceives her without lying to her.

Densher maintains his literal, surface "honesty" to the end, even going so far as to stop in at the Brompton Oratory on Christmas morning, not out of any religious feeling, but because Aunt Maud has suggested that he must be on his way to church, and he has not denied it. In the last chapters, however, this honesty has something frantic about it, a compulsion in Densher to protect himself from his own conscience and from the magnitude of what has happened to him by behaving with exaggerated, strict, legalistic "decency." He is eager first of all to marry Kate and announce the marriage to Milly as soon as possible, lest she die while he is tacitly deceiving her, and so that any gesture she might make will be the result of no deception but of her own sweet will. Kate seems willing, provided Merton "*knows* something," presumably about Milly's testamentary intentions. He will not admit to any such knowledge, however, and Kate will not give her consent without it (II, 349).

Even after Milly's death, Densher strives to prove his own decency and Kate's by sending his friend the unopened letter from Milly's attorneys and so giving her the opportunity to reject the fruits of her victory without even knowing what they are. Kate predictably fails Densher's "test," but she learns from his seriousness about it more of what has happened to him than he himself yet understands. "'I think that what it really is must be that you're afraid,'" she tells him. "'I mean . . . that you're afraid of *all* the truth. If you're in love with her without it, what indeed can you be more? And you're afraid—it's wonderful!—to be in love with her'" (II, 403). "'I never was in love with her,'" Densher emphatically replies, and Kate believes his assertion without renouncing her own insight.

> She took it, but after a little she met it. "I believe that now—for the time she lived. I believe it at least for the time you were there. But your change came—as it might well—the day you last saw her; she died for you then that you might understand her. From that hour you *did*." With which Kate slowly rose. "And I do now. She did it *for* us." Densher rose to face her, and she went on with her thought. "I used to call her, in my stupidity—for want of anything better—a dove. Well she stretched out her wings, and it was to *that* she reached. They cover us."
> "They cover us," Densher said.
> "That's what I give you," Kate gravely wound up. "That's what I've done for you." (II, 403–404)

In Kate's opinion, Densher *understands* more of what has happened to him than he will admit, even to himself. She has accused him of wanting to "escape everything" (II, 402), and she finally understands his desire to marry her as he might have done before the descent of Milly Theale as a desire to deny the experience of the intervening months, to suppress his understanding of Milly's gift. "'I'll marry you, mind you, in an hour,'" he tells her.

> "As we were?"
> "As we were."
> But she turned to the door, and her headshake was now the end. "We shall never be again as we were!" (II, 405)

Kate in her wisdom knows that Milly cannot be denied. Densher, she believes, knows it too, but is not yet aware of his knowledge.

The question before the reader at this point, of course, is just what change has Milly made. The "dialectical," logical, schematic aspect of the text suggests that we see Milly as representing an alternative way of living (dying) and an alternative kind of consciousness to Kate Croy's and Merton Densher's. We have already examined the practical view that Kate Croy takes of life, and while it is difficult not to admit that the handsome girl does see clearly, it is just as difficult to accept her consistently cold-blooded, acquisitive attitude toward life. A choice of world views limited to Densher's dim and passive amorality and Kate's acute, amoral practicality would be dreary indeed. Milly's view of the world suggests another, a richer and a braver possibility, which I call the heroic, but which might as well be called the romantic or the tragic. In fact Milly's simultaneous discovery of the possibility of active life and the inevitability of early death leads her eventually to cast herself in the role of the princess in a romantic tragedy, pacing in black robes the *piano nobile* of her Venetian palazzo, appearing in extravagant white and pearls at her first and only party, shutting herself up in her "'great, gilded shell'" (II, 152), as she calls it, to *live* "as in the ark of her deluge" (II, 143), and finally to die, betrayed. From the first, however, Milly is above all heroic, determined to do her duty to herself and her friends by enduring her lot without unduly upsetting or involving them, without giving death or illness an unnecessary minute or an unnecessary thought.

To her more distant connections, Kate and her Aunt Maud, she at first merely lies. "'Oh, it's all right,'" she tells Kate. "'You mean you've been absurd?'" "'Absurd.' It was a simple word to say, but the consequence of it, for our young woman, was that she felt it, as soon as spoken, to have done something for her safety" (I, 258–59).

Susan Stringham cannot be treated so cavalierly, however, so Milly has Sir Luke Strett talk with her, and then girds herself as for the first battle of a long campaign, and faces her suffering friend herself:

When Kate and Densher abandoned her to Mrs. Stringham on the day of her meeting them together and bringing them to luncheon, Milly, face to face with that companion, had had one of those moments in which the warned, the anxious fighter of the battle of life, as if once again feeling for the sword at his side, carries his hand straight to the quarter of his courage. She laid hers firmly on her heart, and the two women stood there showing each other a strange front. (II, 99)

Together Milly and Susan face their terror, and Milly shows for the only time her anger and her bitterness. "'When I say she knows I should say she's a person who guesses,'" Susan says, referring to Kate Croy, and adds, "'But *she* doesn't matter.'" Milly replies, seeming for a moment to lose her careful self-control: "'Nobody matters, Susie—nobody.'" Her next words, however, contradict her apparent coldness,[28] and she is soon declaring that she, Susan, and Sir Luke will be heroic together. "'I, on my side, will be beautiful too,'" she says, "'and we'll be—the three of us, with whatever others, oh, as many as the case requires, any one you like!—a sight for the gods'" (II, 100, 101).

At the end of Book Seven, the book in which this conversation occurs and the last in which Milly appears as a center, she has a long interview with Lord Mark, during which she admits her illness (II, 154) and asserts both to him and to herself her cheerfulness and her bravery. She declares her intention to live fully, and Mark declares his availability as a wedded adorer. The neat, perfunctory way in which he bids for her hand and her fortune actually amuses them both:

The prompt neat accent, however, his manner of disposing of her question, failed of real expression, as he himself the next moment intelligently, helplessly, almost comically saw—a failure pointed moreover by the laugh into which Milly was immediately startled. As a suggestion to her of a healing and uplifting passion it *was* in truth deficient; it wouldn't do as the communication of a force that should sweep them both away. (II, 157)

Lord Mark is perhaps bitterly amused at his own failure. The reason why Milly can even now afford to laugh, however, only occurs to him as he is leaving the palazzo. Milly has just informed him of what seems to him her rather fantastic belief that Kate Croy does not return Merton Densher's passionate regard. He is pondering this bit of misinformation and preparing to leave when a salver is brought in with a visiting card. "'I'll see him with pleasure,'" says Milly, and adds for Lord Mark's benefit, "'Mr. Merton Densher.'" "'Oh!'" Lord Mark replies, and leaves, carrying the bitterness of his defeat and the seed of his revenge with him (II, 167).

The last time we are taken into Milly's mind, then, she still believes in the possibility of Merton Densher's loving her. She knows she is doomed, but she is genuinely bright and cheerful, determined to be heroic, to provide no unnecessary reminders of her pathetic fate. In his preface to *The Wings of the Dove,* James declares that "the poet essentially *can't* be concerned with the act of dying," and announces that "the last thing in the world" his novel proposes to be is "the record predominantly of a collapse." To avoid the necessity of writing such a record, he moves out of Milly's mind while she is still heroically resisting, and tells the rest of his story through other centers. The effect of this move is not, however, to lessen the reader's, or, for that matter, the other characters' interest in what the poor girl is thinking and feeling, but to heighten that interest by offering external clues to those thoughts and feelings—Milly's appearance at her party, Susan's later reports on her condition—while keeping the narrative center in the pointedly contrasting, unheroic mind of Merton Densher. Milly Theale's sensibility is more present in Densher's Venice and London than the spirit of the fabulously absent Mrs. Newsome in Lambert Strether's Paris, and certainly of more interest to the reader. We would give anything to know what Milly said to Merton in their last interview, and we are as shocked as our journalistic friend when Kate Croy throws the dove's last letter into the fire unopened.

Milly Theale's heroic nature dominates *The Wings of the Dove:* Kate's venality seems shabbier, Merton's passivity more reprehensible in implicit contrast to it. Her appearance in the third book opens such an abyss in the developing novel of manners that all Kate's manipulation can never close it and bring about the requisite happy ending.

In order even to begin to understand Milly Theale's nature rather than simply observe its effects, however, we must turn from the dialectical to the myth-making functions of the text, and the way in which repeated words and images point to meanings without ever clearly delineating them. Kate suggests this course when she again refers to Milly as a dove in her final analysis of the American's effect on Merton Densher. "'She stretched out her wings,'" she says, "'and it was to *that* they reached. They cover us'" (II, 404). The effect of Kate's return to the dove image is of course to send the reader back to the visions James has provided and the theories he has himself developed of Milly as a mild and timid American virgin to be "worked," as a "worker" of her own dovelike appearance, and as a symbol of the grace of the holy spirit. Densher himself, and James through him, add some of their authority to this last interpretation by insisting on the redemptive power of Milly's now unknowable *words*. He will never know, Merton realizes,

> what had been in Milly's letter. The intention announced in it he should but too probably know; only that would have been, but for the depths of his spirit, the least part of it. The part of it missed forever was the turn she would have given her act. That turn had possibilities that, somehow, by wondering about them, his imagination had extraordinarily filled out and refined. It had made of them a revelation the loss of which was like the sight of a priceless pearl cast before his eyes—his pledge given not to save it—into the fathomless sea, or rather even it was like the sacrifice of something sentient and throbbing, something that, for the spiritual ear, might have been audible as a faint far wail. (II, 396)

Milly's nature and her value in the text and in Densher's life are defined not only by her actions and by her intentions, not only by the observable effect of her words, but by her unknow-

able words themselves. Milly makes a difference,[29] a difference
Kate is beginning to understand and Merton can so far only
feel. She does this not by fitting into the argument of the text,
by providing a third alternative to two unsatisfactory views of
the world, but by focusing the words and the images the text
and its characters use, by paradoxically embodying freedom and
servitude, life and death, by personifying the abyss, the holy
spirit, even love itself, by being a princess and representing
those two "things" to which the text so often almost inter-
changeably refers, *everything* and *nothing*.[30]

The meaning of *The Wings of the Dove* cannot be summed
up in a slogan—"Only connect," say, or "Live all you can; it's
a mistake not to." It can't even be summed up in a chapter or
an essay or a critical monograph. More than in any other work
of James, and certainly more than in any work of Balzac, the
meaning of *The Wings of the Dove* is generated by and inseparable from the process of reading. To understand *The Wings
of the Dove* is to experience the buildup and the defeat of generic
expectations, to learn about Merton Densher and Milly Theale
as they learn about themselves and so to participate in their expanding consciousnesses, and to read the text actively, following
up the associations it suggests and allowing them to generate
meanings which are too complex and too personal to be para-
phrased. Milly Theale means everything that the myth-making
and the dialectical functions of the text can induce the reader to
make her mean, every association its words and images trigger
and every conclusion its argument implies. The text itself tells
us something about international life around the turn of the century, a good deal about the drama of developing consciousnesses,
and something about the irony of fate. More importantly, from
a literary-historical point of view, it foregrounds the reading experience it evokes, using generic expectations and repeated patterns of words and images to insist on the ability of the reading
experience to serve as an analogue for our experience of the
world, as a model for the interpretation of life itself.

In *La Cousine Bette* Balzac proposes that we see the world
as a stage, and the stage as a battleground for characters whom

he identifies with various virtues and vices in all their impurity and moral ambiguity. In *The Wings of the Dove* James elaborates on Balzac's vision, not only portraying the clash of egos on the stage of society, but revealing the ordinarily hidden development of egos on the stages of their consciousnesses, and foregrounding the drama of understanding on the stage of the text. Balzacian realism assumes a knowable, representable world. Jamesian realism in its final stage represents what looks like a similar world, while demonstrating both the limits of its knowability and the ways in which writers and readers can compensate for the little they know by the great deal they can come to understand.

CONCLUSION

French avant-garde writers and critics of the last forty years or so have seen their work as a reaction against something they condescendingly refer to as "Balzacian realism." This mythical mode of writing is defined, oddly enough, by reference not to Balzac's fictions, but to his brief "Avant-propos" and to those introductions to the various sections of the *Comédie humaine* composed at his behest by Félix Davin.[1]

When critics of Balzacian realism take the time, as Roland Barthes did, to *read* Balzac, they discover not the transparent reportage that Balzac may have had and that Davin certainly did have in mind, but texts which are *readable* in that they use language referentially, and also highly self-conscious about the literary conventions they deploy and the kinds of readings they are calculated to evoke. Balzacian realism is systematically mimetic in its attempts to represent the appearance of the world and reveal the systems that structure the world. It is also systematically textual insofar as it develops, uses, and criticizes systems of perception and representation. The same is true of Jamesian realism, and of all fiction that aspires both to represent the world and to evoke in words an experience analogous to our experience of the world. The words themselves—taken one by one or sentence by sentence—may seem transparent, may produce icons for the world in the reader's imagination, or refer indexically to actual times and places. The texts, however, are conscious, literary constructions, aware and often critical of their own generic and cultural assumptions.

The Robbe-Grillet who, in *The Voyeur* or *The Erasers* exploits and calls in question the function of interpretation in literary texts is a descendant of the Balzac of *Le Père Goriot,* whether he likes it or not. The Thomas Pynchon who puts his Oedipa Maas on the trail of a revolutionary alternate postal system in a surrealistic but recognizable Southern California has *The Princess Casamassima* as part of his literary heritage, whether he realizes it or not.

Contemporary criticism, in its sophisticated flight from the naive epistemological assumptions it associates with realism, risks promulgating a conception of the novel as ideally and entirely self-reflexive. Fredric Jameson, no naive reader himself, offers the following, practically Dickensian, description of the process:

> In matters of art, and particularly of artistic perception, in other words, it is wrong to want to *decide*, to want to *resolve* a difficulty: what is wanted is a kind of mental procedure which suddenly shifts gears, which throws everything in an inextricable tangle one floor higher and turns the very problem itself (the obscurity of the sentence) into its own solution (the varieties of Obscurity) by widening its frame in such a way that it now takes in its own mental processes as well as the object of those processes. In the earlier, naive state, we struggle with the object in question: in this heightened and self-conscious one we observe our own struggles and patiently set about characterizing them.[2]

Neither the reduction to transparency nor the reduction to self-reflexive textuality can lead to a thorough understanding of the realistic novel. The reduction to transparency is unfaithful to all we know of language, literary conventions, and the phenomenology of perception, while the reduction to textuality is unfaithful to our broadest notion of the novel itself, from Cervantes to Pynchon and beyond. The former is either naive or dishonest. The latter shunts the traditional, readable novel aside in favor of the pure "writerly" text, a legitimate exercise surely, but a faithful account of none but the most radical literary projects: Sollers's *Nombres,* perhaps, but none even Robbe-Grillet's *La Jalousie* or Beckett's *Molloy; Finnegan's Wake,* perhaps, but certainly not *Ulysses.* And not *Gravity's Rainbow* or *Pale Fire* or *The End of the Road,* either, insofar as these texts create iconic representations of physical worlds.

This is not to suggest, of course, that the poetics of realism I have developed to account for the novel-writing practice of Balzac and James would work as well for Beckett and Joyce, but only to emphasize the continuities that are often overshadowed by the very important changes in the history of the novel. The advantage of the several notions I have collated under the rubric of systematic realism is that they foreground the similarities between Balzac and James while allowing for serious differences in emphasis. They have also proved useful to me in establishing, teaching, and contemplating the twentieth-century lines of descent from the great nineteenth-century realists.

Early in this essay I suggested that Balzac and James, for all their differences, would point a single way for the development of the realistic novel of the future. This way is defined by a combination of textual complexity and faithfulness to observed reality. It is the way of Lawrence and Hardy, rather than Gissing and Bennett, of Faulkner rather than Dreiser and Lewis, of Proust at his most objective and of Zola at his best. It is the way of intelligent, critical, literary realism, of storytelling which scorns not the moving accident and yet provides the attentive reader with matter for his reflection and form his thoughts.

4. The classic expressions of the Marxist view may be found in Lukacs's essays on *Illusions perdues* and *Les Paysans,* translated in *Studies in European Realism* (New York: Grosset and Dunlap, 1964). See also the work of Pierre Barbéris in France (e.g., *Balzac et le mal du siècle* [Paris: Gallimard, 1970]) and Linda Rudich in this country (e.g., "Pour une lecture nouvelle du *Père Goriot,*" *La Pensée* 168 [1973]: 73–95). The Baudelairean view has been developed by Albert Béguin in his *Balzac visionnaire* (Geneva: Skira, 1946) and brought up to date in his *Balzac lu et relu* (Paris: Seuil, 1965). See also Per Nykrog, *La Pensée de Balzac dans la Comédie humaine* (Copenhagen: Scandinavian University Books, 1965) and several recent books focusing on *La Peau de Chagrin.* Among the structuralist analyses are Tahsin Yücel, *Figures et messages dans la Comédie humaine* (Paris: Mame, 1972); Bernard Vannier, *L'Inscription du corps* (Paris: Klincksieck, 1972); Roger Kempf, *Sur le corps romanesque* (Paris: Seuil, 1968); and Leo Mazet, "Récit(s) dans le récit: l'échange du récit chez Balzac," *L'Année Balzacienne* (1976): 129–61.

5. Philip Grover, *Henry James and the French Novel: A Study in Inspiration* (New York: Barnes and Noble, 1973), concentrates on technique, while Adeline Tintner's many articles seek out similarities of plot and theme.

6. Christopher Prendergast, *Balzac: Fiction and Melodrama* (New York: Holmes and Meier, 1978), p. 187.

7. John Carlos Rowe, *Henry Adams and Henry James* (Ithaca: Cornell University Press, 1976), p. 173.

8. Peter Brooks, *The Melodramatic Imagination: Balzac, Henry James, Melodrama, and the Mode of Excess* (New Haven: Yale University Press, 1976), pp. 198–206.

9. See, for example, page 167, quoted in chapter two below.

10. Two books, George Levine's *The Realistic Imagination* (Chicago: University of Chicago Press, 1981) and John Romano's *Dickens and Reality* (New York: Columbia University Press, 1978) have influenced my thinking on realism since I finished this essay. If I had the work to do again, this influence would certainly be evident.

CHAPTER 1

1. Several recent writers on realism have developed a theory according to which the novelist does not *observe* reality and then attempt to *reproduce* it in his text. The act of observation is for them inseparable from the act of composition, and the elements of reality which make their way into the text are not unavoidable facts but parts of an interpretive model from which other facts have been excluded. They are, in other words, already textual, elements in a version of reality, a system of characters, themes, images, and words, which stand as a complex sign for reality. Gérard

NOTES

PREFACE

1. See "The Natural History of German Life," in *The Essays of George Eliot*, ed. Thomas Pinney (New York: Columbia University Press, 1963), pp. 266–99.

2. James published five essays on Balzac: "Honoré de Balzac" (1875), "Balzac's Letters" (1876), "Honoré de Balzac" (1902), "The Lesson of Balzac" (1906), and "Honoré de Balzac" (1913). The first two were reprinted in the *French Poets and Novelists* volume (London: Macmillan, 1878). The 1902 and 1913 essays appeared in *Notes on Novelists* (New York: Scribner's, 1914). "The Lesson of Balzac" is included in Leon Edel's collection of James's essays entitled *The Future of the Novel* (New York: Vintage, 1956).

3. On language and narrative technique see for example Seymour Chatman, *The Later Style of Henry James* (Oxford: Basil Blackwell, 1972); David Lodge's chapter, "Strether by the River" in *Language of Fiction* (New York: Columbia University Press, 1966); and Robert L. Caserio's chapter, "The Story in It: James" in *Plot, Story and the Novel* (Princeton: Princeton University Press, 1979). On specific texts see, for example, Christine Brooke-Rose's series of articles on *The Turn of the Screw* ("The Squirm of the True" in *PTL* 1 [1976]: 265–94 and 513–46 and *PTL* 3 [1977]: 517–62). Shoshana Felman's confrontation with the same text in *Yale French Studies*, nos. 55–56 (1977): 94–207; and Donald O'Gorman's "Henry James's Reading of *The Turn of the Screw*," *HJR* 1 (1979–1980); 125–38, 228–56. *The Sacred Fount* has also received some attention (see Shlomith Rimmon, *The Concept of Ambiguity: The Example of James* [Chicago: University of Chicago Press, 1977], pp. 167–226), as have the unfinished novels (see Sergio Perosa, *Henry James and the Experimental Novel* [Charlottesville: University of Virginia Press, 1978]). For reevaluations see, for example, Charles Thomas Samuels, *The Ambiguity of Henry James* (Urbana, Illinois: University of Illinois Press, 1971) and the series of centennial reevaluations in the *Henry James Review*. Charles R. Anderson's *Person, Place, and Thing in Henry James's Novels* (Durham, N.C.: Duke University Press, 1977), a first-rate, full-length general study, is an exception to this trend toward specialization.

Genette, for example, and, influenced by him, Stephen Heath, focus on this complex sign as a linguistically encoded version of whatever a society prefers to believe about itself. For them, the realistic novel reflects not actual phenomena as they occur, but the set and the structure of such events as society has decided in advance to consider "believable" (*"vraisemblable"*) (Heath, *The Nouveau Roman: A Study in the Practice of Reading* [Philadelphia: Temple University Press, 1972], chap. 1, and Genette, "Vraisemblance et motivation," in *Figures II* [Paris: Seuil, 1969], pp. 71–100). "Evidently," writes Heath, "this *vraisemblable* is not recognized as such, but rather as, precisely, 'Reality.' . . . For a particular society, in fact, the work that is realistic is that which repeats" not reality itself, if there is such a thing, but "the received forms of 'Reality'" (pp. 20, 21). Wolfgang Iser, to cite another example, conveniently links Genette's insights (which he seems to have arrived at independently) with his own notions of textual and cultural systems. "No literary text," he writes, "relates to contingent reality as such, but to models or concepts of reality, in which contingencies and complexities are reduced to a meaningful structure. We call these structures word-pictures or systems." And further: "The literary text is also a system, which shares the basic structure of overall systems. . . . However, this structure becomes operative not in relation to a contingent world but in relation to the ordered pattern of systems with which the text interferes or is meant to interfere" (*The Act of Reading: A Theory of Aesthetic Response* [Baltimore: Johns Hopkins University Press, 1978], pp. 70, 71–72).

In order for a novel to be received as realistic, then, it must represent not the uninterpreted surface of reality, but those "models or concepts of reality" which novelist and reader share, or which they can at least pretend to share for the duration of the novel. My goal here is to examine the ways in which two novelists transform the particular "word-pictures or systems" in whose terms they perceive reality into the consciously crafted word-pictures and systems that are literary texts. I do not intend to match text and world or even primarily to show how historically determined notions of "reality" influence the novelists, but to explore the rhetorical process through which a perceived system becomes a textual system which in turn demands to be perceived as congruent with the reader's notion of reality.

2. L'auteur ne sait encore aucun observateur qui ait remarqué combien les moeurs françaises sont, littérairement parlant, au-dessus de celles des autres pays comme variété de types, comme drame, comme esprit, comme mouvement: tout s'y dit, tout s'y pense, tout s'y fait. L'auteur ici ne juge pas, il ne donne pas le secret de sa pensée politique, entièrement contraire à celle du plus grand nombre en France; mais à laquelle on arrivera peut-être avant peu. Le temps n'est pas loin où la duperie coûteuse du gouvernement constitutionnel sera reconnue. Il est

historien, voilà tout. Il s'applaudit de la grandeur, de la variété, de la beauté, de la fécondité de son sujet, quelque déplorable que le fassent, socialement parlant, la confusion des faits les plus opposés, l'abondance des matériaux, l'impétuosité des mouvements. Ce désordre est une source de beautés. Ainsi n'est-ce pas par gloriole nationale ni par patriotisme qu'il a choisi les moeurs de son pays, mais parce que son pays offrait, le premier de tous, l'*homme social* sous des aspects plus multipliés que partout ailleurs.

3. Autrefois tout était simplifié par les institutions monarchiques; les caractères étaient tranchés: un bourgeois, marchand ou artisan, un noble entièrement libre, un paysan esclave, voilà l'ancienne société de l'Europe; elle prêtait peu aux incidents du roman.

4. Aujourd'hui, l'Egalité produit en France des nuances infinies. Jadis, la caste donnait à chacun une physionomie qui dominait l'individu; aujourd'hui, l'individu ne tient sa physionomie que de lui-même.

5. La Société française allait être l'historien, je ne devais être que le secrétaire. En dressant l'inventaire des vices et des vertus, en rassemblant les principaux faits des passions, en peignant les caractères, en choisissant les événements principaux de la Société, en composant des types par la réunion des traits de plusieurs caractères homogènes, peut-être pouvais-je arriver à écrire l'histoire oubliée par tant d'historiens, celle des moeurs.

6. "Un écrivain doit avoir en morale et en politique des opinions arrêtées, il doit se regarder comme un instituteur des hommes; car les hommes n'ont pas besoin de maîtres pour douter," a dit Bonald. ... J'écris à la lueur de deux Vérités éternelles: la Religion, la Monarchie, deux nécessités que les événements contemporains proclament, et vers lesquelles tout écrivain de bon sens doit essayer de ramener notre pays.

7. See David Lodge, *The Modes of Modern Writing* (Ithaca: Cornell University Press, 1977), pp. 73–81 and 93–103, for further discussion of these Jakobsonian terms.

8. Zola, after all, has claimed Balzac as the founder of modern realism (see *Les Romanciers naturalistes* [Paris: Grasset, 1890], pp. 3–73), while James has proclaimed himself a child of Balzac and declared that "the main object of the novel is to represent life" (see "Alphonse Daudet" in *Partial Portraits* [1887; rpt. Ann Arbor: University of Michigan Press, 1970], p. 227).

9. Claude Lévi-Strauss, *The Savage Mind* (anon. trans. of *La Pensée sauvage* [Paris: Plon, 1962]) (Chicago: University of Chicago Press, 1966), p. 23. For *"modèle réduit"* the translator here uses "small-scale."

10. Lévi-Strauss, *The Savage Mind*, pp. 1–16.

11. "Miniature/miniaturization" are terms the translator sometimes uses for *"modèle réduit/réduction."*

12. Martin Price, "The Fictional Contract," in *Literary Theory and Structure: Essays in Honor of William K. Wimsatt,* ed. Frank Brady, John Palmer, and Martin Price (New Haven: Yale University Press, 1973), pp. 168, 170, 171.

13. Lévi-Strauss, *The Savage Mind,* p. 24.

14. Henry James, *The Spoils of Poynton; A London Life; The Chaperon,* p. x.

15. Henry James, *The Ambassadors,* I, x.

16. Henry James, *The Notebooks of Henry James,* ed. F. O. Matthiessen and Kenneth B. Murdock (New York: Oxford University Press, 1961), p. 136.

17. James, *Spoils of Poynton,* p. vii.

18. James, *Notebooks,* p. 137.

19. James, *Notebooks,* p. 137.

20. James, *Spoils of Poynton,* p. vii.

21. See Peter Demetz, "Balzac and the Zoologists: A Concept of the Type," in *The Disciplines of Criticism,* ed. Peter Demetz, Thomas Greene, and Lowry Nelson, Jr. (New Haven, Yale University Press, 1968), pp. 397-418.

22. See David H. Pinkney, "The Myth of the French Revolution of 1830," in *A Festschrift for Frederick B. Artz,* ed. David H. Pinkney and Theodore Ropp (Durham: Duke University Press, 1964), pp. 52-71.

23. "Ainsi, la Banque avait réparé la brèche faite à la Magistrature par la Noblesse."

24. *Une Fille d'Eve* is, I suppose, a sexist work. Balzac's women are not always so submissive (consider e.g., Madame de Beauséant or Valérie Marneffe).

25. See William F. Hall, "James's Conception of Society in *The Awkward Age,*" *NCF* 23 (1968): 28-48.

26. For a different opinion on the relative success and failure of the characters in *The Awkward Age,* see Daniel J. Schneider, "James's *The Awkward Age:* A Reading and an Evaluation," *Henry James Review* 1 (1980): 219-27.

CHAPTER 2

1. In a recent essay in the *Henry James Review* ("Re-Reading *The American:* A Century Since," *HJR* I [1980]: 139-53), James Tuttleton acutely observes that Newman does not wish to break into Parisian society in order to make a place for himself there, but rather in order to make off with Claire de Cintré.

2. . . . il remarqua combien les femmes ont d'influence sur la vie sociale, et avisa soudain à se lancer dans le monde, afin d'y conquérir des protectrices. . . . Elle était d'ailleurs, et par son nom et par sa fortune, l'une des sommités du monde aristocratique.

3. En se montrant dans cette société, la plus exclusive de toutes, il avait conquis le droit d'aller partout. . . . En prononçant le nom du père Goriot, Eugène avait donné un coup de baguette magique, mais dont l'effet était l'inverse de celui qu'avaient frappé ces mots: parent de Mme de Beauséant.

4. "Si vous connaissiez la situation dans laquelle se trouve ma famille," dit-il en continuant, "vous aimeriez à jouer le rôle d'une de ces fées fabuleuses qui se plaisent à dissiper les obstacles autour de leurs filleuls."

5. "Autrefois les dames ne donnaient-elles pas à leurs chevaliers des armures, des épées, des casques, des cottes de mailles, des chevaux, afin au'ils pussent aller combattre en leur nom dans les tournois? Eh bien, Eugène, les choses que je vous offre sont les armes de l'époque, des outils nécessaires à qui veut être quelque chose."

6. See Erich Auerbach, *Mimesis: The Representation of Reality of Western Literature* (1953; rpt. New York: Doubleday-Anchor, 1957), on the notion of the mixing of rhetorical levels.

7. Nicole Mozet analyzes the role of "the truth" in *Le Père Goriot* in her article, "La Description de la Maison-Vauquer," *L'Année Balzacienne* (1972): 97–130.

8. Sans ses observations curieuses et l'adresse avec laquelle il sut se produire dans les salons de Paris, ce récit n'eût pas été coloré des tons vrais qu'il devra sans doute à son esprit sagace et à son désir de pénétrer les mystères d'une situation épouvantable aussi soigneusement cachée par ceux qui l'avaient créée que par celui qui la subissait.

9. Kempf, *Sur le corps romanesque,* p. 70.

10. "Ah! c'est vous, monsieur de Rastignac, je suis bien aise de vous voir," dit-elle d'un air auquel savent obéir les gens d'esprit.
    Maxime regardait alternativement Eugène et la comtesse d'un [*sic*] manière assez significative pour faire décamper l'intrus.

11. A quatre heures et demie la vicomtesse était visible. Cinq minutes plus tôt, elle n'eût pas reçu son cousin.

12. Brooks, *Melodramatic Imagination,* pp. 132–33.

13. Sa figure fraîche comme une première gelée d'automne, ses yeux ridés, dont l'expression passe du sourire prescrit aux danseuses à

l'amer renfrognement de l'escompteur, enfin toute sa personne explique la pension, comme la pension implique sa personne. Le bagne ne va pas sans l'argousin, vous n'imagineriez pas l'un sans l'autre. L'embonpoint blafard de cette petite femme est le produit de cette vie, comme le typhus est la conséquence des exhalaisons d'un hôpital. Son jupon de laine tricotée, qui dépasse sa première jupe faite avec une vieille robe, et dont la ouate s'échappe par les fentes de l'étoffe lézardée, résume le salon, la salle à manger, le jardinet, annonce la cuisine, et fait pressentir les pensionnaires.

14. "Vous voulez parvenir, je vous aiderai. Vous sonderez combien est profonde la corruption féminine, vous toiserez la largeur de la misérable vanité des hommes."

15. "Si vous me la présentez, vous serez son Benjamin, elle vous adorera. Aimez-la si vous pouvez après, sinon servez-vous d'elle."

16. "J'irai!" se disait-il, "et si Mme de Beauséant a raison, si je suis consigné ... je ... Mme de Restaud me trouvera dans tous les salons où elle va. J'apprendrai à faire des armes, à tirer le pistolet, je lui tuerai son Maxime!"

17. Rastignac résolut d'ouvrir deux tranchées parallèles pour arriver à la fortune, de s'appuyer sur la science et sur l'amour, d'être un savant docteur et un homme à la mode.

18. "Je vais vous éclairer, moi, la position dans laquelle vous êtes; mais je vais le faire avec la supériorité d'un homme qui, après avoir examiné les choses d'ici-bas, a vu qu'il n'y avait que deux parties à prendre: ou une stupide obéissance ou la révolte."

19. "Et si la volonté de Dieu était de lui retirer son fils, Taillefer reprendrait sa fille. ... Moi, je me charge du rôle de la Providence, je ferai vouloir le bon Dieu."

20. "J'ai un ami pour qui je me suis dévoué, un colonel dans l'armée de la Loire qui vient d'être employé dans la garde royale. Il écoute mes avis, et s'est fait ultra-royaliste: ce n'est pas un de ces imbéciles qui tiennent à leurs opinions. ... Il remettrait Jésus-Christ en croix si je le lui disais. Sur un seul mot de son papa Vautrin, il cherchera querelle à ce drôle qui n'envoie pas seulement cent sous à sa pauvre soeur, et ..."

21. "Entre ce que je vous propose et ce que vous ferez un jour, il n'y a que le sang de moins."

22. Rastignac shifts his attention from Madame de Beauséant and Vautrin as proposers of plans to Goriot and Vautrin as sponsors of women.

23. La comtesse était magnifique avec tous ses diamants étalés, qui, pour elle, étaient brûlants sans doute. . . .

24. . . . il revit alors, sous les diamants des deux soeurs, le grabat sur lequel gisait le père Goriot.

25. ". . . il n'y a qu'une bosse, celle de la paternité, ce sera un Père Eternel."

26. "Un père est avec ses enfants comme Dieu est avec nous. . . . Eh bien! quand j'ai été père j'ai compris Dieu. Il est tout entier partout, puisque la création est sortie de lui. Monsieur, je suis ainsi avec mes filles. Seulement, j'aime mieux mes filles que Dieu n'aime le monde, parce que le monde n'est pas si beau que Dieu, et que mes filles sont plus belles que moi."

27. " . . . moi, moi qui vendrais le Père, le Fils et le Saint-Esprit pour leur éviter une larme à toutes deux!"

28. Il la regarda d'un air surhumain de douleur. Pour bien peindre la physionomie de ce Christ de la Paternité, il faudrait aller chercher des comparaisons dans les images que les princes de la palette ont inventées pour peindre la passion soufferte au bénéfice des mondes par le Sauveur des hommes.

29. "Vous seriez une belle proie pour le diable."

30. Son regard était celui de l'archange déchu qui veut toujours la guerre.

31. Pierre Barbéris (*Le Pére Goriot de Balzac* [Paris: Larousse, 1972], pp. 260–283) points out the similarities of Delphine's lovenest and the Garden of Eden.

32. Brooks, *Melodramatic Imagination,* p. 137.

33. See ibid.

34. Ah! sachez-le: ce drame n'est ni une fiction, ni un roman. *All is true,* il est si véritable, que chacun peut en reconnaître les éléments chez soi, dans son coeur peut-être.

35. See John V. Antush, "The 'Much Finer Complexity' of History in *The American,*" *Journal of American Studies* 6 (1972): 85–95; and Cornelia Pulsifer Kelley, *The Early Development of Henry James* (1930; rev. ed. Champaign: University of Illinois Press, 1965), pp. 233–44.

36. . . . comme il essaie de représenter les sentiments humains, les crises sociales, le mal et le bien, tout le pêle-mêle de la civilisation.

37. Henry James, *The American* (New York: Scribner's, 1907), p. xxi. James's perception of Newman as an inept interpreter is clearer in the 1907 New York Edition than it is in the original 1877 version. For this

reason, I have chosen to quote from the later text, to follow the quotations with the New York Edition page numbers in parentheses, and to footnote significant variants. For the original text I have used the Norton Critical edition edited by James W. Tuttleton (New York, 1978).

38. Henry James, *The Princess Casamassima* (New York, Scribner's, 1908), p. xii.

39. George Knox, "Romance and Fable in James's *The American*," *Anglia* 83 (1965), rpt. in *The Merrill Studies in The American*, ed. William T. Stafford (Columbus: Charles E. Merrill, 1971), p. 69.

40. James himself recognized the romance elements in *The American* when he wrote the preface for its republication, but he was less concerned with specific archetypal or intertextual aspects of the novel than with broader generic considerations. The character of Christopher Newman may well have been conceived in conformity with a traditional romance model, but this was not what was bothering James when he admitted that he "had been plotting arch-romance without knowing it" (*The American*, p. ix). He was concerned, rather, with the fact that he had allowed his literary enthusiasm to carry him beyond the realm of "the things we cannot possibly *not* know, sooner or later," to that of "the things that . . . we never *can* directly know; the things that can reach us only through the beautiful circuit and subterfuge of our thought and our desire" (*The American*, p. xvi). He had moved, that is, from the inevitability of metonymic relations to the radical unverifiability of metaphoric ones, from storytelling to romance-writing.

41. Charles Feidelson, "James and the 'Man of Imagination,'" in *Literary Structure and Theory: Essays in Honor of William K. Wimsatt*, ed. Frank Brady, John Palmer, and Martin Price (New Haven: Yale University Press, 1973), p. 338.

42. Ibid., p. 343.

43. The earlier version makes less of Newman's linguistic naiveté: "'I can't fancy myself chattering French!' said Newman with a laugh. 'And yet, I suppose that the more a man knows the better'" (24).

44. In the earlier version Newman does not mention the shorthand writer (75), and James declares that his hero has "never read a novel!" (38). The effect of the first change is to emphasize Newman's willful ignorance of some of the mechanics of language. That of the second is to emphasize the romance nature of *The American*.

45. The "thin, sharp eyebeam, as cold as a flash of steel," was originally "a certain delicate glance" (172).

46. Richard Poirier, *The Comic Sense of Henry James* (New York: Oxford University Press, 1960), p. 64.

47. The only changes in this passage are that the words "deep commotion" have replaced the less Wordsworthian "inward tremor" and "recreation" has replaced "diversion" (68).

48. The sentence on Ruskin was added (75–76).
49. In 1877 Newman had written that his two critics "were both idiots" (76), and left no room for the "everything-something" ambiguity.
50. This passage is substantially new in the New York Edition.
51. This passage is an expansion of the following:

> "What you propose to do will be very disagreeable," M. de Bellegarde said. "That is very evident. But it will be nothing more." (288)

52. James has made an important change in this passage in order to emphasize Newman's failure even now to understand what has happened to and around him. It originally read: "The most unpleasant thing that had ever happened to him had reached its formal conclusion, as it were; he could close the book and put it away" (306).
53. Much has been made of the last sentence of the original edition: "Newman instinctively turned to see if the little paper was in fact consumed; but there was nothing left of it." (See, for example, Martha Banta, "Rebirth or Revenge: The Endings of *Huckleberry Finn* and *The American,*" *MFS* 15 [1969]:191–207.) It is, to my mind, a much more effective ending than the later, more protracted one, and Newman's final glance into the fire seems to me to be a glance of farewell evoked perhaps by the last recurrence of the habit of hoping for vengeance, but serving to verify the fact that the episode is finished for ever.
54. Brooks, *Melodramatic Imagination*, p. 167.

CHAPTER 3

1. Charles Sanders Peirce, "Logic as Semiotic: The Theory of Signs" in *Philosophical Writings of Peirce*, ed. Justus Buchler (1940; rpt. New York: Dover, 1955), p. 104.
2. Gaëtan Picon, *L'Usage de la lecture*, vol. 2 (Paris: Mercure de France, 1961), p. 83.
3. Ibid., p. 87. One does wonder, however, how Balzac's metaphysical extravagances, *Séraphita*, for example, fit into this scheme.
4. *All is true*, il est si véritable, que chacun peut en reconnaître les éléments chez soi, dans son coeur peut-être.
5. Les dévorantes presses mécaniques . . .
6. A l'époque où commence cette histoire, la presse de Stanhope et les rouleaux à distribuer l'encre ne fonctionnaient pas encore dans les petites imprimeries de province.
7. Angoulême se servait toujours des presses en bois, auxquelles la langue est redevable du mot faire gémir la presse, maintenant sans application.

Le plateau mobile où se place la *forme* pleine de lettres sur laquelle s'applique la feuille de papier était encore en pierre et justifiait son nom de *marbre*.

Ce Séchard était un ancien compagnon pressier, que dans leur argot typographique les ouvriers chargés d'assembler les lettres appellent un Ours. Le mouvement de va-et-vient, qui ressemble assez à celui d'un ours en cage, par lequel les pressiers se portent de l'encrier à la presse et de la presse à l'encrier, leur a sans doute valu ce sobriquet. En revanche, les Ours ont nommé les compositeurs des Singes, à cause du continuel exercice que font ces messieurs pour attraper les lettres dans les cent cinquante-deux petites cases où elles sont contenues.

8. S'il avait d'abord vu dans David son unique enfant, plus tard il y vit un acquéreur naturel de qui les intérêts étaient opposés aux siens: il voulait vendre cher, David devait acheter à bon marché; son fils devenait donc un ennemi à vaincre. Cette transformation du sentiment en intérêt personnel, ordinairement lente, tortueuse et hypocrite chez les gens bien élevés, fut rapide et directe chez le vieil Ours.

9. Michel Butor, *Repertoire* (Paris: Minuit, 1960), pp. 83–84.

10. For more on this, see Georg Lukacs, *Studies in European Realism,* pp. 47–64.

11. This is all the more interesting in the context of systematic realism in that it quite clearly reflects the economic and technological developments of the years in which the story of *Illusions perdues* unfolds, years which J.-A. Néret describes in his history of the trade as a time of great expansion, when mechanization of printing in Paris did indeed increase demand for paper, and the spread of lending libraries put a premium on potentially popular books. See J.-A. Néret, *Histoire illustrée de la librairie* (Paris: Larousse, 1953), pp. 120, 130, 157.

12. La nature avait fait un chimiste de M. Chardon père, et le hasard l'avait établi pharmacien à Angoulême. La mort le surprit au milieu des préparatifs nécessités par une lucrative découverte à la recherche de laquelle il avait consumé plusieurs années d'études scientifiques.

13. "Où se fait donc le journal?" dit Lucien en se parlant à lui-même? "Le journal?" dit l'employé ... "le journal? ... —broum! broum!—Mon vieux, sois demain à six heures à l'imprimerie pour voir à faire filer les porteurs.—Le journal, monsieur, se fait dans la rue, chez les auteurs, à l'imprimerie, entre onze heures et minuit."

14. "Que voulez-vous être?" "Mais rédacteur travaillant bien, et partant bien payé." "Vous voilà comme tous les conscrits qui veulent être maréchaux de France!"

15. "Je vis en vendant les billets que me donnent les directeurs de ces théâtres pour solder ma sous-bienveillance au journal, les livres que m'envoient les libraires et dont je dois parler. Enfin je trafique, une fois Finot satisfait, des tributs en nature qu'apportent les industries pour lesquelles ou contre lesquelles il me permet de lancer des articles. L'*Eau carminative,* la *Pâte des Sultanes,* l'*Huile céphalique,* la *Mixture brésilienne* payent un article goguenard vingt ou trente francs. Je suis forcé d'aboyer après le libraire qui donne peu d'exemplaires au journal: le journal en prend deux que vend Finot, il m'en faut deux à vendre. Publiât-il un chef-d'oeuvre, le libraire avare d'exemplaires est assommé. C'est ignoble, mais je vis de ce métier, moi comme cent autres!"

16. "Lucien avait un pied dans le lit de Coralie, et l'autre dans la glu du journal . . ." (V, 402). The Balzacian hero as contortionist? Compare *Le Père Goriot* (III, 77–78): "To be young, to be thirsty for the great world, to be hungry for a woman, and to see the doors of two houses open to one's knock! to have one's foot in the faubourg St-Germain, *chez la vicomtesse de Beauséant,* and one's knee in the Chausée d'Antin, *chez la comtesse de Restaud.*"

17. "Le Journal au lieu d'être un sacerdoce est devenu un moyen pour les partis; de moyen, il s'est fait commerce; et comme tous les commerces, il est sans foi ni loi. . . . *Les crimes collectifs n'engagent personne.* Le journal peut se permettre la conduite la plus atroce, personne ne s'en croit sali personnellement." (V, 405)

18. "Lucien! il est beau, il est poète, et, ce qui vaut mieux pour lui, homme d'esprit; eh bien, il entrera dans quelques-uns de ces mauvais lieux de la pensée appelés journaux, il y jettera ses plus belles idées, il y desséchera son cerveau, il y corrompra son âme, il y commettra des lâchetés anonymes qui, dans la guerre des idées, remplacent les stratagèmes, les pillages, les incendies, les revirements de bord dans la guerre des *condottieri.* Quand il aura, lui, comme mille autres, dépensé quelque beau génie au profit des actionnaires, ces marchands de poison le laisseront mourir de faim s'il a soif, et de soif s'il a faim."

19. "Entre nous, vous pouvez m'apporter jusqu'à deux feuilles par mois pour ma Revue hebdomadaire, je vous les payerai deux cents francs. Ne parlez de cet arrangement à personne, je serais en proie à la vengeance de tous ces amours-propres blessés de la fortune d'un nouveau venu. Faites quatre articles de vos deux feuilles, signez-en deux de votre nom et deux d'un pseudonyme, afin de ne pas avoir l'air de manger le pain des autres. Vous devez votre position à Blondet et à

Vignon qui vous trouvent de l'avenir. Ainsi, ne vous galvaudez pas. Surtout, défiez-vous de vos amis!"

20. See V, 518: So the fall of Lucien, of this intruder, of this little clown who wanted to swallow the world, was unanimously resolved and thoroughly thought-out. Vernou, who hated Lucien, undertook to give him no respite. In order to get out of paying three thousand francs to Lousteau, Finot accused Lucien of having kept him from making fifty thousand francs by revealing to Nathan the secret of the operation against Matifat. Nathan, with the advice of Florine, had secured Finot's support by selling him his little one-sixth interest for fifteen thousand francs. Lousteau, who was losing his three thousand francs, never forgave Lucien for the enormous damage done to this interests. Wounded pride becomes incurable once the oxide of money [*l'oxyde d'argent*] gets into it.

[Aussi la perte de Lucien, de cet intrus, de ce petit drôle qui voulait avaler tout le monde, fut-elle unanimement résolue et profondément méditée. Vernou qui haïssait Lucien se chargea de ne pas le lâcher. Pour se dispenser de payer mille écus à Lousteau, Finot accusa Lucien de l'avoir empêché de gagner cinquante mille francs en donnant à Nathan le secret de l'opération contre Matifat. Nathan, conseillé par Florine, s'était ménagé l'appui de Finot en lui vendant son *petit sixième* pour quinze mille francs. Lousteau, qui perdait ses mille écus, ne pardonna pas à Lucien cette lésion énorme de ses intérêts. Les blessures d'amour-propre deviennent incurables quand l'oxyde d'argent y pénètre.]

21. La prétendue trahison du poète fut alors envenimée et embellie des circonstances les plus aggravantes. . . . Tous sentaient instinctivement qu'un homme jeune et beau, spirituel et corrompu par eux, allait arriver à tout; aussi pour le renverser employèrent-ils tous les moyens.

22. Lucien se trouva sur la place Vendôme, hébété comme un homme à qui l'on vient de donner sur la tête un coup d'assommoir. Il revint à pied par les boulevards en essayant de se juger. Il se vit le jouet d'hommes envieux, avides et perfides.

23. En apprenant cette nouvelle, le vieux Séchard pensa joyeusement que la lutte qui s'établirait entre son établissement et les Cointet serait soutenue par son fils, et non par lui.

24. Le nom de *Cointet frères* l'effarouchait, il le voyait dominant celui de *Séchard et fils.* Enfin le vieillard sentait le vent du malheur. Ce pressentiment etait juste: le malheur planait sur la maison Séchard.

25. En province, au contraire, les avoués cultivent ce qu'on appelle dans les études de Paris la *broutille,* cette foule de petits actes qui surchargent les mémoires de frais et consomment du papier timbré.

26. Quatre-vingt-dix lecteurs sur cent seront affriolés par les détails suivants comme par la nouveauté la plus piquante. Ainsi sera prouvée encore une fois la vérité de cet axiome:
Il n'y a rien de moins connu que ce que tout le monde doit savoir, LA LOI!

27. Vous ne sauriez croire à quel point la qualité de banquier, jointe au titre auguste de créancier, change la condition du débiteur. Ainsi, *en Banque* (saisissez bien cette expression?), dès qu'un effet transmis de la place de Paris à la place d'Angoulême est impayé, les banquiers se doivent à eux-mêmes de s'adresser ce que la loi nomme un *compte de retour*. Calembour à part, jamais les romanciers n'ont inventé de conte plus invraisemblable que celui-là; car voici les ingénieuses plaisanteries à la Mascarille qu'un certain article du Code de commerce autorise, et dont l'explication vous démontrera combien d'atrocités se cachent sous ce mot terrible: *la légalité!*

28. Le plus rusé journaliste peut se trouver fort niais en matière d'intérêts commerciaux, et Lucien devait être et fut le jouet de Petit-Claud.

29. "Nous te devons beaucoup," dit Séchard à Petit-Claud.
"Mais je viens de vous ruiner," répondit Petit-Claud à ses anciens clients étonnés. "Je vous ai ruinés, je vous le répète, vous le verrez avec le temps; mais je vous connais, vous préférez votre ruine à une fortune que vous auriez peut-être trop tard."
"Nous ne sommes pas intéressés, monsieur, nous vous remercions de nous avoir donné les moyens du bonheur," dit Mme Eve, "et vous nous en trouverez toujours reconnaissants."

30. V. S. Pritchett, *Balzac* (New York: Knopf, 1973), pp. 67–84.

31. Lukacs, *Studies in European Realism*, p. 48.

32. Néret, *Histoire*, p. 124.

33. Pour être traduite par la voix, comme pour être saisie, la poésie exige une sainte attention. Il doit se faire entre le lecteur et l'auditoire une alliance intime, sans laquelle les électriques communications des sentiments n'ont plus lieu.

34. En effet, ceux qui comprennent la poésie cherchent à développer dans leur âme ce que l'auteur a mis en germe dans ses vers; mais ces auditeurs glacés, loin d'aspirer l'âme du poète, n'écoutaient même pas ses accents.

35. "Après tout, c'est des phrases," dit Zéphirine à Francis, "et l'amour est une poésie en action."

36. "Mais que peut-on dire contre ce livre? il est beau," s'écria Lucien.
"Ha! ça, mon cher, apprends ton métier," dit en riant Lousteau.

"Le livre, fût-il un chef d'oeuvre, doit devenir sous ta plume une stupide niaiserie, une oeuvre dangereuse et malsaine."

"Mais comment?"

"Tu changeras les beautés en défauts."

"Je suis incapable d'un pareil tour de force."

37. Lucien fut stupéfait en entendant parler Lousteau: à la parole du journaliste, il lui tomba des écailles des yeux, il découvrait des vérités littéraires qu'il n'avait même pas soupçonnées.

"Mais ce que tu me dis," s'écria-t-il, "est plein de raison et de justesse."

38. "Nous avons vu Nathan ce matin, il est au désespoir; mais tu vas lui faire un article où tu lui séringueras des éloges par la figure."

"Comment! après mon article contre son livre, vous voulez ..." demanda Lucien.

. . . .

"Tu pensais donc ce que tu as écrit?" dit Hector à Lucien.

"Oui."

"Ah! mon petit," dit Blondet, "je te croyais plus fort!"

39. The question of the origin of language and the possibility of some such "primal" state of linguistic transparency was raised in the eighteenth century by Rousseau, among many others. Jacques Derrida discusses it at length in *De la grammatologie* (Paris: Minuit, 1967).

40. Brooks, *Melodramatic Imagination*, p. 122.

41. Lionel Trilling, Introduction to *The Princess Casamassima*, by Henry James (New York: Macmillan, 1948), rpt. in *Discussions of Henry James*, ed. Naomi Lebowitz (Boston: D.C. Heath, 1962), pp. 31, 32.

42. Henry James, *Letters*, ed. Leon Edel (Cambridge: Harvard University Press, 1980), 3:28.

43. Critics have frequently—and mistakenly—taken James's fastidiousness for prudery. See, for example, Maxwell Geismar, *Henry James and the Jacobites* (Boston: Houghton Mifflin, 1963), or, in a less cranky mode, F. W. Dupee, *Henry James*, The American Men of Letters Series (1951; rpt. New York: William Morrow, 1974), p. 125, who quotes Gide on James's heroines—"'They are only winged busts; all the weight of the flesh is absent, all the shaggy, tangled undergrowth, all the wild darkness'"—and goes on himself with the following: "And James seems himself to acknowledge the limitation, when, at the peril of retroactively compromising his portrait of Isabel he shows her fleeing from Goodwood's kiss. With all his wider experience, James is more Puritan—if not simply less human—than Hawthorne, for whom, in *The Scarlet Letter,* the color of adultery is also the color of life-blood and roses."

44. James, *The Future of the Novel,* p. 91.

45. James, *Partial Portraits,* p. 285.

46. James, *Notebooks,* p. 47.

47. See Clinton Oliver, "Henry James as a Social Critic," *Antioch Review* 7 (1947), rpt. as Introduction to *The Princess Casamassima,* by Henry James (New York: Harper Torchbooks, 1959), p. 12.

48. James, *Future of the Novel,* p. 12.

49. See Leon Edel, *Henry James: The Middle Years* (New York: Lippincott, 1962), pp. 147–48.

50. James, *Partial Portraits,* p. 206, my emphasis.

51. See above, chapter one, and *Partial Portraits,* pp. 227–28.

52. W. H. Tilley, *The Background of The Princess Casamassima,* University of Florida Monographs, Humanities #5, 22 (Gainesville, Florida: University of Florida Press, 1960), p. 22.

53. Lyall Powers, *Henry James and the Naturalist Movement* (n.p., Michigan State University Press, 1971), esp. pp. 19–20.

54. On the effect of the vow see Taylor Stoehr, "Words and Deeds in *The Princess Casamassima,*" *ELH* 37 (1970): 95–135.

55. Cf. William Veeder, *Henry James—the Lessons of the Master* (Chicago: University of Chicago Press, 1975), p. 99: "To regard life as a matter of reading is especially natural to Protestants because the very essence of their religion is (supposedly) the individual's interpretation of The Word. With salvation itself at stake, sign-reading becomes obsessive in popular fiction, as almost any novel of the period will demonstrate."

56. The correlation of *vraisemblance* and interpretability is posited in Julia Kristeva, "La Productivité dite texte," in *Semiotike: Recherches pour une sémanalyse* (Paris: Seuil, 1969), pp. 208–245.

CHAPTER 4

1. See Picon, *L'Usage de la Lecture,* p. 84, on the transition from *Illusions perdues* to *Splendeurs et misères:* "Lucien has died. In wresting him from the hands of death, Carlos is returning him not to life itself but to a life after death, not to the world itself, but to a world beyond the world. The ending of *Illusions perdues* is not just one episode among others: it is the passage from reality—that reality where Lucien lived and lost his illusions—to a fantastic dream-world."

2. Christophere Prendergast, "Melodrama and Totality in *Splendeurs et misères des courtisanes,*" *Novel* 6 (1973):162.

3. Pierre Barbéris, *Balzac: une mythologie réaliste* (Paris: Larousse, 1971), p. 215.

4. Picon, *L'Usage de la lecture,* p. 84.

5. For the story of Balzac and the *roman-feuilleton,* see René Guise, "Balzac et le roman-feuilleton," *L'Année Balzacienne* (1964):283–338.

6. For a discussion of this, see Pierre Citron's comments in the "Inté-grale" edition (IV, 278) and the Guise article just cited.

7. Letter of May 31, 1843, quoted by André Lorant in *Les Parents pauvres d'Honoré de Balzac* (Geneva: Droz, 1967), 1:322.

8. Henry James, *Notebooks,* p. 179.

9. Lorant, *Les Parents pauvres,* 1: 340.

10. Quoted in ibid., 1:323.

11. Picon, *L'Usage de la lecture,* p. 86.

12. It is interesting to speculate, though, on the potential parallel. Both men experienced difficulties with their writing when they were in their mid-to-late forties, and both emerged from their difficulties with a new style. The difficulties and the styles themselves are quite different, but the biographical parallel is striking.

13. Ce ne sera certes pas un hors d'oeuvre que de décrire ce coin de Paris actuel, plus tard on ne pourrait pas l'imaginer; et nos neveux, qui verront sans doute le Louvre achevé, se refuseraient à croire qu'une pareille barbarie ait subsisté pendant trente-six ans, au coeur de Paris, en face du palais où trois dynasties ont reçu, pendant ces der-nières trente-six années, l'élite de la France et celle de l'Europe.

14. Lorant, *Les Parents pauvres,* 1:300–304.

15.   "Vous ne pouvez, dans la situation où vous êtes, marier votre fille que de trois manières: par mon secours, vous n'en voulez pas! et d'un; en trouvant un vieillard de soixante ans, très riche, sans enfants, et qui voudrait en avoir, c'est difficile, mais cela se rencontre. . . . Et de deux! La dernière manière est la plus facile . . ."

Mme Hulot leva la tête, et regarda l'ancien parfumeur avec anxiété.

"Paris est une ville où tous les gens d'énergie qui poussent comme des sauvageons sur le territoire français se donnent rendezvous, et il y grouille bien des talents, sans feu ni lieu, des courages capables de tout, même de faire fortune. . . . Eh bien! l'un de ces *condottieri,* comme on dit, de la commandite, de la plume, ou de la brosse, est le seul être, à Paris, capable d'épouser une belle fille sans le sou, car ils ont tous les genres de courage.

16. Cf. VII, 55–56, 139–40.

17. Christopher Prendergast provides a subtle, lucid analysis of the way Balzac turns the conventions of allegorical melodrama back on them-selves, to create a text which, like *Le Père Goriot* and *The American,* criticizes its own apparent generic assumptions. Although I wrote this chapter before Prendergast's work was published, readers of both will find significant agreement between them. Whereas I grant a little more credence to the face value of allegorical labels than Prendergast does, we

both value Balzac's dynamic way of using them, whether as self-decon-struction (Prendergast, *Balzac: Fiction and Melodrama,* chap. 8) or as elements in a textual drama (below, this chapter).

18. "Adeline! . . . Adeline, je te verrai dans la boue et plus bas que moi!"

19. Lisbeth, déjà bien malheureuse du bonheur qui luisait sur la famille, ne put soutenir cet événement heureux. Elle empira si bien, qu'elle fut condamnée par Bianchon à mourir une semaine après, vaincue au bout de cette longue lutte marquée pour elle par tant de victoires.

20. Pour Adeline, le baron fut donc, dès l'origine, une espèce de Dieu qui ne pouvait faillir; elle lui devait tout:. . . .

21. La férocité du Vice avait vaincu la patience de l'ange, à qui, sur le bord de l'Eternité, il échappa le seul mot de reproche qu'elle eût fait entendre de toute sa vie.

22. "Vraiment!" s'écria Crevel ouvrant des yeux animés autant par le désir que par ce mot magique: *Une femme comme il faut.*

23. "Valérie," disait le Brésilien à l'oreille de la jeune femme, "je te re-viens fidèle; mon oncle est mort, et je suis deux fois plus riche que je ne l'étais à mon départ. Je veux vivre et mourir à Paris, près de toi et pour toi."
"Plus bas, Henri! de grâce!"

24. "Mais pourquoi ne quittez-vous pas tout pour moi, si vous m'ai-mez?" demanda le Brésilien. . . . Ce naturel de l'Amérique, logique comme le sont tous les hommes nés dans la Nature, reprit aussitôt la conversation au point où il l'avait laissée, en reprenant la taille de Valérie.

25. "Je la tuerai!" répéta froidement le Brésilien. "Ah ça! vous m'avez appelé Sauvage! . . . Est-ce que vous croyez que je vais imiter la sot-tise de vos compatriotes qui vont acheter du poison chez les phar-maciens? . . . J'ai pensé, pendant le temps que vous avez mis à venir chez vous, à ma vengeance, dans le cas où vous auriez raison contre Valérie. L'un de mes nègres porte avec lui le plus sûr des poisons animaux, une terrible maladie qui vaut mieux qu'un poison végétal et qui ne se guérit qu'au Brésil, je la fais prendre à Cydalise, qui me la donnera; puis, quand la mort sera dans les veines de Crevel et de sa femme, je serai par-delà les Açores avec votre cousine que je ferai guérir et que je prendrai pour femme. Nous autres Sauvages, nous avons nos procédés! . . ."

26. "Laissez-moi toute à l'Eglise! je ne puis maintenant plaire qu'à Dieu! je vais tâcher de me réconcilier avec lui, ce sera ma dernière coquet-terie! Oui, il faut que je *fasse le bon Dieu!*"

27. "Voici quarante ans, monsieur, que nous remplaçons le Destin," répondit-elle avec un orgeuil formidable, "et que nous faisons tout ce que nous voulons dans Paris."

"Moi, je me charge du rôle de la Providence, je ferai vouloir le bon Dieu."

28. Elle fut la Haine et la Vengeance sans transaction. . . .

"Je viens de voir le désespoir de la Vertu! . . ."

"Madame, je vous témoignerai par avance la reconnaissance profonde que je vous garderai de l'honneur que vous m'avez fait, en ne montrant pas la cantatrice Josépha, la maîtresse du duc d'Hérouville, à côté de la plus belle, de la plus sainte image de la Vertu."

"Je veux devenir méchante, à la fin! Ma parole d'honneur, je crois que le Mal est la faux avec laquelle on met le Bien en coupe."

Prendergast points out Lisbeth's shabby treatment and Adeline's prudish naiveté, arguing against identifying them with Evil and Virtue. I agree to the extent that they are not simple allegorical representations of pure qualities, but I think their effectiveness in the novel depends on their power to represent moral qualities in their necessary complexity. This kind of allegory produces the effect that Prendergast and I both value in *La Cousine Bette,* the true picture of the dramatic interaction of moral qualities in real people and situations.

29. E.g., VII, 142; 357.

30. Elle monta donc résolument, non pas chez elle, mais à cette mansarde. Voici pourquoi. Au dessert, elle avait mis dans son sac des fruits et des sucreries pour son amoureux, et elle venait les lui donner, absolument comme une vieille fille rapporte une friandise à son chien.

31. Quand, à Paris, une femme a résolu de faire métier et marchandise de sa beauté, ce n'est pas une raison pour qu'elle fasse fortune. On y rencontre d'admirables créatures, très spirituelles, dans une affreuse médiocrité, finissant très mal une vie commencée par les plaisirs. Voici pourquoi. Se destiner à la carrière honteuse des courtisanes, avec l'intention d'en palper les avantages, tout en gardant la robe d'une honnête bourgeoise mariée, ne suffit pas. Le Vice n'obtient pas facilement ses triomphes; il a cette similitude avec le Génie, qu'ils exigent tous deux un concours de circonstances heureuses pour opérer le cumul de la fortune et du talent.

32. F. R. Jameson, "*La Cousine Bette* and Allegorical Realism," *PMLA* 86 (1971):247.

33. See, for example, *La Peau de chagrin.*

34. Compare, for example, the theme of the "drama" and the dramatic conceptions of scenes in *Le Père Goriot* and the descriptions of the theater in *Illusions perdues*.

35. "Nous devons quatre termes, quinze cents francs! notre mobilier les vaut-il? *'That is the question!'* a dit Shakespeare."

   "Vous ne vous ressemblez plus, vous êtes parti avec la physionomie du More de Venise et vous revenez avec celle de Saint-Preux!"

   "Avec toi, mon cher confrère, Gubetta, mon vieux complice, je pourrais accepter une situation *chocnoso* . . . non, philosophique; mais un Brésilien qui, peut-être, apporte de son pays des denrées coloniales suspectes . . ."

36. "Tiens la petite en bride, sois Bartholo! Gare aux Auguste, aux Hippolyte, aux Nestor, aux Victor, à tous les *or!*"

37. Chapters 47 and 49 in editions, such as the "Intégrale," which give chapter titles.

38. I count five allusions to Racine, two each to Corneille, Shakespeare, and Rossini, and one each to Molière, Voltaire, Beaumarchais, Meyerbeer, and Adam.

39. Jean Racine, *Phèdre*, in *Théâtre complet*, ed. Maurice Rat (Paris: Garnier, 1960), I, iii. Subsequent references to *Phèdre* will be followed by act and scene numbers in parentheses.

40. "Toi! Tu n'as ruiné que les tiens, tu n'as disposé que de toi! et puis tu as une excuse, et physique et morale . . ."
   Elle se posa tragiquement et dit:
   C'est Vénus tout entière à sa proie attachée.

41. Ici se termine en quelque sorte l'introduction de cette histoire. Ce récit est au drame qui le complète ce que sont les prémisses à une proposition, ce qu'est toute exposition à toute tragédie classique.

42. Jameson uses the division of the text marked by this passage as a sign which leads him to its underlying concerns. His analysis of these concerns is totally convincing, but I clearly disagree with his statement that the "theatrical terminology" of the passage is "deceptive." See "*La Cousine Bette* and Allegorical Realism," p. 243.

43. P. Barrière, *Honoré de Balzac et la tradition littéraire classique* (Paris: Hachette, 1928), p. 225.

44. Ibid.

45. "Ma femme n'a pas longtemps à vivre, et si tu veux tu pourras être baronne." Adeline jeta un cri, laissa tomber son bougeoir et s'enfuit.

46. Brooks, *Melodramatic Imagination,* p. 31.

47. Ibid, p. 32.

48. "Je suis un épicier, un boutiquier, un ancien débitant de pâte d'a-
    mande, d'eau de Portugal, d'huile céphalique, on doit me trouver
    bien honoré d'avoir marié ma fille unique au fils de M. le baron
    Hulot d'Ervy, ma fille sera baronne. C'est Régence, c'est Louis XV,
    Oeil-de-Boeuf! c'est très bien . . ."

49. "Ma fille Hortense a pu se marier, le mariage dépendait entièrement
    de vous, j'ai cru à des sentiments généreux chez vous, j'ai pensé que
    vous auriez rendu justice à une femme qui n'a jamais eu dans le coeur
    d'autre image que celle de son mari, que vous auriez reconnu la né-
    cessité pour elle de ne pas recevoir un homme capable de la compro-
    mettre, et que vous vous seriez empressé, par honneur pour la famille
    à laquelle vous vous êtes allié, de favoriser l'établissement d'Hortense
    avec M. le conseiller Lebas. . . . Et vous, monsieur, vous avez fait
    manquer ce mariage . . .

50. "Sortez, monsieur," dit Mme Hulot, "sortez, et ne reparaissez ja-
    mais devant moi. Sans la nécessité où vous m'avez mise de savoir le
    secret de votre lâche conduite dans l'affaire du mariage projeté pour
    Hortense . . . Oui, lâche . . . ," reprit-elle à un geste de Crevel. "Com-
    ment faire peser de pareilles inimitiés sur une pauvre fille, sur une
    belle et innocente créature? . . . Sans cette nécessité qui poignait mon
    coeur de mère, vous ne m'auriez jamais reparlé, vous ne seriez jamais
    plus rentré chez moi. Trente-deux ans d'honneur, de loyauté de
    femme ne périront pas sous les coups de M. Crevel . . ."

51. La majesté de la vertu, sa céleste lumière avait balayé l'impureté
    passagère de cette femme, qui, resplendissante de la beauté qui lui
    était propre, parut grandie à Crevel. Adeline fut en ce moment sub-
    lime comme ces figures de la Religion, soutenues par une croix, que
    les vieux Vénitiens ont peintes; mais elle exprimait toute la grandeur
    de son infortune et celle de l'Eglise catholique où elle se réfugiait par
    un vol de colombe blessée. Crevel fut ébloui, abasourdi.
    "Madame, je suis à vous sans condition!"

52. Qui voyait la Bette pour la première fois, frémissait involontairement
    à l'aspect de la sauvage poésie que l'habile Valérie avait su mettre en
    relief en cultivant par la toilette cette Nonne sanglante, en encadrant
    avec art par des bandeaux épais cette sèche figure olivâtre où bril-
    laient des yeux d'un noir assorti à celui de la chevelure, en faisant
    valoir cette taille inflexible.

53. "Attendez-vous à lire quelque jour le nom de mon pauvre cousin à
    l'article Tribunaux."

54. The relation of her eventual fate to the intensity of the exercise of her will might well be studied in the context of the Balzacian "philosophy" suggested by *La Peau de chagrin,* and by Per Nykrog's book on *La Pensée de Balzac.*

55. Tout était péril pour Valérie, qui, prévoyant une explication avec Crevel, ne voulait pas Hulot dans sa chambre où il pourrait tout entendre. Et le Brésilien attendait chez Lisbeth.

56. The pun is perpetrated in the headings to chapter 69 ("Second père de la chambre Marneffe") and chapter 71 ("Troisième père de la chambre Marneffe").

57. Chapter 75.

58. En ce moment, Victorin et la cousine Bette entrèrent, et restèrent hébétés de ce spectacle. La fille était prosternée aux pieds de son père. La baronne, muette et prise entre le sentiment maternel et le sentiment conjugal, offrait un visage bouleversée, couvert de larmes.

59. "Hector!"
Ce cri fit retourner le baron, et il montra soudain un visage inondé de larmes à sa femme, qui l'entoura de ses bras avec la force du désespoir.
"Ne t'en va pas ainsi . . . ne nous quitte pas en colére. Je ne t'ai rien dit, moi! . . ."
A ce cri sublime les enfants se jetèrent aux genoux de leur père.
"Nous vous aimons tous," dit Hortense.
Lisbeth, immobile comme une statue, observait ce groupe avec un sourire superbe sur les lèvres. En ce moment, le maréchal Hulot entra dans l'antichambre et sa voix se fit entendre. La famille comprit l'importance du secret, et la scène changea subitement d'aspect.

60. La porte s'ouvrit. La majestueuse loi française, qui passe sur les affiches après la royauté, se manifesta sous la forme d'un bon petit commissaire de police, accompagné d'un long juge de paix, amenés tous deux par le sieur Marneffe.

61. Martin Kanes, *Balzac's Comedy of Words* (Princeton: Princeton University Press, 1975), pp. 167–88.

62. "Mais votre cousine Hortense possède le groupe de Samson dont voici la lithographie publiée par une Revue; elle l'a payé de ses économies, et c'est le baron qui, dans l'intérêt de son futur gendre, le lance et obtient tout."
"De l'eau! . . . de l'eau!" demanda Lisbeth après avoir jeté les yeux sur la lithographie au bas de laquelle elle lut: *groupe appartenant à Mlle Hulot d'Ervy.* "De l'eau! ma tete brûle, je deviens folle! . . ."

63. "Vous êtes-vous bien amusé hier?" dit Hortense, car Wenceslas n'est revenu qu'après une heure du matin.
"Amusé? . . . pas précisément," répondit l'artiste qui la veille avait voulu *faire* Mme Marneffe. "On ne s'amuse dans le monde que lorsqu'on y a des intérêts. Cette petite Mme Marneffe est excessivement spirituelle, mais elle est coquette . . ."

. . . .

Hortense devint pâle comme une accouchée.
"Ainsi, c'est bien . . . chez Mme Marneffe . . . et non pas . . . chez Chanor que vous avez dîné . . . ," dit-elle, "hier . . . avec Wenceslas, et il . . ."
Stidmann, sans savoir quel malheur il faisait, devina qu'il en causait un. La comtesse n'acheva pas sa phrase, elle s'évanouit complètement.

64. La baronne vint sur la pointe du pied, Hector n'entendit rien, elle put s'approcher, elle aperçut la lettre, elle la prit, la lut, et trembla de tous ses membres. Elle éprouva l'une de ces révolutions nerveuses si violentes que le corps en garde éternellement la trace. Elle devint, quelques jours après, sujette à un tressaillement continuel; car, ce premier moment passé, la nécessité d'agir lui donna cette force qui ne se prend qu'aux sources mêmes de la puissance vitale.

65. "Elle paraît avoir des armes contre vous! . . ." répondit-elle. "Je ne sais pas encore de quoi il s'agit, mais je le saurai . . . Elle a parlé vaguement d'une histoire de deux cent mille francs qui regarde Adeline."
La baronne Hulot se renversa doucement sur le divan où elle se trouvait, et d'affreuses convulsions se declarèrent.

CHAPTER 5

1. Henry James, *Roderick Hudson* (New York: Scribner's, 1907), p. xvii.
2. See Leon Edel, "Henry James: The Dramatic Years," Introduction to *Guy Domville,* by Henry James (London: Rupert Hart-Davis, 1961), pp. 13–29.
3. See the Introduction to *Guy Domville,* cited above, and the third volume of Edel's biography, *Henry James: The Middle Years.*
4. James, *Notebooks,* p. 99.
5. Henry James, *The Scenic Art: Notes on Acting and the Drama, 1872–1901,* ed. Allan Wade (London: Rupert Hart-Davis, 1949), esp. pp. 164–65, 209, 230–31, 296.

6. Henry James, *Letters,* ed. Leon Edel (Cambridge: Harvard University Press, 1980), 3: 452.

7. The "discovery" has been of the greatest importance for the modern novel. Gérard Genette in his objection to the distinction between pictorial telling and dramatic showing, and his substitution of the distinction between the "récit de paroles" and the "récit d'événements" seems to me narrowly literal in his interpretation of James and unnecessarily obfuscatory in his multiplication of distinctions. (This last does not apply, however, to the rest of Genette's very useful essay.) See "Discours du récit" in *Figures III* (Paris: Seuil, 1972), pp. 67–282.

8. James, *Notebooks,* p. 263.

9. James, *Scenic Art,* pp. 250–51.

10. See Leon Edel, *Henry James: The Treacherous Years* (New York: Lippincott, 1969), p. 114.

11. James, *Scenic Art,* p. 257.

12. Ibid., p. 259.

13. Edel, *Treacherous Years,* p. 114.

14. Henry James, *The Wings of the Dove* (New York: Scribner's, 1909), I, 4. Subsequent references to this edition will be followed by volume and page numbers in parentheses.

15. Here is James's description of Lionel Croy's room:

> It was at this point, however, that she remained; changing her place, moving from the shabby sofa to the armchair upholstered in a glazed cloth that gave at once—she had tried it—the sense of the slippery and of the sticky. She had looked at the sallow prints on the walls and at the lonely magazine, a year old, that combined, with a small lamp in coloured glass and a knitted centre-piece wanting in freshness, to enhance the effect of the purplish cloth on the principal table; she had above all from time to time taken a brief stand on the small balcony to which the pair of long windows gave access. The vulgar little street, in this view, offered scant relief from the vulgar little room; its main office was to suggest to her that the narrow black house-fronts, adjusted to a standard that would have been low even for backs, constituted quite the publicity implied by such privacies. One felt them in the room exactly as one felt the room—the hundred like it, or worse—in the street. Each time she turned in again, each time, in her impatience, she gave him up, it was to sound to a deeper depth, while she tasted the faint flat emanation of things, the failure of fortune and of honour. (I, 3–4)

16. For an ingenious, but, to my mind, extravagant, comparison of *The Wings of the Dove* to the Tristan story, see Oscar Cargill, *The Novels of Henry James* (New York: Macmillan, 1971), pp. 338–47.

17. The parallels with *The Marble Faun* have been discussed by Marius Bewley in *The Complex Fate* (London: Chatto and Windus, 1952), pp. 31–54.

18. Robert L. Caserio has recently argued, for me most convincingly, that in *The Wings of the Dove* James rejects pictures in favor of action, rejects princesslike "being" in favor of participation in the world. See his *Plot, Story, and the Novel,* pp. 211ff.

19. *William Shakespeare: The Complete Works,* ed. Alfred Harbage (Baltimore: Penguin Books, 1969), III, iv, 101.

20. Austin Warren, "Myth and Dialectic in the Later Novels," *Kenyon Review* 5 (1943): 551–68. Leo Bersani takes up Warren's point in his article, "The Narrator as Center in *The Wings of the Dove,*" *MFS* 6 (1960):131–44, and suggests further that the characters "live their experience as if they were writing about it" (134). I might add that they write about it as if they were composing the same text.

21. Warren, "Myth and Dialectic," p. 556.

22. Quentin Anderson, for example, has based an elaborate interpretive scheme for the novel as redemptive allegory partly on this identification. See *The American Henry James,* (New Brunswick, N.J.: Rutgers University Press, 1957), pp. 233–80.

23. See F. O. Matthiessen, *Henry James: The Major Phase* (New York: Oxford University Press, 1944), pp. 68–69.

24. See, for example, Cargill, *The Novels of Henry James,* pp. 343–47; Matthiessen, *The Major Phase,* pp. 68–73; Anderson, *The American Henry James,* pp. 233–80; Laurence Holland, *The Expense of Vision* (Princeton: Princeton University Press, 1964), pp. 303–313.

25. Matthiessen does comment briefly on this. See *The Major Phase,* p. 69.

26. Edel, *The Middle Years,* p. 386.

27. Frederick Crews, *The Tragedy of Manners* (New Haven: Yale University Press, 1957), p. 66.

28. II, 100–101: "'Nobody matters, Susie. Nobody.' Which her next words, however, rather contradicted. 'Did he take it ill that I wasn't here to see him? Wasn't it really just what he wanted—to have it out, so much more simply, with *you?*'"

29. John Carlos Rowe discusses his notion of Milly as a creator of *difference* in *Henry Adams and Henry James* (Ithaca: Cornell University Press, 1976), p. 176.

30. See I, 130–31; II, 51–52, 155, 197, 292–93, 349.

CONCLUSION

1. See, for example, Heath, *The Nouveau Roman,* pp. 15–19.

2. Fredric R. Jameson, "Metacommentary," *PMLA* 86 (1971):9.

INDEX

LIBRARY OF CONGRESS CATALOGING IN PUBLICATION DATA

Stowe, William W., 1946–
Balzac, James, and the realistic novel.

Includes bibliographical references and index.
1. Fiction—19th century—History and criticism.
2. Realism in literature. 3. Balzac, Honoré de, 1799–
1850—Criticism and interpretation. 4. James, Henry,
1843–1916—Criticism and interpretation. I. Title.
PN3499.S78 1983   809.3′1   82-61388
ISBN 0-691-06567-5

WILLIAM W. STOWE is Assistant Professor of English at Wesleyan University. He has published articles in *Texas Studies in Literature and Language, Reader, Philological Quarterly*, and *Comparative Literature*.